This Book Belongs to the Library of

_____

_____

_____

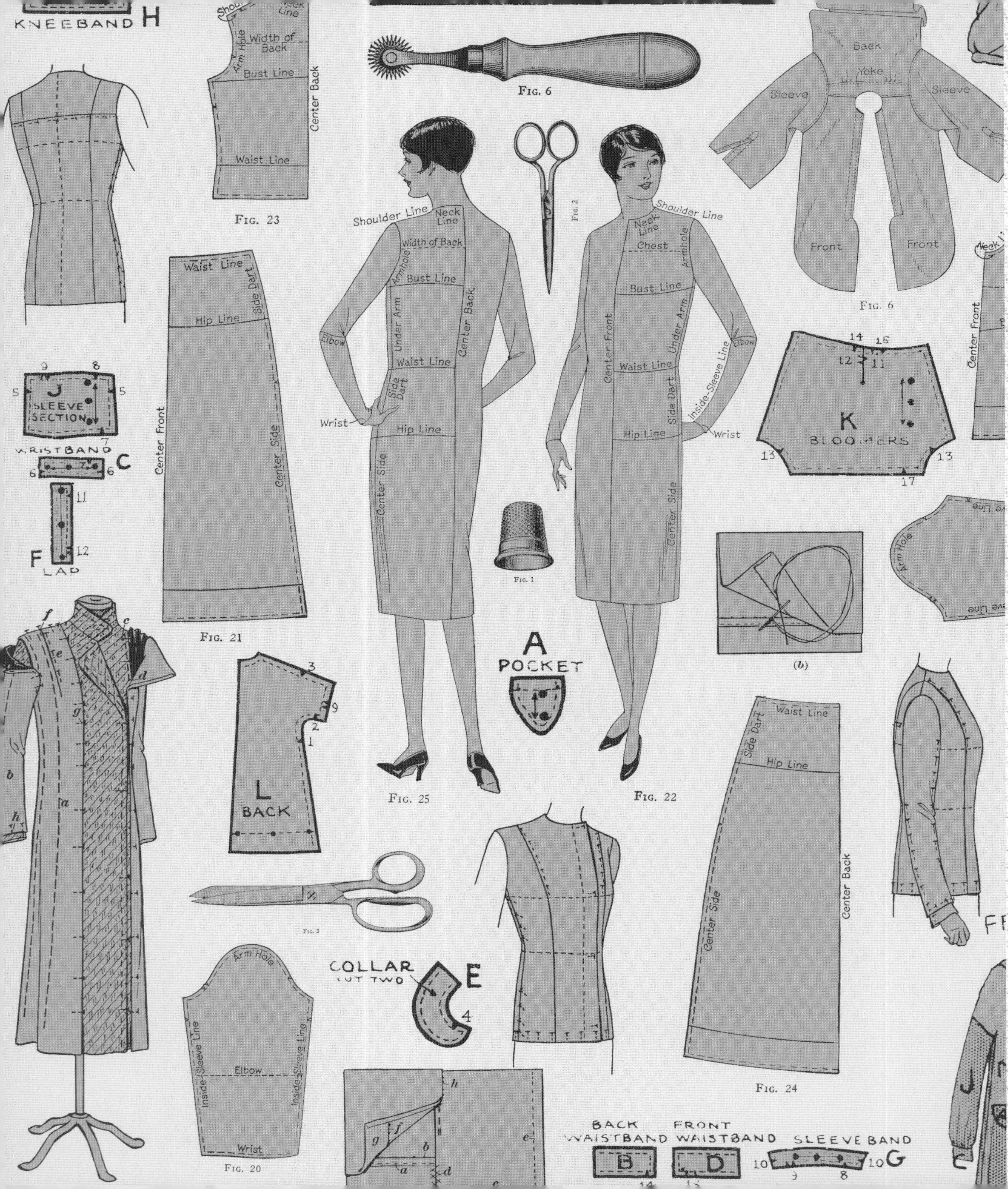

KNEEBAND **H**

Width of Back

Bust Line

Shoulder Line

Arm Hole

Center Back

FIG. 23

FIG. 6

Waist Line

Side Dart

Hip Line

Center Front

Center Side

FIG. 21

9   8
J
5   5
SLEEVE SECTION

WRISTBAND
6   7   6   **C**

11

F   12
LAP

Back
Yoke
Sleeve   Sleeve

Front   Front

FIG. 6

Neck

Center Front

14   15
12   11
K
BLOOMERS
13   13
17

Shoulder Line
Neck Line
Width of Back
Arm Hole
Bust Line
Under Arm
Center Back
Waist Line
Side Dart
Wrist
Hip Line
Center Side

Shoulder Line
Neck Line
Chest
Armhole
Bust Line
Under Arm
Center Front
Waist Line
Side Dart
Inside-Sleeve Line
Elbow
Hip Line
Wrist
Center Side

FIG. 2

FIG. 1

A POCKET

Arm Hole
Sleeve Line

Sleeve Line

(b)

3
9
2
1
L BACK

FIG. 25

FIG. 22

Side Dart
Waist Line
Hip Line
Center Side
Center Back

FIG. 24

f   e
e
d
g
a
b
h

Arm Hole
Inside-Sleeve Line
Elbow
Inside-Sleeve Line
Wrist
FIG. 20

COLLAR
CUT TWO
E
4

h
g   f
a   b
c   d

BACK   FRONT
WAISTBAND   WAISTBAND   SLEEVE BAND
B   **D**   10   **G**

Amy Barickman's
VINTAGE NOTIONS

An Inspirational Guide to
Needlework, Cooking, Sewing,
Fashion, and Fun

ab

amy barickman

Kansas City

For information write the publisher:
Amy Barickman, LLC
P. O. Box 30237
Kansas City, Missouri 64112
www.amybarickman.com
amyb@amybarickman.com

Third Printing
Library of Congress Control Number: 2010900744

ISBN: 10: 0982627009
ISBN: 13: 978-0-9826270-0-6

The material, both editorial and artwork, first appeared in various publications of The Woman's Institute of Domestic Arts and Sciences, located in Scranton, Pennsylvania. Most of it appeared in periodical newsletters and magazines published under the names *Fashion Service* and *Inspiration*, between the years 1916 and 1934. Many of the essays reprinted here first appeared in the book *Thimblefuls of Friendliness* by Mary Brooks Picken, copyright © 1924.

We take great care to ensure that the information included in our publications is accurate and presented in good faith. No warranty is provided nor results guaranteed. For your convenience, we post an up-to-date listing of corrections on our website www.vintagenotions.com. If a correction is not noted, please contact our customer service department through our website or call 913-341-5559. You may also write us at P.O. Box 30237, Kansas City, MO 64112.

Dedication

To Mary Brooks Picken, and all of the women at The Woman's Institute of Domestic Arts and Sciences, whose work inspires me today. Their entrepreneurial spirit led the way for millions of women to exercise their creativity, business, and leadership skills. The message embodied in their work at the Institute continues to empower women today. The lessons they taught and those handed down to me by my grandmother, Mildred Conrad, and my mother, Donna Martin, inspired my own career and the journey that has led me to publish this book.

I will always be grateful to the fabric and quilt shop owners who have supported my businesses, Indygo Junction and The Vintage Workshop, over the past twenty years. Their hard work and dedication to the fabric arts industry has kept the love of sewing and its rewards alive and thriving. Thank you!

This book is also dedicated to the new generation of creative spirits. I encourage you to seek the knowledge and wisdom that previous generations have to offer.

Another Year

For every Winter there's a Spring—
   Oh, that's the beauty of the thing!
For ev'ry midnight there's a morn,
   For ev'ry loss a hope is born,
For ev'ry sultry day the dew,
   For ev'ry old year there's a new!

Yes, buds for all the leaves that fall—
   That is the beauty of it all,
New dreams for all the dreams that die,
   For ev'ry night a dawning sky—
For ev'ry heartache, failure, fear,
   Another chance, another year!

—Douglas Malloch
Excerpted from Inspiration, 1923

Contents

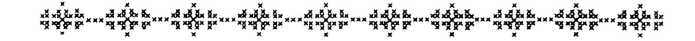

Introduction

Mary Brooks Picken

When given the opportunity to introduce a wildly-talented, intelligent, creative, and courageous woman to a new audience, it is hard to know where to begin. The woman I am writing about is the sole inspiration for this book. She is an American heroine to those who know of her, and someone worth getting to know if you are new to her history. Her name is Mary Brooks Picken.

Mary Brooks Picken, a granddaughter of pioneers, was born in a Kansas farmhouse in 1886. As a small child, Mary's sewing and design talent was apparent and at a young age, she set off for a career in fashion that took her to Kansas City and later Boston, where she further refined her dress-making skills. As was the custom, she married young and began a traditional home life that would later directly influence her career path as the first American authority on home arts and founder of The Woman's Institute of Domestic Arts and Sciences in Scranton, Pennsylvania. The school, founded in 1916, was the heart and soul of Mary's vision and combined correspondence courses with classroom instruction in dressmaking, millinery, cooking, fashion design, beauty, and homemaking. It attracted students from around the world as enrollment climbed to almost 300,000 women, making it the largest school in history devoted solely to the education of women.

Keep in mind that women could not yet vote, less than ten percent of women worked outside the home, and very few went to college. Vocational schools were thriving for young men, but women remained an afterthought in the American workforce. It was nothing short of amazing that Mary Brooks Picken founded an educational institution that was affordable for these women, generated income for them immediately, and elevated the value of their work.

> *In sympathetic understanding of the needs of the home, in experience, in practical knowledge of her art, no woman in America is better qualified to head a great school for women.*

Discovering Mary's Work

So where do I fit into this story? I'll start at the beginning. In the summer of 2008, while returning from a creative workshop in Omaha, Nebraska, I began reviewing several vintage newsletters and magazines that I had collected along the way as I was hunting for artwork for my company, The Vintage Workshop. All I knew about the newsletters was that they were published under the titles *Inspiration* and *Fashion Service* by The Woman's Institute of Domestic Arts and Sciences in Scranton, Pennsylvania, between 1916 and 1934, and that they were inspiring. Combing through the aged pages of these wonderfully illustrated and beautifully written publications, I realized that much of the information and wisdom in the pages was still relevant for women today and provided a blueprint for living a simple, fulfilling life.

I began to research the Institute further, scouring flea markets, antique shows, and the Internet for more material. I learned that Mary Brooks Picken was a pioneering businesswoman who was considered the international authority on dressmaking. She was the author of the popular textbook *The One-Hour Dress and How to Make It*. It was a bestseller that brought national attention to Mary and the Institute. She eventually went on to write nearly 100 books on sewing, dressmaking, needle arts, and fashion, including *Thimblefuls of Friendliness*, a popular book published in 1924 that contains Mary's timeless wisdom and everyday philosophy on life. She taught at Columbia University, was the first woman to be named a trustee of the Fashion Institute of Technology, and was one of five original directors of the Costume Institute, now part of New York's Metropolitan Museum of Art. Her accomplishments introduced her into the most prominent circles of her day and made her a celebrity in her own right.

About *Vintage Notions*

I conceived of this book, *Vintage Notions,* to rescue Mary Brooks Picken from obscurity and to reintroduce the inspirational essays, clever sewing patterns, cooking basics, and beautiful illustrations from the Institute's newsletters with a fresh and modern voice. The book is organized seasonally—each chapter represents a month of the year—because our lives are keenly connected to the change of seasons, from the food we eat to the clothes we wear.

Thimblefuls of Friendliness
By Mary Brooks Picken

For years you have been reading Mrs. Picken's cheering, comforting articles and editorials in INSPIRATION. This year Mrs. Picken has consented to the publication of her choicest writings, assembled in a single volume, attractively bound. Her only condition is that the book be offered at a price so low that every student may be able to secure a copy. It is 48 pages, 7 by 10 inches in size, with attractive cover.

SPECIAL OFFER!

The price of the book is 75 cents, but if you order four copies for gifts, Mrs. Picken will include free one extra copy autographed for you. Remember—single copies 75 cents, postpaid. Four copies, $3.00, postpaid, with an extra copy autographed, free.

Each chapter opens with *Modern Notions*, my thoughts about the relevance of the everyday wisdom offered for each month. Each season has its own storage pocket, a clever place to stash away clippings, fabric swatches, and any little notion that inspires you in your domestic pursuits. When I comment on the material with a modern tip or technique, this symbol 🪡 will appear in the text.

Articles and instructions from the authors and editors who contributed to the original newsletters and magazines are featured throughout the book. The text is true to the original source material and edited for inclusion in this book so that the authentic voices of the writers come through and the charm of the language is preserved as much as possible. I have chosen the best material to share with you, combining stellar content with charming artwork, and adding vintage textiles and needlework from my personal collection. I hope you feel the sense of excitement and inspiration I felt as I discovered Mary's work for the first time.

Timeless Inspiration

As the founder of The Vintage Workshop and Indygo Junction, companies dedicated to the creative arts, I have spent my twenty-year career immersed in the world of crafts and the domestic arts. My goal has always been to provide artists with imaginative and inventive information that allows them to perfect their talents and skills. Like the newsletters of The Woman's Institute, the various websites and books I have written have all been the result of the collaboration of women working together toward a common goal.

And while my endless collecting and hunting for great vintage material will never stop, I understand the drive behind it now in a way I did not before encountering the work of Mary Brooks Picken. It seems that all along, part of me was searching for the answers that Mary and her work provided. She has become a beacon for me, both personally and professionally, and I want to share some of her light with you. Her work shows that dignity, joy, and meaning can be derived from the home arts, whether it is cooking a meal for one's family, mending a child's romper, making a cute apron as a gift, indulging oneself with a fashionable kimono, or just trying to be a better friend, neighbor, wife, daughter, sister or mother.

At heart, this book is a celebration of what women can do, with just

their own two hands and together as a united community, reaching across great divides. Mary's work and legacy inspired women to form "Institute Clubs" all over the world as women found one another through classified ads. They wrote independently to the Newsletter's editors to request introductions to other women so that they could learn from each other, share experiences and find valuable business contacts (our modern Facebook). Mary's example encouraged these women to look inside their lives, take the skills that they had developed (the only skills that at the time were available to many of them), and use those talents to broaden and enrich their lives. Despite the many opportunities that are now open to us, the desires of American women today are surprisingly in tune with our female forebears: family, friends and fulfilling work—and maybe a good lipstick and the perfect dinner dress!

In this book, I have recaptured a period of time when women used sewing as the springboard to independence, financial security, and self-esteem. In the process, they discovered self-confidence in their work, a wealth of resources and common bonds with women all over the world, and a simple philosophy for living a fulfilling life. While we have come a long way since these magazines went to press in the 1920s, that does not mean we have moved beyond what the women in these pages have to offer; in fact, we are lucky to follow in their footsteps. Each department in *Vintage Notions* tells a different side of the story of what it means to be a busy, creative woman, then and now, with the similarities far outweighing the differences.

I hope that the body of Mary Brooks Picken's work—and the philosophy and wisdom behind it—will resonate in your life the way it has in mine.

Enjoy!

Amy B.

Mary Brooks Picken and the Woman's Institute

1850 Sewing machines become available for home use with the American invention of the hand-cranked (and later the foot-powered) machines, introduced by F. Elias Howe, Jr., and a few years' later perfected by Isaac Merritt Singer.

1860s Tissue paper patterns are commercially introduced by Ebenezer Butterick, the tailor behind the famous Butterick patterns. A decade later his company produced almost six million patterns annually.

1870 Eight western colleges open their doors to women; as a result, female enrollment in public universities increases by 1000 percent—which still only comes out to about 7.6 percent of all women being educated at the collegiate level.

1877 Sewing machines begin to become affordable for the first time—in 1856, a Singer cost about $125 when the average annual income was $500. By 1902, consumers could purchase a Minnesota brand machine for $23.20 from Sears, Roebuck and Co.

1886 On a farm near Arcadia, Kansas, an ingenious little seamstress named Mary Brooks is born. Her grandmother taught her sewing at a very early age. Her youth and young adulthood are spent with needle and thread in various sewing classes. From girlhood on, she was intensely interested in sewing and decided to make sewing and the teaching of sewing her profession. She attended and graduated from seven schools of dressmaking in Kansas City, Boston, and New York.

1890 The Women's Suffrage Movement begins with the formation of the National American Women Suffrage Association (NAWSA) under the leadership of Elizabeth Cady Stanton.

1891 Thomas J. Foster founds the International Correspondence Schools (ICS), making the postage stamp a new form of tuition, and education a new possibility for students all over the United States.

1906 Mary Brooks officially begins her firsthand domestic education when she ties the knot to Harry Picken; the newlywed settles in Kansas City and teaches sewing courses at the YWCA and to female inmates at the Leavenworth Penitentiary.

1911 Big changes for Mary Brooks Picken when she is suddenly widowed and appointed instructor at the American College of Dressmaking in Kansas City; by this year, over 632 high schools in America had incorporated domestic courses into the curriculum as the female equivalent of industrial education; the ICS follows suit with plans to develop domestic courses as part of its curriculum.

1914 Mary Brooks Picken packs her bags (perfectly, we're sure) for Scranton, PA, after being recruited by the ICS; always a busy bee, within two years Picken has written 64 textbooks and developed two dressmaking courses. In 1916 Dorothy Harmeling (shown below) is the first of 3,022 students to enroll in the newly established Woman's Institute in Scranton. The Institute has its first advertisement in *McCall's* magazine—and 4,000 women immediately respond. The Institute's mission is stated to be "for the purpose of making a practical knowledge of the domestic arts and sciences available to every woman or girl, wherever she may live."

1918 The first Woman's Institute book, *The Secrets of Distinctive Dress* by Mary Brooks Picken is published and sells more than 125,000 copies.

1920 A monthly newsletter, *Inspiration*, a "magazine devoted to the advancement and encouragement of the students," is introduced. Mary Brooks Picken is the editor and the magazine was free upon enrollment. It is shortly joined by its sister publication *Fashion Service*, a quarterly illustrated guide to current fashion. She edited these magazines from 1920 to 1925, contributing numerous articles and essays.

1920 We get the vote! Women receive the right to vote as the Nineteenth Amendment to the Constitution. Despite these advancements, less than ten percent of married women work outside the home.

1921 Educators, artists, and the governor himself gather in Scranton, Pennsylvania, for the dedication of The Woman's Institute's new million-dollar structure, calling it the "largest Woman's college in the world"; more than 125,000 women from the US, Canada, and abroad are now enrolled.

1920s The Woman's Institute continues to flourish with Mary Brooks Picken as vice president and director of instruction overseeing three hundred teachers and the only woman on the board of twelve. By this time, the Institute had enrolled more than 253,000 women and girls in one or more of its courses in sewing, dressmaking, designing, millinery, and cookery. This is close to the same amount as the total number of women enrolled in all American colleges and universities.

1925 Picken leaves the Woman's Institute for New York to work as a dressmaking editor for a popular magazine, *Pictorial Review*. She makes frequent trips to Europe to report on Paris fashion openings, filing her stories by telegram. After her departure, the Institute experiences a downturn in her absence.

1926 The number of home seamstresses continues to grow, as 98 percent of rural and 92 percent of urban households polled this year now own sewing machines; with this growth, the Institute club programs are growing all over the world, with the city of Chicago boasting the most home clubs.

Tenth Anniversary of The Woman's Institute 1916 - 1926

1928 Picken establishes a studio where she holds classes on fashion and fabric styling for employees of department stores and fabric manufacturers. In the same year, it is announced by The Woman's Institute that the Institute's "two splendid magazines will be rolled into one."

MARY BROOKS PICKEN
Fashion and Fabric Studio
16 Park Avenue
New York, N. Y.

1930s The crisis of the Great Depression and war shortages renew interest in sewing; however, these changes aren't lasting, as women continue to work outside the home and ready-made clothing becomes the timesaving solution for busy women.

1931 Mary Brooks Picken remarries, to former Woman's Institute vice president G. Lynn Sumner. She leaves the Institute to begin a brilliant career in advertising with clients including Singer Sewing, Dennison Crafts, and The Spool Cotton Company.

1937 The Woman's Institute officially closes its doors, drawing to a close one of the most remarkable periods in domestic arts education of American women.

1939 Picken founds the Mary Brooks Picken School on Madison Avenue in New York. In the same year, she publishes *The Language of Fashion: A Dictionary and Digest of Fabric, Sewing, and Dress*, the first comprehensive guide and reference book on fashion.

1949 Mary Brooks Picken authors her most widely distributed book, *The Singer Sewing Book*, and over the years sells more than 8 million copies.

1960 Mary's weekly syndicated column reaches 300 newspapers.

1981 Mary Brooks Picken passes away.

Modern Notions

There's nothing so wonderful as a fresh start. For me, ringing in the New Year, with all its attendant streamers and confetti, is more about the chance to recommit to the life I want to lead than a night of wild revelry. So it heartens me that in these pages Mary Brooks Picken consistently advises her students that do-overs *do* apply and that our happiness is not contingent on getting things right the first time.

Just like remodeling a worn-out shirt into an apron (this month's *Magic Pattern)*, January resolutions offer us the chance to refashion our lives. The business I am in relies on constant reinvention and the creative process is never perfect, but always evolving. As the busy mother of grade-school-age children, the same formula is true—children will make many mistakes along the way and it's up to me to retain a sense of calm and happiness when faced with the "do-overs" of the younger set, since everything is a fresh start in their lives.

So many women found in the correspondence courses of-fered by The Woman's Institute that *exact* fresh start they needed in life. Some found not a second chance but a *first* chance, their very first opportunity to work and provide for their families and themselves, and all under the gentle, guiding hand of Mary Brooks Picken and her instructors.

Like Mary, my own career path has been in publishing material related to the domestic arts, especially needle-crafts and sewing. The advancement of modern technology in my business has connected me to a large universe of women who enjoy the same things I do. Just like the women who communicated with each other and the Institute regularly, I also receive modern testimonials from women who enjoy my publications and offerings—it's just that today their messages arrive instantly.

In these pages we celebrate all the best things about the domestic arts. In January, the Institute instructors teach us how to make the perfect soup stock for those cold Winter afternoons. Follow easy instructions to make your beauty ritual salon-worthy and learn how to remodel men's shirts into useful, colorful aprons. Mary Brooks Picken also reminds us in her essay *A Thimbleful of Happiness* that being grateful should always be a part of our plan for happiness: "For surely, when we are happy, we are successful, at least in that little domain where we are queen." How grateful I am for the path forged by Mary Brooks Picken and the feeling of empowerment that I've inherited from her.

Happy New Year,

Amy B.

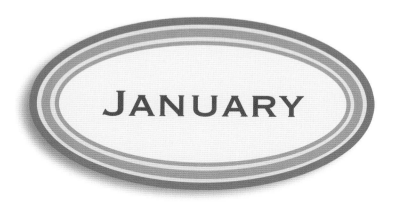

JANUARY

Happiness needs no accessories,
for it is in itself omnipotent.
It takes hold in the heart,
builds its nest, and brings forth
its own birds to sing for you.

—*Mary Brooks Picken*

A Thimbleful of Happiness

Builders for Eternity
A New Year's Message

by Mary Brooks Picken
From *Thimblefuls of Friendliness*, January 1924

"Isn't it strange that Princes and Kings
And clowns that caper in sawdust rings,
And just plain folk like you and me,
Are builders for Eternity?
To each is given a bag of tools,
A shapeless mass and a book of rules;
And each must make ere life is flown,
A stumbling block or a stepping stone?"

I heard a young woman say the other day, "Oh, I give up. What's the use of my trying to be anybody or trying to have nice things? My ambitions only make me restless and miserable."

But we all know that ambitions once entertained are hard to lose. The farther you come from attaining them, the more miserable you will be. Hence the need of continual effort.

To the woman who says, "What's the use?" one might say: "What's the use of working, of washing the dishes, of getting up in the mornings, of liking air and sunshine and pretty things?"

There isn't any real use, perhaps, in it all, but it is oh so satisfying, to go into a kitchen to cook dinner where everything is happily clean and in place.

What a satisfying, luxurious feeling it is to crawl into a well-made cozy bed.

What a delight it is to don fresh, clean clothing.

What a self-respecting feeling one has when one puts on a well-made dress that is appropriate and becoming.

All these things take time and effort, but they pay double in sheer pleasure.

And we should use our energies to make happiness come for every effort, pleasure for every thought that we give to family, home, or clothing, and thus make of all our responsibilities stepping stones to success, via happiness.

For surely, when we are happy, we are successful, at least in that little domain where we are queen. No matter what our environment, no matter what our circumstances—a singing tea kettle, a cozy fire, some one to care for, some one to care, a conscience that does not disturb—all these help in our walk up the steps to divine contentment.

For some of us it may seem a long journey, but trying makes it interesting. And we have the satisfaction all the way of having done our best with our "bag of tools," our "shapeless mass," and "book of rules."

So let's make a new start, filled with joy and anticipation of the year ahead, determined to face those stepping stones and stumbling blocks that come our way, and to try to do our best.

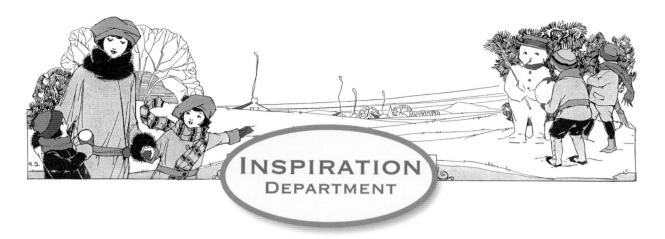

Getting A New Start

by Gustave L. Weinss, *Inspiration*, January 1920

"The determination to try again is without doubt the greatest factor for success in the lives of all whose achievements are noteworthy."

The courage, indomitable spirit, to start again after disappointments, losses, failures, and disasters has made possible the success of individuals, the perfection of institutions, the reconstruction of cities, the restoration of nations.

So we can do well to bear these things in mind as we make our pilgrimage through life, for just as an oasis permits the desert traveler to refresh himself on his way, so will a new start enable us to go on our way encouraged, reinvigorated, and determined to dare and do.

So, as the New Year advances, let us all try to recognize and utilize the wonderful possibilities of getting a new start. A new start will help us to bear our trials and tribulations and overcome them. It will soothe and conquer our fears and worries. It will help us deliver ourselves from indifference and inspire us to real endeavor. It will instill in us the courage and determination to win. It will urge us on in the performance of acts and deeds that will be for the betterment of ourselves and thereby for the betterment of those who associate with us.

Model 3

3 C

Hats for the Season

by Mary Mahon, *Inspiration*, 1928

A medium roseglow Bakou body with a notched brim, is trimmed with ornate designs of several tones of brown, a touch of red, and a tracery of gold thread applied on its side crown and top brim.

The staple combination of satin and pedaline, with floral spray of brilliants, occurs in this hat for immediate wear. The pedaline brim droops low on the left side and turns up against the crown on the right.

In designing a successful hat, the principle requirements are that it shall be comfortable, easy to wear, well balanced from every angle, appropriate for the occasion, and suited to the figure of the wearer. Then comes the adjuncts of style, becomingness, and beauty. While each of these elements figures largely in the development of a hat, suiting the hat to the figure probably deserves the greatest attention. The shape, size, and line should be decided on while one is standing before a mirror large enough to reflect the entire figure. Then the hat may be studied from all angles—straight front, profile, side back, direct back, and side front.

3 A

Cote de toile, a crocheted yedda body in Lucerne blue, has crown incrustations of taffeta and a narrow brim, slashed and draped in a smart over-one-eye movement, drawing the side close to the head.

This large cart-wheel felt capeline partakes of two shadow tones of green, the darker making the brim flange and cutout oak-leaf design of the crown. A tiny scarf of chiffon encircles the crown base.

3 B

| (a) | (b) | (c) | (d) |

FIG. 2

Practical lines in hats for unusual types; (a) and (b), the tall, thin type, and (c) and (d), the large, stout type

INSTRUCTION DEPARTMENT

Accessories of Fur or Fabric

Fashion Service, January 1929

The softening touch of fur characterizes the newest costume accessories. Nor need it be real fur, for, following the fashion for coats of fur fabrics, the smartest shops are showing scarves, muffs, and hats of good imitation pelts along with the real. These accessories will be very useful, too, in the spring with suits and dresses.

Almost every one has a few scraps of fur left from trimmings or good parts from a worn coat that can be utilized for accessories, such as those pictured here. The furs that are appropriate and have style value at present are mole, black, gray, or tan caracul, krimmer, barunduki, ermine, summer ermine, curly caracul, squirrel, leopard, shaved lamb, American broadtail, and nutria. Notice that all of these are comparatively flat furs. In the absence of these, use smart fur fabrics.

The diagrams show the shapes of these accessories, all of which are lined with matching silk crepe. The new muffs are very small, nine to eleven inches across. They are padded slightly, but not heavily as in the past. Wool batting, such as is used for comforters, is excellent for this use.

4 D

4 E

4 C

4 B

4 F

Be the Best of Whatever You Are
Inspiration, 1923

If you can't be a pine on the top of the hill,
    Be a scrub in the valley—but be
The best little scrub at the side of the hill;
    Be a bush if you can't be a tree.
If you can't be a bush, be a bit of the green,
    Some highway to happier make,
If you can't be a muskie, then just be a bass—
    But the liveliest bass in the lake.
We can't all be captains, we've got to be crew,
    There's something for all of us here;
There's big work to do, and there's lesser to do,
    And the task we must do is near.
If you can't be a highway, then just be a trail,
    If you can't be the sun, be a star;
It isn't by size that you win or you fail—
    Be the best of whatever you are.

—**Douglas Malloch**

Those who win are those who work and keep on trying. They are just average persons like you or me, or, as Charles Bartlett says, they are "not built on any particular plan nor blessed with any peculiar luck; they are just steady and earnest and full of pluck." But those who win must work for their success. That is the secret. So, you see, no person has a monopoly on the ability to be successful. This is as free as the air we breathe.

New Year's Resolutions
by Barbara Ellison, *Inspiration, 1920*

Buy wisely, and unless you have definite use for an article, do not buy it. Wait until your wardrobe is definitely assembled in your own mind and everything "fits in," hat, shoes, gloves, purse, not to mention stockings and slips.

Be slim by being trim, be attractive by being immaculate. See that the seams of your stockings run straight and the heels of your shoes never run over. Keep your gloves clean. Never allow spots to mar your clothes nor perspiration to deface a gown. And never allow your shoulder straps to protrude. You can keep them out of sight by sewing one end of a ribbon or a piece of bias tape to the shoulder. Fasten it with a snap at the other end; then snap it around the straps of your undergarments.

One of the greatest virtues of the right clothes, rightly worn, is that they enable us to forget them and ourselves. When they are right enough for us to do this, we become our most likable and natural selves and, even if your features are not perfect nor perfectly assembled, we may some day hear of ourselves in one of those sibilant whispers that so audibly clothe a spoken confidence, "What a charming woman!"

Soup-Making Secrets

by Laura MacFarlane, *Inspiration*, 1923

Soup has its place in the meal in that it stimulates the appetite and aids in the flow of digestive juices.

It was the coldest day of the season up to that time. All the way home in the car, remarks about the weather could be heard floating back and forth . . . Some persons were happy about it, and others, of course, were very much annoyed. But the remark that appealed to me most came from a high-school girl who, in the midst of the discussion about the merits of the high-school play that had been presented, burst out with "Gee, I hope mother has soup tonight. I just love hot soup on a night like this, don't you, Frances?"

When I stopped to think it over, I realized that she was right. When the mercury is hovering around the zero mark, nothing seems to "touch the spot" like a bowl of steaming, appetizing soup. So this month I decided to discuss with you some of the secrets of successful soups, so that if that high-school girl was yours, she would not be disappointed when she returned "hungry as a hound" at the end of her strenuous day.

Without doubt, the soup course of a meal is neglected oftener than any other. Many housewives omit soup altogether, which is indeed unfortunate, for soup has its place in the meal, in that it stimulates the appetite and aids in the flow of the digestive juices. And appetizing soup is not at all difficult to make if one just understands the underlying principles and applies them properly. In addition, soup is often a real economy, for it can utilize materials that might otherwise be wasted.

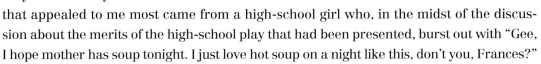

Basics

1. If one intends to serve soup often, a stock pot made of either enamel or earthen-ware should be procured.

2. Here should be put the bones from the cooked roast, the trimmings cut from it before it was put in the oven, the tough ends and bones of beefsteak, the carcasses of fowls, together with any remains of stuffing and tough or left-over bits of meats, left-over vegetables, any gravy or unsweetened sauces used for meats and vegetables, the water in which rice, macaroni, or certain vegetables have been cooked, and so on.

3. Great care should be exercised, however, to keep the stock pot scrupulously clean, for nothing is more undesirable than a utensil of this kind if proper attention is not given to it. Frequently, it should be thoroughly emptied, thoroughly washed, and then exposed to the air to dry.

4. Should meat be purchased expressly for soup making, the tough cuts, such as the shin, the shank, the lower part of the round, the neck, the flank, the shoulder, the tail, and the brisket are preferable to the tender ones.

5. As far as vegetables are concerned, those which provide the most flavor should be selected, and these include cabbage, cauliflower, asparagus, corn, onions, turnips, carrots, parsnips, tomatoes, beans, peas, lentils, salsify, potatoes, spinach, celery, mushrooms, and okra.

6. The flavoring of the stock is an extremely important part of soup making. Cloves, peppercorns, red, black, and white pepper, paprika, bay leaf, sage, marjoram, thyme, summer savory, tarragon, celery seed, fennel, mint, and rosemary are the flavorings most desired. In addition, Worcestershire sauce is a very valuable flavoring, and celery, parsley, and onions are much used.

7. As a greasy soup is always unpalatable, an effort should be made to remove as much of the grease from it as possible. If the soup is hot, a large part of the grease may be skimmed off with a spoon and the rest then removed with clean blotting paper, tissue paper, or absorbent cotton. If the soup is allowed to become cold, the fat, which collects on top, will harden and it can then be removed by merely lifting off the cake that forms.

8. And soups, regardless of their nature, should never repeat any of the foods of your menu. For instance, don't serve chicken soup if chicken is your entrée meat, nor tomato soup, if this is the basis of your salad or vegetable course.

Stocks

The foundation of the majority of soups is known as stock. Every one who aspires to the making of appetizing soups should therefore be familiar with several kinds of stocks. A stock that is suitable for *clear soups or bouillon* has beef for its basis, is flavored with such flavorings as onion, cloves, peppercorns, parsley, celery and bay leaves, and contains the usual flavorings, salt and pepper. A somewhat more economical stock, called *household stock*, is made from merely the trimmings of fresh meat, bones, and tough pieces from roasts, steaks, etc. Then there is *white stock*, which is made from veal and fowl and seasoned with onion, celery, and mace, and which is used for soups that you wish to be particularly dainty and delicious.

Some time ago, I attended a luncheon at which such delicious cream-of-tomato soup was served that the memory of it still lingers with me. Soup of this kind—and in fact all cream soups—are so easily made that no one needs to forgo the pleasure of starting a meal with one of them. They consist merely of a thin white sauce, which is properly seasoned and to which are added such vegetables as potatoes, corn, asparagus, peas, onions, or tomatoes in the form of puree or cut into small pieces.

Quick Tomato Soup

To one pint of stewed tomato, add one pint of water, one slice of onion, a level teaspoonful of salt and a half teaspoonful of pepper. While this is coming to a boil, rub smoothly together one tablespoonful of butter with two of flour. Stir this into the boiling soup, let boil up again, strain and serve.

Cream of Tomato Soup

(serves 4)

1 cup canned tomatoes
1 pt. milk
3 tbls. flour
3 tbls. butter
1 tsp. salt
1/8 tsp. pepper

Force the tomatoes through a sieve and heat them. Make white sauce of the milk, flour, and butter. Pour the tomatoes slowly into the white sauce, stirring rapidly. If the sauce begins to curdle, beat the soup quickly with a rotary egg beater. Add the salt and pepper and serve.

The ABC's of Good Looks

by Marilyn Madison, *Inspiration*, January 1925

When we are sixteen, we desire prettiness; ten years later, good looks. A refreshing appearance, however, is much more essential than either, and if we would present ourselves to the world, as all-around, modern women, we must keep up on all matters of dress and personal grooming, as well as on home arts, children, literature, politics, etc. In our innermost hearts, however, it is the personal element that counts, and we would much rather have compliments for our attractiveness than for our brilliancy any day. And why not? There are yet a few old-time feminine sentiments left, and that's one of them.

I know you have all read the advertisement which reads: "Your complexion tomorrow is a result of the three minutes you devote to it tonight." Whoever inspired that line actually knew of the merits of three minutes' night-time care, for it's wholly true.

All the beauty specialists with creams and lotions to sell insist on: "No soap, no water, just delicate creams gently rubbed in and off and then a skin tonic to freshen."

This is fine for train travel or for camping, but when you want to look "fit as a fiddle," give your face a good scrubbing the night before and use a barrel of water to rinse the soap off.

When you have finished cleansing the face, have an orange stick handy; wrap one end with cotton, dip it in cuticle remover, and run it around the base of and underneath the nails, pushing the cuticle back and cleansing the nail thoroughly. Then rub on a little white Vaseline to make them smooth and shiny.

With the hands taken care of, pat the face gently with a bit of cold cream, and remember that housework and soft white hands keep company only when the latter are rinsed and softened by a suitable hand lotion after each adventure into pan or tub. Before sleeping, brush the hair, be it short or long, at least fifty times. That's only half as many strokes as most beauty doctors recommend, but positively no less will do if your hair is to look alive and clean.

In the morning, wash the face with cold

water for color and wide-awakeness. Clean the teeth thoroughly. Pat in a little cold cream all over the face and neck, wiping any surplus away and then rinsing the face again with cold water. Dust the body with talcum, and you will be ready to sit down in front of your mirror to make your face and hair ready for the day.

A delicate use of cosmetics is desirable; a burlesque-type use is vulgar and detracts a hundred times more than it adds. Too much rouge, too much powder, like chewing gum, is seldom evidenced by a woman of refinement. Keep folks guessing; don't tell your secret. Rouge so cleverly that every one will wonder whether your color is real.

 ## Here are some basics to follow:

1. Comb out your hair and brush it lightly. If you have curlers in the night before, the amount of combing and brushing should be measured by the length of hair and the "permanency of the wave." Next, pin the hair back out of the way and give attention to the face.

2. A little rouge, oh, so little, is allowable. A tangerine color, the best beauty folks say, is good for all complexions. If the skin is very white, the chin may also have a little.

3. Now powder the face and neck thoroughly, but don't "load" the powder on. Dust it smoothly just as though you were putting sugar on a jelly roll, and not as though you were icing a cake.

4. Then, if your eyes need it, touch a wee, wet brush to a little pad of mascara and brush the eyelashes lightly.

5. Put your clothes on carefully, stockings straight, corsets well-pulled down with plenty of supporters, and be sure that your shoes are neat and well kept.

6. After breakfast, brush your teeth again, wiping the mouth very clean, and apply a little lip rouge as needed. Always apply it with the tip of your finger, for then you will not be liable to use too much.

7. Finally, brush your clothes and step out into the world, full of assurance that you are a good example of a type of woman worthy of the deference accorded your sex and a credit to your sisters, no matter where or how you meet them.

RE-MODEL,
RE-CYCLE, RE-USE:

How to Remodel Past-Season Frocks

by Alwilda Fellows,
Inspiration, 1923

A season or more ago, a mere scanning of a fashion magazine would oftentimes suggest a number of remodeling possibilities for a dress. For the thrifty and clever home dressmaker, makeovers are never out of the running. She is well aware of the fact that there is almost always use for good materials in pieces of any appreciable size and is not content to lay away a garment for another season until, by careful planning, she is convinced that the result will not justify her effort. And this is a point well worth considering. Do not remodel a dress simply for the sake of using the material; rather, consider how well satisfied you will be with the result and whether you will get sufficient wear and enjoyment from the dress.

Sometimes a dress that has a bedraggled and ordinary appearance needs but a thorough cleaning and one or two up-to-the-minute touches to give it a new lease on life. A bertha collar, such as the one shown at the upper left in the illustration, or lace or lingerie panel-collar pieces are bound to make a decided change in the appearance of a costume. The addition of lower puffed-sleeve sections of net, chiffon, Georgette, or lace, or a fabric or novelty girdle would also prove effective.

One means of overcoming the handicap of a short skirt that has not sufficient hem allowance to provide the desired length, is to split the skirt crosswise in one or more places and insert pin-tucked or plain bands of material or a wide band of lace. The manner in which lace is oftentimes employed in bouffant evening frocks is shown in the sketch just below the bertha collar.

A means of converting a two-piece suit into a so-called three-piece model is suggested by the design at the upper center. By cutting the skirt off at the top, you may dispose of pocket slits, or if the skirt, even with a facing, has not sufficient length to permit this, you may extend the braid or embroidery design over the slits in the material. Crepe de Chine or Canton crepe in a light or bright color or one that matches the suit would be a good selection for the contrasting material.

Possibilities for the ever-popular combination of blue and black wool and black satin are offered in the model at the lower left, although any other pleasing combination of colors and materials might be employed to advantage in this same design.

A one-piece evening wrap or a street coat made up in a suitable material might be converted into a very smart frock similar to the one shown at the lower right. The front opening may be cleverly disposed of in the skirt by parting the edges ever so slightly to reveal a band of contrasting material. This same material might provide a narrow vest and sleeve trimming in the waist portion as well as an inserted band to lengthen the skirt portion. Tinsel embroidery in darning- or couching-stitches decorates the contrasting material and may be likewise used to cover a pocket slip, as shown. If you follow these suggestions for remodeling a coat or dress, it will be necessary to make the sleeves and armhole portions in accordance to the original cut of the garment, or to supply sleeves of a new material.

At the lower center, portions of a dress which are too small to be used to advantage with another material in the making of an entire frock have been put to good service in the development of a blouse. A style of special make-over merit shows the upper sleeve portions, collar and reverse facings, narrow side panels, and hip band being of plain material and the remainder of the blouse of a figured fabric.

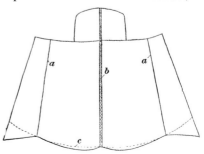

Magic Pattern

Men's Shirts Put to Feminine Use

by Margaret Murrin, *Inspiration*, 1925

When remodeling, the end in view is the accomplishment of something of use or beauty, but when use and beauty are combined, the result is doubly worth the effort put toward it. Such a result may be had in making use of the unworn parts of the discarded shirts of the masculine members of the family for aprons cut, trimmed, and finished as shown.

 See Notes, on page 232, for modern tips and techniques.

Perhaps many of you have already made one apron from a shirt without realizing that careful planning will make it possible to cut two plenty large enough for the average woman. To do this, make use of the sleeves for one apron and the body of the shirt for another.

The apron shown at the upper center of the illustration is made from the sleeves. To make this, rip the sleeves out of the shirt, but do not rip the sleeve seams. Instead, cut the sleeves directly up from the placket opening so they may be laid out flat, as shown in Fig. 1, where the seams are represented by *a*. Then join

Fig. 1

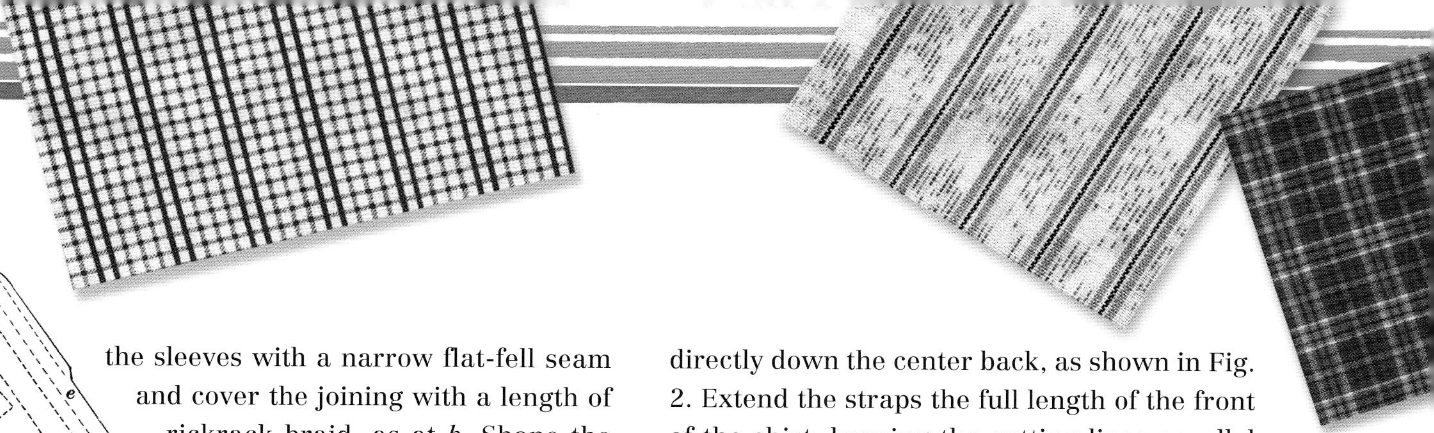

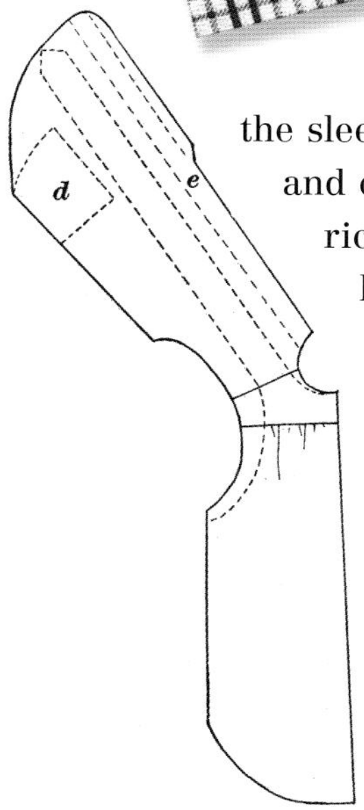

the sleeves with a narrow flat-fell seam and cover the joining with a length of rickrack braid, as at *b*. Shape the lower edge by trimming off the bottom to form a curve, as at *c*. Cut a bib from the lower part of the fronts of the shirt, as indicated in both Fig. 2 and Fig. 3 by the sections marked *d*, and attach this as shown in the diagram, using a flat-fell seam covered with rickrack.

If you do not care for rickrack as a means of finishing the outer edge of the apron, use bias tape applied as a facing. If you use the rickrack, make a very narrow turn to the right side, on the edge of the apron, and baste it in place; then baste and stitch the rickrack over it, concealing the raw edges.

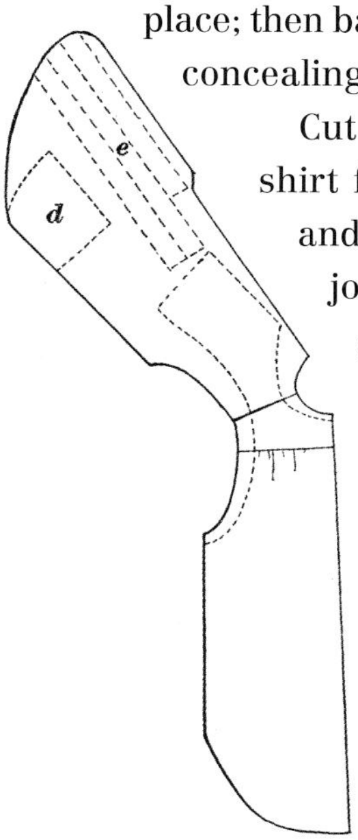

Cut strings for this apron from the shirt fronts, as at *e*, Fig. 2 and Fig. 3, and after stitching and turning them, join them securely to the apron. The garment is then complete and ready for wear.

In order to make the apron shown to the left of the group, rip the sleeves out of the shirt and rip the underarm seams of the shirt, and spread it flat on your cutting table with a fold

FIG. 2

FIG. 3

directly down the center back, as shown in Fig. 2. Extend the straps the full length of the front of the shirt, keeping the cutting lines parallel with the center-front line, and trimming off the ends in a point as shown.

Still another type of apron, one that has a back section extending to the waist line and that can be cut from the body part of the shirt without ripping the shoulder seams, is shown at the right of the group. This apron is preferred by many women, since it is buttoned on the sides.

In preparation for cutting, rip the underarm seam of the shirt after removing the sleeves, and place it flat on the table as shown in Fig. 3. Adjust your pattern with its center-front on the center-back fold and cut. Notice that the center-back line of the apron pattern is on a slant, making a bias seam at this point. Use a French seam for this joining, and finish the outer edges of the apron in any of the ways described. Or use a bias facing in a contrasting color, first stitched with its right side to the wrong side of the apron, then brought over to the right side so that the seam line is directly on the edge, and, with the raw edge turned in, stitched down flat.

Dressing Up Your Wintertime Table

by Laura MacFarlane, *Inspiration*, January 1923

It's all well and good to say that if you serve good, hot food, your table will be a popular place. But how much more charm and individuality your meals will have and how much more real enjoyment you'll afford your family and your guests if you dress up your table for your everyday as well as your company meals.

Orange Baskets

When invited to participate in the table arrangement contest at a flower show, the orange baskets we created for the luncheon table drew the most attention. We chose fruit for our first course and served it in these orange baskets on very unusual pottery plates. Passersby wanted to know just how these fruit baskets were made. To make them, choose rather large oranges and arrange them to have the ends of the orange as

1.   2.

the top of your baskets. Cut around the sides, a little above the center and leave at opposite sides about 1/2-inch of fruit uncut to form the handle. Cut from this point on each side over to the other side, where you have left the side uncut. Repeat on both sides to form the handle. Strip off the two wedges of skin and loosen the pulp very carefully from the skin, removing it in sections. Scallop the edges of the basket with a pair of scissors. Add an airy bow of tulle to carry out the desired color scheme of your table. When ready to serve, fill the bowl of the basket with fruit cocktail, using the pieces of orange, banana, pears, pineapple and a hint of lemon juice and powdered sugar mixed in to the fruit. Top with a Maraschino cherry.

Testimonials

Remodeling Pays Her Back

A woman from Idaho wrote this inspiring letter to the *Fashion Service* editors:

"My husband has been foreman on a large stock ranch while the cooking and cleaning were left to me. I have also raised a nice flock of poultry, besides keeping a large house in order and caring for two small children, and in addition I have made $30 sewing for others. I think I have done splendidly for one year's work. But I've been happy and content though it all.

"You should see the remodeling I have done. I took an old worn coat of mine, cleaned it and used the under side as the right side and made a nice warm, good-looking overcoat for my six-year-old school boy. I also remodeled a crepe dress for myself, and I have made several men's shirts this year. I am getting so I can put one together in a very short time, and they are as neat and correctly made as the ready-made shirts in the store."

Yet another student writes from Massachusetts:

"My sewing is coming along better every day. I have done a little outside work and had only pleasant returns from it. If I could only sew all day, I would be perfectly happy.

"As we are going on a short vacation soon, I am making clothes for Sonny and for myself, and my old cast-offs are coming in very handy to make him some lovely little overalls, and a brown velvet blouse of mine, out of style completely, is going to make him a nice coat.

"Whenever I see some one cast aside a garment, I want to say, 'Give it to me; I can use it some way,' for nothing goes to waste now."

Modern Notions

Valentine's Day has always been one of the leading paper craft holidays—and who knew you could have so much fun with just a few paper doilies and red construction paper! At my grade school it was tradition to take an afternoon off just before the holiday to hand-make each and every card we delivered, as well as a personalized valentine "shoebox" made of construction paper, magazine clippings, glue and glitter. In those days, the joy of giving a valentine was equal to the joy of receiving one—well, most of the time.

One of my favorite things about valentine exchanges is the rich history behind the holiday. I just adore that a day is devoted solely to the celebration of love and continues to thrive in a country busy with so many other everyday activities. With the fast pace of modern life, we all know the exchange of a valentine can be as easy as a trip to the local supermarket—but love is just too special to be left to the manufacturers. While evidence of valentine exchanges goes all the way back to the 1400s, it wasn't until the 1800s that commercial valentines were manufactured en masse. I often see remnants of these early keepsakes at antique stores and auctions and marvel at the artisan quality that seemed to be the norm then.

So grab your sweethearts, whether they are great gal-pals or the little ones in your life, and get snipping and gluing—Cupid is ready for his annual entrance. When it comes time to pass your work on to your special someone, they'll appreciate the extra time it took you to truly give a little of your own heart.

Speaking of hearts, in this month's *A Thimbleful of Love*, Mary Brooks Picken celebrates love of a non-romantic kind—the love and adoration of a family member whose steadfast kindness left a lasting impression on young Mary. She recalls an uncle nicknamed "Uncle Like," who gave his love with such abandon and in such abundance that Mary recalls how she and her sisters could be open and honest with him.

Other things that may come in handy when it comes to matters of the heart? Lingerie, perfume, and homemade pie are all part of this month's offerings. As the *Department of Fashion* says, "Every woman has a warm place in her heart for pretty under things." I'm fairly certain members of both sexes hold a warm place in their hearts for pretty under things. For this Valentine's Day, see the instructions in this chapter on creating your own charming lingerie. Check out the *Department of Good Looks*, for the virtues of perfumes and the *Department of Cookery* for the "Secrets of a Perfect Pie." Pies are definitely a way of showing love in my family. My son Jack can't get enough of my mother's wonderfully tart Michigan Cherry Pie. When she makes this family favorite we all appreciate her love for the domestic arts—and her fondness for pleasing those she loves.

Yours,

Amy B.

FEBRUARY

The language of the heart—
the language which "comes from the heart"
and "goes to the heart"—is always simple,
always graceful, and always full of power...

—Bovee

A Thimbleful of Love

The Understanding Heart

by Mary Brooks Picken
Excerpted from *Thimblefuls of Friendliness*, 1924

Emerson wrote, "Oh, the comfort, the inexpressible comfort of feeling safe with a person—having neither to weigh thought nor measure words, but pouring them all right out just as they are, chaff and grain together, certain that a faithful hand will take and sift them, keep what is worth keeping, and with the breath of kindness blow the rest away."

How many people do you know who are like that? How many have we ever known with whom we felt entirely free, with whom we could think aloud, with whom we could talk without being misunderstood, challenged, or discountenanced. But how we do cherish those friendships which have for their basis that perfect understanding which makes guarded expressions and tedious explanations unnecessary.

Nothing influences the soul for good more than an understanding heart. In my life the finest example of this is a great uncle, the good man who brought up my mother. It was not his experience in living, his money, nor his ability that caused my grandmother to ask him, her brother-in-law, in his youth, to look after her six children when she knew the end was near. It was because she knew his heart that she left him such a trust. He accepted it and never married, but devoted his life to bringing up these children. My mother was the baby, and when she grew up and married, this dear old uncle lived with her and my father.

Many remarked on the unselfishness of this man, on how much he, as an individual, sacrificed in giving his life to these, his older brother's children. But he never seemed to sense any sacrifice, and no man ever had children or grandchildren of his own who loved him more devotedly than did my brothers and sisters and myself.

He was the only elderly person in our family, aside from my grandmother, and when I see old people outliving their usefulness and being tolerated by their children, when I see middle-aged people growing older and considering only their own selfish interests or inclinations, I realize more and more the greatness of the man we lovingly called "Uncle Like."

Often, as a little girl, I thought of him and what it was about him that we all loved so much. As the years pass, I realize that it was his understanding, his concern for our feelings, his appreciation of our weaknesses. When we were rebuked at school, were "spelled down," when we stubbed our toes, skinned our knees, it was his often unspoken, understanding friendliness that helped us adjust ourselves to the humiliation or the pain.

It was his interest in our good grades and his excuses for our poor ones that made us run to him with our report cards and led us to be honest in reading the percentages, which he could not see. It was his understanding that made us feel free to tell him that we were afraid to put the worm on the hook when fishing and ask him to do it, to feel free to go to him with an empty cup when wild-strawberry hunting and confess that the reason we did not have any was that we had eaten all that we picked.

This uncle has been gone many years; yet even now, when our family is together, we talk of him longingly, for the principles that he believed in are in our hearts, and his friendship still inspires and directs us. He never scolded nor spoke unkindly, never criticized; yet we knew that his standards meant that every piece of candy, every apple, should be equally shared; that a lie never could be hidden, that we must confess before we could be absolved. When we were in trouble, he was willing that we should hide behind his chair, but his lap always invited us to come around front, and we knew that the only way we could do that was to tell him all about it. The life of "Uncle Like" to me is proof that good does not die.

"The influence of an understanding heart will live forever because through such influence comes the permanence of life and love."
—Mary Brooks Picken

Every Woman's House...Her Castle

by Mary Brooks Picken, 1924

Not long ago I went to visit a woman who lived in what she called her "little shotgun house"—three rooms straight in a row like the barrel of a gun—and I have never been more sincerely and joyously welcomed. I never saw a cleaner house, or two happier people than my friend, Ella, and her husband, Jim.

Ella is a plump little creature with a generous waist line, made more generous looking by a bountiful checked-gingham apron, the border of which was 10 or 12 inches deep, representing three pairs of birds, each carefully cross-stitched in with white thread. The day I was there she had used the apron to dress up for me, wearing it over a spic-and-span clean dress. Ella had used her Sunday dishes because I was there, and with great pride she showed me her sixty-three-piece set. Jim earns a nominal wage running an elevator, their two children have married and gone, and here these twin-hearted souls are living on, happy and proud of each other. They have found richness of life. When ten minutes after six came, Ella was eagerly listening for the one step that spelled completeness of life for her. Her Jim was there—he was hers completely and entirely. She believed in him more than in herself.

When I look from within myself at these good friends, their simple little house, their unaffectedness, I rejoice in their peace. No matter to them if it storms outside or the streetcar men strike or the papers cry hard times. These two people will love on, trust on, and daily grow more firmly attached to God and Truth . . . A splendid house is not necessary for the happiness of these good people. They know no conveniences, yet they have peace within for they know industry, kindness, and love, and these have provided treasured wealth.

". . . We must measure our lives in terms of what gives us joy. When we do that, we build up happiness in our lives out of what we do. Then, with the advance of our years, we can say, as did Julia Ward Howe, when asked if it wasn't harder to grow old, "No, the deeper I drink the cup, the sweeter it grows. The sugar is all at the bottom."
—*Inspiration*, 1921

Undergarments:
Corsets Play An Important Role

Fashion Service, 1926

To be well dressed consists not alone in wearing becoming and appropriate outer garments but in selecting lingerie and corsets that provide the proper foundation for the right effect. Such phrases as "nipped-in waistline" and "molded silhouette," constantly seen in the dispatches from the style centers, should awaken us all to a realization of what a properly fitted corset can mean to our general appearance.

The term corset covers a wide range of garments nowadays, for whatever the demands of the figure, they have been met by manufacturers. Not only in the corset, but in its necessary accompaniment, the brassiere, they provide the proper design and weight for all types. The illustration here shows two types of corsets, the one at the left providing restraint but also ease for the stouter figure, and that at the right of the clasp-around type, without lacing and with only enough boning to flatten too obvious curves.

Corsets have three functions—only two if slenderness is the asset and exercise and much walking are the habit. These are, respectively, to hold up the stockings and to make for a neat waistline. The third reason is that a corset helps to confine the hips and to control a surplus of flesh. Women everywhere realize that a corset should be worn for neatness and not for support. A back that cries for a corset needs, instead, waist and back exercises that will overcome the sense of fatigue when a corset is not worn.

In the choice of a corset, height must be considered as well as breadth. The corset suitable for the tall figure is never right for the shorter one, and vice versa, because the boning appropriate for one will not only prove uncomfortable on the other but will not fulfill its proper function, that of a support to muscles and flesh. In fitting a corset, try it on in sitting and standing positions before a mirror, noticing the length particularly, both of the corset and the boning. Make sure, too, that the corset is plenty large, since it is a very easy matter during the fitting to feel satisfied with a small size, which when worn, will slip up and prove very uncomfortable.

With the corset properly chosen, you are ready to give attention to other articles that contribute to a correct foundation.

Fragrances for My Lady Fair

by Barbara Ellison, *Fashion Service*, 1927

Next time you pass a toilet goods counter, sniffing the delicious odors of lavender and jasmine and a host of flower fragrances, and your hand instinctively reaches for your purse and then draws back in a Puritanical prejudice against perfumes, just remember that, in addition to being no longer in ill-repute, they are even considered medicinal.

In France, the perfume oils generally used in toilet waters are antiseptic, and, like many fragrant oils, they give off oxygen. The alcohol, too, in which the perfumes are dissolved, is a sterilizing agent and a mild antiseptic to the skin, preserving it against ordinary local infection.

And now that we've established such a good cause for perfumes, how shall we use them never to offend but to give a suggestion of fragrance as delicate as it is delicious, as indefinable as it is charming? Of course, you never mean to use them too lavishly, but there may be danger that you don't realize when you have used too much, so a safe rule is to always use a little less than seems necessary.

Perfumes have their personalities and there are times and places for perfumes of every sort. You seldom get a true idea of the odor of a perfume by smelling it in the bottle. It will help you, therefore, in choosing your perfumes, to place a drop in the palm of the hand, rubbing it hard. This will dissipate the alcohol, leaving only the true fragrance of the essence, which is then readily distinguishable. If you are a blonde or medium-blonde, select the flower fragrances, the fresh odors of spring blossoms being especially suitable if you are a charmingly youthful person. If you are a brunette, on the other hand, particularly of more mature years, the more complex or sophisticated scents are better in keeping, and quite as charming in their own way. Or you might follow the lead of the smart Parisian women who prefer the floral types for daytime use and will use blends only at night.

The Month of Hearts & Heroes

Fashion Service, 1929

February, the month of red-letter days, so short and fleeting, and yet so full of fun and frolic! And to the usual occasions for festivity—Lincoln's Birthday, St. Valentine's Day, and Washington's Birthday—and some years give us an extra day for Leap Year parties. Surely, this is the Mardi Gras month of the year and should be celebrated in the true spirit of gaiety.

On St. Valentine's Day, dedicated to the little God of Love, Cupid plays a stellar part in every celebration. So hearts and bows and arrows dominate the decorations and menu.

The mere mention of Valentine or Washington's Birthday party suggests fancy costumes. Attractive ones for both occasions are shown here.

If the party requires a centerpiece, you should choose nothing more appropriate or graceful than the heart bouquet shown below, for here, out of a mound of green, spring countless sprays of many-colored hearts. An easy way to produce this effect is to paste small hearts to stems of fine green wire and insert these stems in a large flower holder, covering the holder with real moss, feathery fern, or green crepe paper, crumpled and arranged in a mound.

Place cards, a red heart pierced with an arrow and surmounting a white card, continue the ideas and flower candy favors add their delicate touch.

George Washington

The quaint charm of Colonial times fittingly characterizes the George Washington Party when old blue china may be brought forth and used with red and white food to complete a patriotic color scheme.

The table decorations shown here, a Jerusalem cherry plant surrounded by a mound of moss and small cardboard hatchets, recalls the famous deed, while place cards, featuring the Father of This Country guarding the fallen tree, complete the familiar picture.

When Hearts Are Trumps

by Mary Gilgallon, *Inspiration*, 1927

When February comes, with its wealth of "party" days, one is never at a loss to decide which will appeal most to children, from tiny girls and boys to those who have almost reached the portals of the realm of grown folks. St. Valentine's Day, with its characteristic symbols—hearts and flowers—is the one day in the year when sentiment reigns supreme. Games and decorations may be timely and amusing, and most attractive and appetizing menus may be planned to carry out an appropriate color theme.

Entertainment

A most appropriate game for St. Valentine's Day is a hunt for hearts. The children are first divided into groups of five, and each group forms an animal family. They may be cats, dogs, roosters, ducks, cows, horses, donkeys, or any animals or birds with which children are familiar. Each group chooses a leader, and the signal for the hunt is given. When a member of one of the "family" finds a heart, he must put his finger on it and call for his leader by means of the call characteristic of the animal he represents. The leader so called immediately responds and picks up the heart, none but the leader being allowed to do this. After a short time, the call is given for counting, and the group which found the most hearts has the privilege of acting as audience while each of the other groups in turn gives its animal call for the amusement of the rest.

Refreshments

The following menu will amply satisfy the most discriminating person under five:

Ice Cream or Fruit Gelatin
Jelly Sandwiches
Sugar Cookies or Sponge Cake

If ice cream is allowed, by all means have it, for no other dessert takes its place in childish hearts, but be sure to have it homemade (see pages 130-131) and of a very simple nature. The gelatin may be poured into a long, rather shallow pan to set, and then cut with a heart-shaped cookie cutter. Sandwiches of white bread with a red filling can easily be prepared. Use any jelly or marmalade that has a distinct red tint.

Sweet Sandwiches

1 lb. cinnamon candies
1 cup whipped cream

Put the candy through the food chopper, making sure that it is ground up thoroughly. Then whip it into the cream. Spread this mixture on thin buttered slices of white bread. Have your ingredients ready and kept chilled ahead of time. At the last minute, whisk the sandwiches together and serve.

The Secrets of a Perfect Pie

Not long ago, I heard a woman say, "It seems strange that while so many women can make good cake, so few of them can make good pie." And as I thought it over I realized that there was so much truth in what she said.

This is unfortunate indeed, for if a dessert contest were held, there's no doubt that pie would lead all the other varieties in popularity. So let's look into the matter of pie making in order that we may learn for all time the secrets—they're only a few in number—that will enable all of us to supply our home folks with pies which they will enjoy and of which we may be proud.

Ingredients and How to Combine Them

Only four ingredients are necessary in the making of light, airy pastry, and they are flour, fat, salt and water, but it is the quantity and the way they are put together that really count. Some recipes call for baking powder, and while this adds to the lightness of the pastry, it is not essential. The following proportions are sufficient for a one-crust pie.

Pastry

1 cup flour	1/2 cup shortening
1/2 tsp. salt	1/4 cup water

Have the ingredients ready before you start to work and have them cold. Some persons are able to make a good piecrust with hot ingredients, but the old rule of having the fat hard and the water ice cold should never be overlooked.

Today's food processor mixes dough in a few seconds.

Sift the flour, measure a cupful into a sifter, add the salt, and then sift into the bowl. Add the shortening and work it into the flour by cutting it in with two knives or working it in with a fork or a perforated spoon. The idea is not to mix the fat in too thoroughly, but rather to have it in tiny lumps that will roll out and make layers or flakes.

Then, add the water, a little at a time. And here is where the real trick comes. No more water than is necessary to make the dough clean the bowl should be used. Wait long enough between the additions to make sure that the flour and the shortening need more water, from what is given in the recipe.

Sift just a light dusting of flour on the board, turn the ball of pastry on to it, and work lightly and quickly with the fingers until all the ingredients are well blended. Allow the pastry to stand for a few minutes and then roll out, using a quick, light movement of the rolling pin. Place on a pie plate, cut off along the edge, flute the edge or mark as desired, and then either bake in readiness for a filling or fill at once.

Baking the Pie

It is in the baking of the pie where so many cooks fail. Pastry needs a hot oven, 450 to 500 degrees for large pies and small ones and tarts. The layers of cold air that have been incorporated into the crust in the mixing expand quickly in a hot oven and make the crust light. After a light brown color appears, the oven should be cooled to 400 degrees for large pies and 450 for small ones.

 Circle aluminum foil around the edges to prevent burning.

If you are merely baking a crust, 12 minutes will be sufficient time, but a filled pie requires from 30 to 45 minutes or longer. Be sure that your pie, if it contains a top crust, is sufficiently browned, for nothing is more insipid than a pie that is pale in color. A top crust should always be cut to enable the steam to escape, and a crust for a cream pie should be pricked on the bottom so as to prevent bubbles.

Meringue for Pies

Many pies call for meringue, so one should be prepared to make a meringue that will stand up well. The whites of 2 eggs and 2 tablespoonfuls of sugar are sufficient for the average-size pie. Whip the whites until almost stiff and then fold in the sugar, a little at a time, whipping all the while. Flavor with vanilla. Drop on the pie in spoonfuls and connect the spoonfuls, or put into a pastry bag and decorate in any desired way. Place in the oven and brown slightly for 12 to 15 minutes.

Lemon Pie

1 pint milk	2 eggs	Scald the milk in the upper part of a double boiler. Mix the
1 cup sugar	1 lemon	sugar, flour, and salt and add to the grated rind and the
4 tbls. flour	Pinch salt	juice of a lemon. Stir into the milk. Beat the egg yolks and
		add to the mixture. Cook until thick.

Canned Cherry Pie

Add 1/2 cup of sugar to a 16-ounce can of cherries. Pour into a pan lined with pie dough over which a little flour has been sprinkled. Sprinkle a little more flour over the top. Cover with a top crust or with strips of dough in lattice effect. Bake 45 minutes. See baking instructions in copy above.

We suggest following the instructions on the back of the can.

Simplicity Lends Charm to the Newest Lingerie

Inspiration, 1923

Every woman has a warm place in her heart for pretty under things. And half of the joy of owning them comes from making them. They are so simple now, too, that a satisfying array of dainty garments is the reward for only a few hours' work.

So far as nightgowns are concerned, sleeves either are considered of so little importance that they are omitted altogether or they are made fascinating in design or trimming and are one of the most interesting details of the garment. An extended band at each armhole edge of the nightgown shown in Figure 1 might be termed as sleeves. For under dresses that are not confined closely at the waistline, the costume slip has proved so thoroughly comfortable and satisfactory that it is displacing petticoats to a very great extent. For wear under dainty or light-colored dresses, any of the usual lingerie materials may be employed and trimming of lace applied as shown in Figure 2. In order to make the shoulder straps very dainty, provided you use lace, roll the edges of the material and whip the lace to the rolled hem, as shown in *a*.

An utter lack of sleeves characterizes the low-cut nightgown of crepe shown in Figure 3. Bindings of turquoise-blue finish the edge of the shoulder straps, an enlarged detail of which is shown in *b*, and the upper and lower edges of the gown. Ribbon bows and a distinctive monogram provide additional touches.

A combination of colors, such as yellow and orchid, gray and rose, would be delightful for the combination suits of abbreviated chemise and drawers illustrated in Figure 4. The narrow ribbon straps, which cross at the shoulder, match the trimming material. Another attractive way of using narrow ribbon is shown at *c*, fagoting stitches being used to join the ribbon. An enlarged detail of the embroidery design is shown at *d*. Consisting

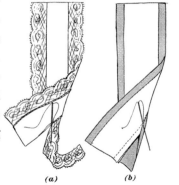

(a)   (b)   (c)

merely of lazy daisies, French knots, and darning stitches, this may be easily developed without a pattern.

Tiny tots "undies" come in for a bit of consideration in Figure 5. These little drawers show an interesting detail—plaits laid in the back portion at the side seam to provide a little extra length and incidentally, more freedom.

Experience has proved that the most satisfactory sort of brassiere to produce a low-bust effect is one having hose supporters attached which will hold the brassiere down in its original position on the figure. The brassiere shown in Figure 6 combines this feature with a cut that is also an assurance of holding the bust in a low position.

Dark-colored knickers as shown in Figure 7 are another reason for the decline of petticoat favor, as they are ideal for wear under a dark dress or suit. Knickers may be finished with simple chatting below the knees or in a more interesting effect, as shown in the fashion pictures and the enlarged detail at *e*. To make such a finish, form double headings of self-material and insert a strip of contrasting material between them. Then stitch these together to form casings.

Changeable taffeta or satin makes an ideal fabric for a négligée of the type illustrated in Figure 8. The trimming is of picoted strips of self-material gathered in scalloped fashion, as shown in *f*, and then the gathering drawn up to form a purled effect.

Although of simple kimono cut, the nightgown shown in Figure 9 gains the much-coveted individuality by its sleeves, which are slashed their entire length and finished with bindings extended from the gathered neckline, and by dainty cross-tucked medallions edged with lace. The application of the medallions, as in *g*, is not at all tedious. Turn under the edges of the cross-tucked circles, baste and stitch them flat. Then cut away the surplus material underneath, stitch the hem flat, and whip the lace in position so that it just covers the two rows of stitching, as the illustration shows.

Orchid crepe and cream-colored lace combine with delectable results in the combing or bed jacket illustrated in Figure 10. This would make an especially acceptable gift or would be cherished as a hope-chest treasure by a bride-to-be.

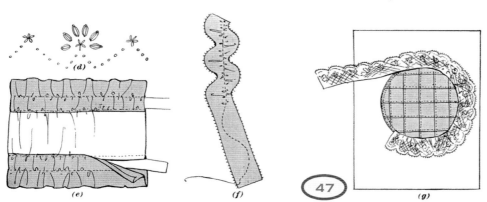

(d)

(e)

(f)

47

(g)

Magic Pattern

A Magic Lingerie Set

So often we hear folks say, "I always buy my lingerie for I never can find time to make it." What a shame, when there are such charming styles to be developed, and when so little actual time is required for even the smartest ones, if one's spare moments are used rightly. This ensemble shown above, suitable for a gift, for sale, or for one's self, may be made in 36 size from 4 yards of voile, crepe de Chine, or Georgette, in just a few hours' time.

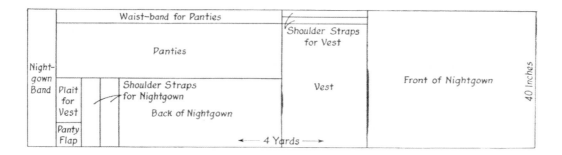

Night-gown Band	Waist-band for Panties			Shoulder Straps for Vest		40 Inches
	Panties					
	Plait for Vest	Shoulder Straps for Nightgown		Vest	Front of Nightgown	
		Back of Nightgown				
	Panty Flap					

← 4 Yards →

Cutting

Follow the diagram above, making the nightgown lengths 48 inches, with a 20-inch back, the vest, 24 inches, and the panties 64 inches. Along the selvage, cut two 2-inch strips from the vest section and a 4-inch band from the panty section. Then cut, as shown, two 5-inch nightgown shoulder straps, a vest side plait, 6 x 12 inches, a panty flap, 6 x 8 inches, and an 8-inch nightgown band.

Making

Insert the vest plait in the seam from the bottom. Cross-stitch hem on all edges, make and apply the shoulder straps. French seam the panties, made on the cross, and join to the band with slight fullness and a 10-inch drape on each side. Cross-stitch hem all edges. Insert the flap in slashes at the center front and back as long as half the finished flap width. Shirr the nightgown front, lay plaits at the seams, and attach to the band. Make and apply the double shoulder straps. Draw up the band in draped effect with a ribbon bow, one end attached inside, the other, outside, above the shirring.

 See Note, page 232, for modern tips and techniques.

Testimonials

Study-to-Sew Club

Not long ago a fat letter postmarked Canton, Ohio, was brought to me, and I lost no time in tearing it open, for I anticipated a great treat. A number of closely written sheets fell out of the bulging envelope, and before I had finished reading the first page my desk and surroundings had disappeared and I, too, was on my way to Mrs. Gaskell's for the all-day sewing meeting of the Study-to-Sew-Better Club of Canton, Ohio. Personal notes were included from those who attended the Club meeting that day.

—*Alice H. Stone, editor*

"Have had a wonderful time today; made a costume slip and collected some new patterns for undies."

—*Mrs. Pearl F. Beck*

"The Study-to-Sew-Better had a lovely time today. I received instruction on the One Hour Dress and cut out a bit of lingerie under the guidance of one of the Club members. The Club is going to be a wonderful help to me."

—*Mrs. Anna Rose*

"Our Club had the pleasure of meeting for an All-Day Sewing Bee at the pleasant home of Mrs. Gaskill, who was a delightful hostess and has the happy faculty of making every one feel at home. Four of our little ones also were made welcome—otherwise the mothers could not have come."

—*Mrs. Seibert*

"Have had an excellent time. Received instruction on the different interpretations of the One Hour Dress and have cut various apron patterns. I think these meetings are wonderful and I know I am going to enjoy my Course more than I ever dreamed."

—*Mrs. Hannah Johns*

$50 Négligée for Only $14

"I have finished my négligée about which I wrote you, and it is perfectly beautiful. Everyone who sees it thinks it is perfectly wonderful the way I have learned to sew so well, and in such a short time. This négligée would cost at least $50 if bought ready-made. The materials cost about $14. I had made seventeen pieces of silk underwear, most of which have some embroidery on them, three silk shirts with embroidered monograms, and two cotton shirts of striped materials."

—*Miss Barbe, Texas*

Spring

Modern Notions

Looking over the magazines in my archives, I'm often struck by how the concerns of women of yesterday often overlap with what we consider our more "modern" notions about life and womanhood. From hobbies to a sense of style to personal goals, this book serves as a generous portion of proof that we're more similar to women of a century ago than we might think. Editors and students of The Woman's Institute maintained a keen eye for what mattered to the fairer sex, regularly publishing material that appealed to the body and soul, whether it was advice on fresh foods for dieting and tricks for disguising generous proportions, or an article on the perfect bath and the allure of spa life.

Speaking of fresh, this month's *Department of Cooking* even features an entirely vegetarian menu—how much more modern can it get? When the vegetarian movement really hit the states in the early 1990s, of course we patted ourselves on the back for our ingenuity and hip little nod toward health, but apparently, meatless meals and vegetarian cooking have been in for longer than we thought.

The *Department of Sewing* advises on the art of creating personalized linens for your home by exploring the art of monogramming. I, too, love adding my initials to home accents, from hand towels to napkins. I know of many women today who use stamps to make personalized stationery, clothing, and handbags—all very "in" and all very timeless. For the needlewoman, small napkins can be monogrammed in an instant for an over-the-top table setting. The font chosen can also take your monogram work from a little bit antiquated to very up-to-date, with certain fonts being appropriate for certain occasions—see the *Department of Sewing* to find out which font is most suited to a ladies' luncheon.

So what difference does it all make to us now, running ourselves ragged, right? Wrong. This thread connecting us to women of yesterday, above all, illustrates the importance of living in the moment. Just think, every concern and worry you carry today has been faced head-on and dealt with in a previous generation. And often those problems, small or large, have been resolved with the utmost grace and beauty, leaving a model to which we modern gals can aspire. If your problems aren't the center of the universe, what is? It's a good question, and one the editors of *Inspiration* and *Fashion Service* strive to answer with every issue. After all, striving for the good life never goes out of style.

Yours,

Amy B.

MARCH

Cheerfulness is much more to be desired than riches. Those who possess it have something riches cannot buy—a great possession because it creates goodwill and makes for real happiness.

— Mary Brooks Picken

A Thimbleful of Cheerfulness

Honest Purpose
"The Road to Progress"

by Mary Brooks Picken
Excerpted from *Thimblefuls of Friendliness*, 1924

On my desk stands a most comforting calendar quotation—the inscription reads:

> Whate'er the hidden future brings,
>   Is helped by hands divine.
> Through all the tangled web of things,
>   There runs a clear design.
> What, though the skies are dark today,
>   Tomorrow's may be blue,
> When every cloud has rolled away,
>   God's providence shows through.

Someone seeing this and catching an optimistic remark that I made, said: "You are a cheerful sort of fatalist—you just seem to know that everything will come out all right."

This was a rejoinder I did not expect, and I had to hesitate a little before admitting that I am inclined that way. But, in defense, I made a declaration to the effect that I never let Fate paddle alone in Mr. Wish's leaky boat. I learned long ago that a happier, safer ride could be had in the good substantial boat, "Honest Purpose," especially when I was helping with the oars. I do actually hold that clouds roll away, that Good is more powerful than Evil and in every circumstance Good will eventually assert itself. I say, always, that sincere desire is unworded prayer and that if we are earnest and have an honest purpose, our prayer will be answered, and answered wholly in accord with our own sincerity and unselfishness. Wishing for things and praying for them are vastly different.

Every day is ours to mold as we will. If we waste it in idle wishing, we must pay. If we build for the future by being faithful to our desires, we lay paving stones that make a safer and more comfortable road for the rest of our lives.

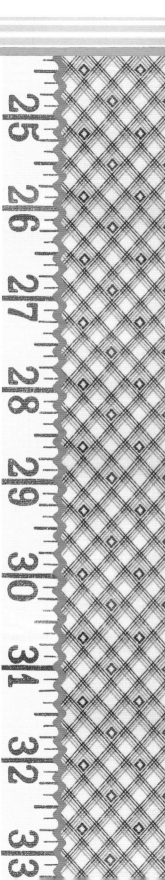

I used to think that "laying aside funds for a rainy day" meant only money; but I have learned that there are several kinds of rainy-day funds. Knowledge of any constructive kind, any educational or human hobby, is a rainy-day fund. It makes life interesting, develops appreciation, and teaches us the virtues of fidelity to honest purpose. Pioneering children along life's pathway establishes at least a contented heart with which to visit on rainy days, just as one does being a good neighbor. Every day we should accomplish something in a constructive way. Study, work, thinking—they all help roll the clouds of unappreciation away and let God's providence shine through.

I heard a wise old philosopher say, "If you want to keep young, don't let your troubles settle in your knees. Sure 'n you can tell the unhappy women by the way they lift their feet. There's no spring in their knees; they drag themselves about, no force within amovin' them."

The force within must be one's very own heart. Don't put weights on your knees. Keep your heart young and free and happy. Look for the good in people, in conditions, in surroundings. Learn to explore a little deeper into the soul of man. Interest yourself in the heart next to you, and your own troubles will melt away like icicles in the sunshine.

Roses Every Day

Excerpted from *Thimblefuls of Friendliness*, 1924

"**I**f you have any roses for me, let me have them now" is a saying that has much merit. How quick we are to complain of faults, a little slight, a little thoughtlessness. A little grievance grows as we think about it and as we talk about it, and that we are sure to do.

But let something good happen, something thoughtful, something that was a real help, and we accept it as a matter of course and say little about it. And day after day we go along accepting the good as a natural consequence with little appreciation, and then are ready to fight over the least little awkward or thoughtless thing.

We forget to say the good things about folks until they are gone, and then angels they actually seem. We never realized before how wonderful, how kind, how unselfish they were. We surround them with roses whose petals fairly flutter with praise, yet nary a one would we have given them if they had lived and helped and befriended us in that unselfish way we recognize so definitely when they are gone.

Let's give the roses every day. A petal of cheer now is worth a dozen roses after awhile.

Disguising Generous Proportions

Inspiration, 1923

Almost all present-day fashions are illustrated on slender figures having little apparent difference in the size of the bust, the hips, and the waistline. I wonder whether this might explain why we receive so many letters complaining that magazines are neglecting the clothes problems of the woman of generous proportions. In the struggle to keep young, women often view the approach of flesh with something like despair. But good, firm flesh, rightly distributed, makes a woman look younger after she has passed thirty-five. Instead of regarding it as a calamity, then, be thankful for it just so long as you keep it within bounds.

It should be unnecessary to warn any woman against the risks of the taking of drugs to reduce flesh. Reduce in safe, sane, and natural ways; or, better still, don't put on flesh that will be a burden to you and that you must fight to get rid of. Begin a regime of self-control before you reach such a stage.

You ask how is it possible for you to recognize features that are either desirable for or unbecoming to the stout figure. These rules will make it possible for you to determine at a glance whether or not a style is correct for a woman of rather large proportions. In simple form, the rules may be given as follows:

- Select dark, inconspicuous colors, usually of plain weave. Hairline stripes and small-figured materials are permissible, but wide stripes, plaids, and large-figured materials are objectionable.

- Choose soft, medium-weight fabrics that do not have a high luster. Transparent materials and fabrics having a heavy pile are extremes that should be avoided.

- Give preference to lengthwise or diagonal lines in order to emphasize the height of the figure and incidentally draw attention from the round measurements. Crosswise lines apparently cut the height of the figure and should, in most instances, be shunned.

- Arrange the trimming according to the general principles of line, remembering that long, single rows of trimming of the same color as the dress will prove a virtue while trimming arranged in patch effect will merely emphasize the unusual proportions of the wearer.

Bathing

Fashion Service, 1928

Baths have many functions aside from their avowed intention of keeping the body clean. There is the early morning bath of warm water or tepid water followed by a cooler spray and a brisk rub that brings a healthy glow to the skin and sets you up for the day.

There is the relaxing bath to be taken just before going to bed. A tepid bath is most relaxing if you're tense and tired, for water that is too hot is likely to be more stimulating than soothing.

Then there is the warm, luxurious bath that draws all the ache out of tired muscles, that gently soothes and restores ragged nerves and frayed dispositions. The ideal time for this is in the afternoon or evening, especially if

Of all the feminine charms, cleanliness should be the most universal, for unlike other charms, it plays no favorites, being the possession of any woman simply for the taking.

one is going out afterwards and wishes to feel particularly fit and relaxed.

Of all the baths, I think I enjoyed the salt rub most. You can have a salt rub right at home if you wish, and you'll find even the home-made variety very awakening and stimulating. Dissolve one cupful of salt in a quart of hot water. Soak a Turkish towel in this until the salt has become thoroughly embedded in the fibers. Then lift it out and hang it up to drip and dry. In the morning, rub yourself vigorously with this towel and you will wonder whether you were ever really alive and thoroughly awake before. The towel may be used until the salt is all removed.

Of course, follow your salt rub with a tepid or cold shower.

Monograms Make Linens Distinctive

Inspiration, 1926 and Fashion Service, 1931

A woman's appreciation and love of the finer things can be expressed in no better way than by the quality and beauty of her linens. And monograms give them character and individuality that make them highly treasured possessions.

So many attractive and dignified styles of letters are offered for your selection that you should have no difficulty in finding a type that will express your own individuality and still be in keeping with the linen on which it is used.

While cut-work monograms are distinctive, they are much more difficult to make than others, which are usually done in satin-stitch. Drop-style monograms, illustrated on the plate doily, can be arranged with any kind of letter. The clever needlewoman can create from these and the many other types of letters individual and artistic monograms.

In selecting the thread, remember that mercerized cotton is most satisfactory, for it works up evenly and smoothly. Be sure that the thread and needle are of the correct size. A needle that is too large makes noticeable holes in the linen, and one too small draws the work out of shape because of the necessity of pulling it through the material.

Mercerized cotton thread, usually white, is the most satisfactory for monogramming. Size 18 or 30 of a smooth, single-stranded thread is best unless the design is very delicate, when one strand of a 6-strand cotton is used. In the case of cross-stitch, two or three strands of a 6-strand floss or size 16 or 18 single strand, give the best effect. Monograms in satin stitch should be highly padded in most cases and very smoothly worked. An embroidery hoop should always be used.

Whenever possible, monograms and initials should be placed on a straight grain of the material, for they hold their

In any monogram, the last name is given the place of prominence. This is, as a rule, the center letter of a three-letter style because it is so often larger and differently marked.

shape and launder better than when worked on the bias. When the linen is of a very fine, firm quality, the letters may be placed diagonally across a corner.

The choice and arrangement of the letters of a monogram are important. The unmarried woman or the bride-elect uses her own initials, making a three-letter monogram if she has a middle name and a two-letter one if she has not. The two-letter monograms are simple, with the letters usually of equal size placed side by side, or that of the given name above that of the surname. The three-letter monogram, however, is governed by definite rules. If the letters are of equal size, they are arranged in consecutive order, horizontally, vertically, or diagonally. But if a diamond, round, oval, or rectangular-shaped monogram is used, the central letter is necessarily largest, thus receiving the greatest emphasis, and so this position is regarded as correct for the initial of the surname.

When a woman who is planning to be married is marking her linens, there can be no question of the impeccable taste displayed when she uses her own initials, for they are her "very own" just as the linens are, while she has no real right to use her fiancée's name until he becomes her husband. After marriage, a woman uses the initials of her maiden name in combination with her husband's surname; or, if she prefers a single-letter monogram, the first letter of his surname is correct.

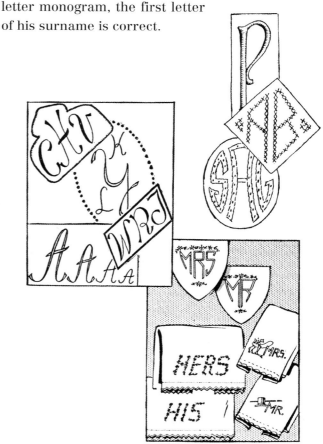

Planning Meals Without Meat

Fashion Service, 1928

No matter how well-balanced our winter menus have been, we all feel hungry for the fresh growing things of Spring, which tone up the system and help to ward off that most undesirable of troubles—Spring Fever. The foods best suited to supply this element are those which contain minerals and vegetable acids.

Two of the most necessary minerals are iron, which assures good rich blood, and lime, which builds and hardens bones. Iron is found in whole-cereal grains and in green vegetables, especially in spinach. Lime abounds in milk, and it is also found in certain greens, in whole wheat, and in nuts.

Fruits and vegetables are such a very necessary part of the diet that they should be assigned a definite place in every meal. The list in the box on this page shows some of the fruits and vegetables that are our best sources of minerals and vegetable acids.

Meat, the food highest in protein value, while appealing to the appetite and very wholesome, is not really essential to a well-balanced meal. However, since protein is the element that provides material for building bone and muscle and repairing worn-out tissue, one must be careful, in planning menus, that food which is to take the place of meat be high in protein.

Fish is a splendid substitute, but it cannot, of course, be served as frequently as some other foods because the majority of persons tire of it very quickly. Beans and peas contain a large percentage of protein and consequently are excellent meat savers, but as their protein is not in just the same form as that of meat, milk, and eggs, these vegetables should seldom be used to the entire exclusion of meat. Cheese and eggs are both high in the necessary food element, and as they lend themselves to many and varied ways of preparation, they very easily replace fish and meat in the diet.

Mineral & Vegetable-Acid Foods	
Fruits	Vegetables
Apples	Greens, lettuces, celery
Pears	Cress, spinach, endive
Bananas	Potatoes
Berries	Root vegetables
Melons	Green beans, beans
Citrus Fruits	Tomatoes, squash

In the daily routine of a household, it helps considerably to have a week's menu planned at one time. Following are six suggested menus of meatless dinners. They are simply to serve as a guide in planning a meal when one must, either of necessity or choice, eliminate meat.

One
Cream of Celery Soup
Cheese Cutlets with Horseradish Sauce
Fried Carrots
Apple, Orange, and Date Salad
Chocolate Bread Pudding

Two
Spanish Omelet
Creamed Asparagus
Glazed Sweet Potatoes
Grapefruit and Celery Salad
Prune Whip with Custard Sauce

Three
Cream of Spinach Soup
Bean Croquettes with Tomato Sauce
Scalloped Potatoes
Peach and Cream Cheese Salad
Gingerbread with Whipped Cream

Four
Fruit Cocktail
Italian Baked Rice
Green Peas
Carrots
Lettuce Salad with French Dressing
Chocolate Cream Pie

Five
Cream of Tomato Soup with Croutons
Asparagus Loaf
New Potatoes with Parsley and Butter
Cabbage Salad with Sour Cream Dressing
Orange Custard

Six
Casserole of Vegetables
Sweet Potato Puffs
Celery and Pineapple Salad
Lemon Sherbet
Sponge Cake

Cream of Spinach Soup

2 tbls. butter
2 tbls. flour
1 pint milk
1/2 cup spinach puree
1 tsp. salt
1/8 tsp. pepper
Cream as desired

Make white sauce by mixing the butter, flour, and milk over medium heat until thickened. Add the puree, which is made by forcing freshly cooked or canned spinach through a sieve. Season with salt and pepper, heat thoroughly, and serve. Cream may be added just before serving in any quantity up to one-eighth of the amount of the soup. Heat the cream and serve as soon as it is added.

Italian Baked Rice

4 cups cooked rice
1/2 cup grated cheese
1/2 cup chopped pimiento
1-1/2 cups tomato juice
2 tsps. salt
1/2 tsp. pepper

Mix the ingredients and pour into a baking dish. Cover the top with the pulp from the tomatoes, and bake for 30 minutes in a moderate oven (350 degrees). Serve hot.

Magic Pattern

The Slip-Over Apron

Fashion Service, 1929

An attractive print, bias tape in a harmonizing color, and less than an hour's time will produce a practical and becoming apron if the simple directions on this page are followed. As the illustration shows, this apron fits well because of its bias cut. It also has smart lines, its short, slightly full back being very fashionable. The neckline permits slipping this over the head readily. For the average figure, provide 1 yard of 36-inch fabric; for smaller sizes, when short, a 32-inch length of 32-inch fabric is better. For each provide about 5 yards of bias-fold tape.

Cutting the Apron

Straighten the cut edges of your material and then fold on the diagonal and place it on your cutting table, all edges even, having the two open edges next to you and the diagonal fold to your right.

Consider the corner at the lower right a. From this point measure along the fold a distance of 4-1/2 inches and place point b and along the open edges 2-1/2 inches and place point c. Join b and c with a straight line.

From b measure along the fold about 9 inches and place point d. At right angles to the fold from d measure 2-1/2 inches and place point e, joining the two with a straight line. From e toward a and parallel to line ad, indicate a straight line for a distance of about 6 inches and mark its termination f. From f indicate a curve to b, as shown.

From f, at right angles to line ef, measure 3-1/4 inches and place point g. Join g and c with a curved line, equidistance from fb at all points.

From ga indicate a line to the left, parallel to the open edges of the material, as shown, and mark its end h. From h measure the right about 6-1/2 inches to 8 inches, depending on the depth you wish the back, and mark point i. Measure the distance between i and g and, midway between them, mark point j. Indicate a dotted guideline from j at right angles to line ig, making it 4 inches long, and mark its end *k*.

At right angles to line *hg* at point *i* measure 2 inches and mark point *l*. Draw a straight line from *i* to *l*, curve it from *l* to *k* and then from *k* to *g*, as shown.

Mark the corner opposite *a*, point *m*. From this point measure along the fold a distance of 8 inches and place point *n*. Along the open edges from *m*, measure 12 inches and place point *o*. Join points *n* and *o* with a curved line, as shown.

When using 32-inch fabric, follow the same plan except for the location of point *d* which should be 7-1/2 inches from point *b*, and of *i*, which should be 6-1/2 inches or less from *h*.

The diagram, shown at the left, illustrates the method of cutting the Magic Slip-Over Apron without a pattern.

To cut the apron, start at *h* and cut to *i*, then to *l*, through *k* to *g*, from *g* to *c* on the curved line, from *c* to *b* and to *e* through *f*, and then to *d*. Use the straight sections between line *hg* and the open edges for the tie.

Cut the curved line from *n* to *o* to form the curved edge on the front of the apron.

Making the Apron

Join the center-back line below the neck opening with a French seam and baste the binding around the neckline. Next, pin in two 3/8-inch folds on each side of the center back in the skirt section of the apron, making them 3-1/2 inches long. These will narrow the back and provide fullness, as shown in the small back view. Stitch and turn the ties and pin in place, locating them just beyond the folds, as shown.

Slip the apron on. If it appears to bulge at the armhole edge, fold in darts on each side about 1/4-inch deep and 2-1/2 inches long, tapering to nothing at the points. Remove the apron and stitch the darts and the folds at the back. Then baste the binding around all unfinished edges, and stitch accurately. Stitch the ties securely in place.

If you wish a pocket, one may be cut from the section *b, e, d* remaining after cutting out the neck opening.

"The ensemble dominates the mode. Not to have a coat that will make of each frock a costume is not to be in Fashion's favor."

The Ensemble Dominates

Fashion Service, March 1929

The ensemble idea grows every day to the satisfaction of those women who wish to appear smartly dressed with as little expenditure of time and money as possible. Business women, who must look their best but have little time for planning costumes with the proper harmonizing accessories, and home women who feel the need of a small but well-balanced wardrobe, are grateful for the emphasis placed on the composed outfit and the ensemble.

The way in which the ensemble dominates the mode this season is the subject of much fashion conversation, and the part played by the coat in the ensemble cannot possibly be overlooked. Every costume, whether for sports, travel, afternoon, or evening, has a coat, and quite unmistakably its own coat. The separate coat and dress as such are seldom in the picture.

Ensemble coats vary in length from the short box coat to full-length, including the fingertip, the three-quarters, and the seven-eighths lengths. In general, one may say that the formality of the costume increases with the length of the coat.

Materials and color combinations form the critical factors in ensemble suits. The wise woman decides on a definite scheme and selects her dresses, wraps, hats, and accessories with this in mind. Those who have been in the habit of building up their entire wardrobe around a single becoming color will find that the compose idea is not entirely new to them, but those who like variety will have to exercise care in selecting harmonizing shades of the same color, or possibly of two in the three-piece ensemble, in order to achieve a unified effect.

Accompanied by a becoming felt or straw hat and a tailored blouse worn over the skirt in the fashion of a two-piece costume or tucked in "tomboy" style, it expresses the tailored mode perfectly.

Blouses have become important once more with the return of the ensemble that is made up of matching coat and skirt and harmonizing blouse. Every frock must have its coat, whether it's the little pique or gingham for morning shopping, the afternoon silks for church and social affairs, or the printed chiffon for evening functions.

Testimonials

Made Her Own Trousseau

Here is a busy office worker who determined to learn to be her own dressmaker, although she had very little time for study.

"Before taking the course I couldn't make an apron. Now, I'm not afraid to try anything. After finishing my tenth lesson, I made all of my trousseau, except my dress, including ten chemise and step-ins of crepe de Chine and batiste and six gowns. A white satin skirt with net and lace ruffles and rosebuds cost me $5.19, an exact duplicate from our best store is priced at $25. One pair of old rose satin pajamas, embroidered in blue yarn cost me $5.65. At the store their price was $25. I have also made one satin kimono, one breakfast coat of crepe de Chine and lace, one sports skirt, and several pretty blouses, and have just finished three summer dresses for the office. I wouldn't take $500 for what your wonderful course has taught me."

—*Miss Janet O'Neill, Dayton, Ohio*

Magic Aprons

"May I tell you of an idea I found very practical and useful as well as pretty? The best of it is that even the woman with the least bit of sewing knowledge can follow it. I made several magic aprons in neat prints and plain colors and gave them as gifts. I supplied an extra 1/4 yard of the material, and from it I fashioned cuffs to match. I used the lower end of a tight-fitting sleeve pattern and cut the cuffs from 7 to 8 inches deep, and from 3 to 4 inches larger than the finished sleeve. Each cuff was cut double and had an inner lining of muslin. The edges were straight or scalloped and bound with matching or harmonizing tape. On the underside of the cuff, I put snaps in such a way that the edges did not overlap but came together as if cuff links were used, although this is a matter of personal preference. Out of the piece remaining from the apron, I fashioned a holder or two, bound to match. The sets are really very pretty and I have been asked to make several as orders."

—*Mrs. E. B. Minnesota*

A Monogram Specialist

"Brides, college girls, expectant mothers, bring garments and household linens for me to add the distinctive, individualizing touch that sets their things apart. For school girls, I make monograms on plain, serviceable dresses with contrasting threads, using the back-stitch, filling in with a seed- or brier-stitch or some other simple stitch that can easily and rapidly be made. For these I receive twenty or twenty-five cents. My monograms are placed by the dozens on shirts, handkerchiefs, laundry bags, pillows for swings and spreads. But I have received from $10 to $50 for work on bridal linens and baby layettes."

—*Mrs. J. R. McLemore, Texas*

Modern Notions

April is one of the most stunningly beautiful months in my Midwestern town, and also happens to be my birthday month. We all know that birthdays can get a little less exciting year after year and the focus has shifted for many of us from celebration to anxiety and dread. But if I've learned one thing from the wise women of these pages, it's that who I am and what I do are the true determining factors in how others see me, crow's feet or no crow's feet. In addition, the process of aging is as natural as it gets, with the changing of the seasons acting as a guide for us as we navigate our own cycles of growth.

As a little girl I looked forward to Easter Sunday as much for the Easter bunny as the new Spring fashions I'd get to wear—new shoes and a unique hat always made me feel so grown-up and ladylike. I have fond memories of the chalkware chicks and ducks that would reappear each year in my Easter basket. Those are now part of my children's baskets along with several glass eggs that my grandmother Mildred had beautifully painted. While reading the Institute material, I am constantly reminded of my grandma's amazing creative spirit. She taught me many valuable lessons including seeing the incredible beauty in nature for which I attribute my love for photography. Her can-do attitude to any challenge (particularly in the creative arts) and her thirst for learning always kept her young at heart. I can only wish to live up to her fine example.

Since meeting my husband, it's also been a seasonal tradition for me to usher in Spring each year by attending opening day at Kauffman Stadium to support our Kansas City Royals baseball team. We take the afternoon off and head out to the stadium for a little quality time as a family. Several years ago, I was lucky enough to have opening day fall on my fortieth birthday. Unfortunately, that year Spring had not quite arrived. Several dear friends along with my family were "good sports" and shared a freezing, but fun day at the ballpark. I am already looking forward to this year's birthday at the ballpark and hoping for a warm day. I also plan to throw a party that includes trying the layer cake and fluffy icing recipe from this month's *Department of Cookery*.

As Laura MacFarlane writes in this month's *Department of Inspiration*, "In this glorious springtime, let's not miss one single minute of its happiness, nor one item of its inspiration. When the arbutus first perfumes the air, let's be up and doing. Plan your wardrobe with the thrill and ecstasy so characteristic of the season. Refurbish what you can, buy new what you must, but in all events, get in tune with the new and budding season." I don't know about you, but that's advice I can wholeheartedly embrace.

Yours,

Amy B.

APRIL

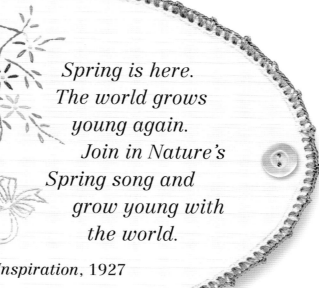

Spring is here.
The world grows
young again.
Join in Nature's
Spring song and
grow young with
the world.

—*Inspiration*, 1927

A Thimbleful of Youthfulness

ALICE SEIPP

Counting Aright: Measure Birthdays by the Heart

by Mary Brooks Picken
Excerpted from *Thimblefuls of Friendliness*, 1924

When are we old?

I know two women—one whose birthdays number seventy, the other, thirty-three. The seventy-year-old one reads, studies, enjoys, goes when she can, delights in a new dress, has a host of friends, and is genuinely happy. And folks just make excuses to visit her because of her keen interest, her joy in good news, her mental alertness, and her whole-hearted friendship. The little school girl, the grandmother of eighty, the boy home from college, the new daddy, all go to see her for contact with that current of friendship that helps them to believe in themselves and stimulates within them a new interest that is joy in itself.

The woman of thirty-three is married, and has "enough to do without that." "No, I didn't read about it; books don't interest me much." "No, I don't read the papers; you never can tell whether they're telling the truth." "Oh, that's all right for those girls that aren't married, but I'm too old to be interested." "Yes, I like music, but I'm too old to take lessons now." Imagine! And only thirty-three!

When do we stop? When does the etiquette of age bid us stop learning, stop being interested, stop growing in mental attainments? Surely, not until we shut our own minds and hearts against the idea.

What can we give our friends when we have shut all doors and put in storage all desire for progress? Nothing. Just nothing. And friends are entitled to more than that. Friendships, to remain permanent, must grow and thrive on interest in the new conversation, on growth in ideas, achievements, and mental alertness. No matter how many birthdays we have, we can be made young again by a new realization that mind development, intelligence, and the ability to make progress are matters of interest, not age; of incentive, not years; and that we must build our own generating plant and work to achieve, to grow, to learn, to find good everywhere, to find delight in the every day.

Some people treasure life so much that they are afraid to use it but with life, as with happiness, the more we use the more we have, for where is there a calendar or a clock big enough to mark for any individual the length of his day?

So let's forget the years and realize for our very own selves that our fountain of youth, our joy-well of living, our power to do things, lies deep in our own hearts, where neither years nor handicaps can interfere. We—you and I—are the only ones who can dip deep enough to get the full value of every day. So why cheat ourselves?

Live life today as though today were all—
As though this very morning you were born.
Your yesterdays are days beyond recall;
Tomorrow does not come until the morn.
Rest not upon the victories you have won;
Because you lost, surrender not to fear.
Your yesterday was ended with the sun.
Tomorrow has not come. Today is here.

—Douglas Malloch

Grow Young with the World

by Laura MacFarlane, *Inspiration*, 1927

Have you ever had the joy, and the thrill, too, of picking arbutus in the springtime? That beautifully delicate little blossom that trails along under the cover of fallen brown leaves and dried up grasses. Whose flowers in their rarest beauty are soft, lovely pink, and whose fragrance is delicacy itself?

One of the pleasantest recollections of my school-going days is of the trips we took on Saturdays to the nearby woods in search of these blooms. I can remember how a few warm days would remind us that we must soon be going for it was surprising how early those dainty buds would peep out from under their Winter bed. And sometimes we'd be caught in a snowstorm after we'd started, so variable was our weather, but that made the trip and our prize all the more coveted, for the difficulty we had in finding the blossoms seemed to increase their value.

So a Spring that came and went without a bunch of arbutus, which we had gathered ourselves, was indeed lacking in its chief charm. And to this very day, though now we've given up picking it in order to preserve the supply, there's nothing that arouses quite the same feeling as the sight of those sweet-smelling buds. They are the real signal of the awakened season. They cry out that Spring is here. That the world grows young again. That we should join in Nature's Spring Song.

So, in this glorious springtime, let's not miss one single minute of its happiness, nor one item of its inspiration. When the arbutus first perfumes the air, let's be up and doing. Plan your wardrobe with the thrill and ecstasy so characteristic of the season. Refurbish what you can, buy new what you must, but in all events, get in tune with the new and budding season.

Growing Old Graciously

Fashion Service, 1929

"There may be beauty in growing old if one learns to do so graciously, not striving to make of oneself a poor counterpart of women twenty years one's junior, but realizing that each age has its charm and being content to express such charm in the best way that one can."

—*Inspiration*, 1926

There is something very fine to me about a woman who grows old graciously and with dignity. I'm not for a return to bonnets and black silk dresses, but I do like to see a woman with such a fine sense of fitness in dress and in her whole mode of self-expression that she is always in harmony with her years.

Everything that a woman can do to make herself look naturally lovely, it is right for her to do; but anything that makes her unnaturally young or unnaturally bright is wrong for her. Just that added touch of rouge gives her face a hardened look and, instead of detracting from her years, adds to them.

And the same is true of dyed hair that is plainly dyed. Women who have dispensed with artificial coloring have found that their features become softened and attractive when framed naturally. In the most picturesque age of the world's history, women purposely donned white wigs or powdered their hair, knowing what a beautiful frame white hair makes for the face.

It is almost inconceivable that a woman of years and judgment should have her face lifted, and yet the plastic surgeon flourishes. But every operation is attended with a risk, for if it is not a success, it may be beyond the power of any surgeon to repair the damage that is done. True, such operations are often successful, but they must be performed again in six or eight years. And, in the meantime, the face has been robbed of its character. It either has an unnatural smoothness that is a bit uncanny or it is like a clock that has stopped.

The form of youth without youth itself must always be a misfit. And why should one wish it since all ages have their beauty for women?

I wish that every woman, as she grows older, might sift her values and feel that she would not change places with younger women if she could. She's come a long way since the days of pink-and-white youth. She ought to be just a little proud of all she's lived and learned and just a little sorry for Youth, still struggling and striving and bruising itself.

If she's accepted the changing seasons gracefully, she's found that, with their passing, her outlook has widened, she's become less self-centered, she is less disturbed by this and that, more at one with the other lives around her.

The Story Your Hands Tell

by Barbara Ellison. *Fashion Service*, 1929

As the days lengthen and old Sol begins to send out a warmer ray, housewives turn speculative eyes toward closets and bureau drawers, and men sigh heavily, for they know that campaigns of house cleaning are about to descend upon their households. Since the hands must bear the brunt of the wear and tear of this spring upheaval, suggestions for their care may be timely.

First, try to feel pride in your hands. If they are not small and shapely, be glad that they are fine and large and capable. A woman's hands are an expression of herself, and if they say to the world, "I am strong and useful and you can depend on me," she has reason to be proud of them.

Housework never has been kind to women's hands and the busiest housewives are the very women who have little opportunity for specialized help. It is only sensible for the housekeeper to avail herself of every method to save her hands.

She may like old ways best, but with her hands so much of necessity in hot water, she will do well to wear rubber gloves for her dishwashing or use a long-handled dish mop. She should wear old gloves, too, when she sweeps or does any sort of rough work. Too often, unfortunately, she does nothing of the sort, but after washing the breakfast dishes, hastily dries her hands and sweeps the floor, raising a dust that settles in the open pores of the skin. Day follows day and then when she is invited to a bridge party or some social affair where she is thrown into contact with women whose hands are better cared for, she is embarrassed over the condition of her own.

To wash the hands, use warm, not hot water, softening it if necessary with just a pinch of powdered borax, and use a good soap that is free from alkali. To use after washing, keep on hand a soothing lotion. There are many good commercial preparations and equally good homemade remedies that are not at all expensive. An ounce of glycerin and the juice of a lemon agree with some hands; glycerin and rose water with others. Pure almond or olive oil is excellent, too, with the addition of a few drops of perfumed water.

"The housewife of pioneer days whose interests were centered mainly in the house regarded her stores of bedding as her chief pride and asset; it was something that was definitely hers."
—The Patchwork Book

Patchwork and Appliqué

by Clarice Carpenter, *Fashion Service*, 1928

Patchwork quilt-making has an aristocratic ancestry and is closely interwoven with the economic and social growth of our country. In early days of America, the French women settlers received new designs for quilts from friends in the old country, who in turn had them handed down to them from the Middle Ages. In Colonial times, the art of patchwork quilt-making reached a high perfection in America. As our grandmothers were forbidden to wear bright colors, patchwork quilts became the medium of expression for their love of them, and into their fine stitches they wove their dreams, their aspirations. These hard-working women put their richest thoughts into their needlework.

How eagerly the women of those days must have looked forward to the infrequent occasions when long distances were traveled to meet together. These opportunities for companionship became the bright spots in their lives. All brought their patchwork, patterns were eagerly exchanged, and originality was greatly prized. The designs were most carefully and skillfully cut out, filled under with wool, appliquéd to form the pattern and then quilted down to the body of the quilt. The lines of the quilting were made to bring out the design created by the appliqué. At these "patchwork meetings" the political and social ques-

Closely spaced blanket-stitches give a lovely finished effect.

Reversed blanket-stitch is worked toward the motif, just catching the edge.

Satin-stitch is used on fine fabrics.

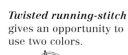

Twisted running-stitch gives an opportunity to use two colors.

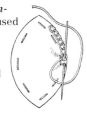

The chain-stitch is used very near the edge of the appliquéd motif.

tions of the day were discussed, as well as the pros and cons of the parson's sermons. The flavor of them has come down to us in story and song as well as history. It may be truly said that these earnest quilters were our first clubwomen.

This was especially true when she had spun the thread and woven the material for the blankets, sheets, and coverlets, had pieced the quilt tops and had perhaps herself done the quilting. To be worthy of note, a quilt should be made in a design that is beautiful, unique or interesting in some particular; of colors which are pleasing or effectively used; and more than anything else, beautifully quilted.

There are two definite methods of making quilt tops, piecing and appliqué, and frequently the two methods are combined in one quilt. The work is generally done in blocks, which afterward are sewn together. A quilt may also be made in one piece. The designs for pieced quilts are mostly in geometric figures. The square, triangle and diamond are the most common shapes, although other straight-line as well as curved-line patterns are used.

Piecework and Appliqué

Piecework consists of small pieces of cloth of different colors sewed together with fine running stitches to form a design. These stitches may be made on the wrong side, leaving a 1/4-inch seam, or the pieces may be over-handed on the right side. Nowadays piecing is frequently done on the sewing machine, which saves much time. The old-time appliqué had a narrow hem turned all around its edge, and was hemmed with a fine almost invisible hemming stitch. In using a perforated quilt pattern, if the design is for an appliqué block, it can be stamped onto the foundation block itself, giving the exact position for the placing of each part of the appliqué figure.

 "Stamped" describes a design transferred to fabric.

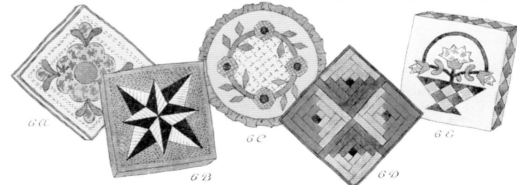

Model 6A—This pillow for an early American bedroom or cottage living room uses very bright colors and is finished with harmonizing bias tape on the edges.

Model 6B—This pillow is an example of true pieced patchwork, the sections of the star being joined to each other rather than applied to a foundation. Plain and striped gingham are used in developing it.

Model 6C—Appliquéd patches of checked and plain gingham on muslin make this round pillow, which is not boxed, but finished with a ruffle of the materials used for the leaves and stems. For a quilt, use the design on square blocks, alternating plain and patchwork.

Model 6D—The log cabin motif used on this pillow was a favorite with our great-grandmothers, perhaps because it could be made from very small pieces. Start each of the four small blocks with a 1-1/4 inch square, so that after seams are removed, it is a 3/4-inch square. Build onto this with stripes of material in two tones, each being longer than the previous one.

Model 6E—Plain and printed cottons on unbleached muslin work well on this design. Though the basket appears to be pieced patchwork, it is simpler to appliqué the dark triangles, since all of the flower motifs must be applied. The patchwork side consists of squares or diamonds and triangles made of the muslin and the material of the basket.

When Birthdays Come Around

Fashion Service, 1928

Whether we're six or sixty or at any of the milestones between, there's one day in the year that stands out from all the rest—our birthday. And on that day, we like to celebrate, and we welcome any plans, simple or elaborate, that our families or friends arrange. Besides giving so much pleasure, birthday celebrations are not hard to plan and carry out, for there are so many little traditional touches that can be called on to aid, chief among them being the birthday cake.

Whether the day is to be marked by a party or just a quiet home celebration, the centerpiece for the table on this particular occasion should be a birthday cake, decorated with candles, one for each year that has passed and, if desired, one to "grow on." The candles may be lighted just before the guests come to the table. Then, when they have burned a little time, the guest of honor is allowed to determine her period of single blessedness or other important matters by blowing them out. This time-honored custom always causes a great deal of merriment.

To make cakes successfully—and this is one of the ambitions of the modern housewife—there are a few principles that should be faithfully observed. Cake making has been defined as the art of combining flour, sugar, butter, eggs, milk, etc., in such a way as to produce a palatable, delicious, yet nourishing article of food. A lack of knowledge of the "art of combining" has been the cause of many cake failures, even though the proper ingredients have been used.

The mixing of the cake should be accomplished as quickly as possible. Cake is never so light and feathery when partly mixed ingredients are allowed to stand for several minutes before others are added. All ingredients of a cake should be assembled before the mixing is started. More flour than any other ingredient is used in a cake, and the texture, lightness, and color of the cake depend greatly on the flour used. To secure the best results, a pastry, or cake flour, which is whiter than bread flour, looks more like starch, feels soft and smooth in the fingers, and holds together when squeezed in the hand, should be used.

Layer Cake

1/2 cup butter
1 cup sugar
2 eggs
2/3 cup milk
2 cups flour
3 tsp. baking powder
Pinch of salt
1/2 tsp. vanilla
1/2 tsp. lemon juice

Grease two layer-cake tins. Cover only bottom of tins with waxed paper, grease again, and set tins aside until they are needed. Sift flour once and then measure 2 cupfuls. Add 3 level teaspoonfuls of baking powder and a pinch of salt, and sift three times. Set aside until needed. Measure 1 cupful of granulated sugar. Roll and sift the sugar until all grains will pass through the sieve. Set aside until needed. Separate the yolks and whites of 2 eggs and set aside in a cool place until needed. Measure 2/3 cupful of milk and set aside until needed.

Now cream the butter until it is soft and white around the edges. Add the sugar gradually, creaming the mixture meanwhile. Beat the egg yolks until thick and lemon-colored. Add them to the butter-and-sugar mixture. Beat well.

Alternate adding a little of the dry mixture ingredients—the flour, baking powder, and salt—and a little of the milk until all are used. Beat the batter hard after each addition of the flour and milk. Add the flavorings and beat the batter very hard. Beat the eggs whites until stiff but not dry, and carefully fold them into the mixture.

Pour the batter into the tins, spreading it high on the sides and at the corners and leaving a slight depression in the center.

Bake in a moderate (350°F) oven from 20 to 30 minutes. When the cake is done, it will shrink from the sides of the tins. It may be tested by inserting a broom straw in the center. If no particles of dough adhere to the straw, it is done.

When cool, the layers may be put together with the fluffy icing or a filling, and then the entire cake covered in icing.

 Today we use toothpicks in place of broom straws.

Fluffy Icing

1-1/2 cups of granulated sugar
3/4 cup water
2 egg whites
1 tsp. vanilla
1/2 tsp. almond extract

Boil sugar and water without stirring until the syrup spins a hair when dropped from spoon. Pour syrup slowly on stiffly beaten egg whites, beating constantly until stiff enough to spread. Add vanilla and almond extract and mix.

Model 10

10 C

10 D

House Dresses

by Mary Brooks Picken,
Inspiration, 1923

"When Fifth Avenue becomes interested in a home frock, that's news! News of a sort that means something, especially when we know that it is being displayed in all the smart shops."

MODEL 10D: *A simple, little kimono-sleeve dress with a removable bib-like panel in the front of the waist is this brown-white-and-blue gingham with rickrack trim. The panel may be unbuttoned at the shoulder and omitted when desired. It is held down securely at the lower end by the sashes, which are fastened to it and tie in a bow in the center back.*

MODEL 10C: *For the figure that requires a little more than the usual fullness over the bust, this model of blue-and-white cross-barred gingham, with its square yoke and gathers, will be admirable.*

MODEL 10 (Center): *A dress that measures up to the ideal in every way is this One Hour type. Made from such a fabric as cretonne, gaily sprigged with more or less conventional flowers in sunny gold, however, any favorite color may be used. The fitted bands at the neck and sleeves and the plain-color pocket flaps are bound with a darker tone than the blouse. The hip fullness is confined under narrow sashes, which are secured by large buttons and then tie in the center back.*

Clothes have a way of reflecting on both the wearer and her associates to such an amazing degree that she who prizes harmony as a part of the daily life of her home will not begrudge the little additional time necessary to plan and make a home dress worthy of expressing her personality. The great proportion of time spent in home dresses by home women causes them to assume marked importance. Not only must they be becoming, but they must be comfortable and practical as well.

Mornings are brighter, household tasks easier, and dispositions happier when home frocks are attractive and becoming; and, while simplicity is a valuable feature, certain concessions to charm must be made if the finished outfits are to be decorative. The models illustrate the types of designs and colors that combine suitability with effectiveness.

In the matter of home dresses, appropriate serviceability is of first importance, but becomingness and fashion should be carefully considered. After a while, one usually finds a type of house dress that is becoming, but one need not get a regulation "blue-and-white stripe" and wear it year after year. One's pride has little part in such uniforms and one's ambition always to appear at one's best receives no stimulus. One woman is frank enough to say, "I look actually ordinary in plain house dresses, so I usually select soft gray or quiet blue and make dainty lawn collars and cuffs and put a wee bit of colored embroidery in them just to make them less ordinary." This is pride, but a wonderfully commendable kind. And her attractiveness repays her a thousand times for the time and thought given to the planning of her clothes. "The foundation of pride is in the heart, and only there, and if not there, it is neither in the look nor in the clothes."

There is no lovelier picture than that of a home woman dressed in an attractive, serviceable, and comfortable dress, one that speaks of cheeriness rather than drudgery, of happiness rather than duty. On days that are stormy or too cold for neighbors or friends to drop in—on such a day, a dress can be almost entirely completed. If hand decoration is used, it can be done as pick-up work after dinner or on an afternoon when some one drops in for a visit.

In considering materials for home dresses, remember that fast colors should be purchased even though they cost a little more per yard. Neatness should dominate in every seam and line to insure that ever-admirable freshness. A niceness should be evident in the size of collars, pockets, facings, and bindings, as well as in belts and hems, so that they look right for the material and are becoming to the individual. Collars can be smart, yet of a neat width and shaping. Belts are often very attractive if they are dainty. Proportion of trimming is ever important in all sewing, but especially so when two colors or kinds of materials are used in combination, for they must appear to balance harmoniously.

The Colorful Easter Holiday

Inspiration, 1920

Well does Easter deserve its recognition as the most joyous holiday of the year. The long, hard winter is past. Spring is at hand. Everywhere flowers are budding and trees are bursting into life. Old Mother Earth is garbing herself anew in the gayest and brightest of colors. And so, if Nature can conquer death in this splendid manner, how much more significant becomes the great story behind Easter.

A number of very delightful customs are connected with the celebration of Easter and observed by old and young alike. The sending of colored eggs to one's friends as gifts is perhaps the most popular of these. This has come down to us through the ages from such peoples as the Egyptians, Persians, and Romans who regarded the egg as the emblem of the universe.

In more recent years, we have added the legend of the eggs being the gift of the Easter rabbit, so small bunnies have become as popular as eggs and chickens. Surely every one of us grown-ups can recall how eagerly we scampered downstairs on Easter morning to see what the Easter rabbit had left for us. And now what pleasure we find in preparing little gifts for the young folks about us, for they should never be overlooked in this joyous, gladsome time.

Dyeing or staining hard-cooked eggs is the general custom, but if one has a little time to devote to Easter preparations, gifts that will please the most fastidious child can be made with very slight effort. Instead of boiling the eggs, the contents can be removed and the empty shells then used as a foundation for all sorts of attractive little novelties. To empty the shell, make a small hole in each end, and then, with the shell held gently between the thumb and forefinger, put one end to the lips and blow through the hole until the contents have run out of the other end. On the empty shells paint little faces and complete the effect by adding cunning dresses and bonnets of crepe or tissue paper in pretty colors. There is no end to the ideas that can be carried out in this way.

Another charming Easter gift can be made by using egg shells as receptacles for a few tiny flowers, such as crocuses. For these, make a rather good-sized hole in the small end of the egg and remove the contents through this opening. Then dye the shells, using purple dye for some and yellow for others. Put tiny flowers in the dry shells.

Charming Hats for the Rosebud Age

They are delightful, the new hats for the kiddies, simple in contour and faultlessly youthful, as is essential for this type of millinery, but developed with such care and such exquisite workmanship that they are a joy to the eye. From the vast assortment of children's imported models, the sextet at the top of the page was selected, each hat embracing a style feature of the season and each suitable for the many occasions that a child might need a hat. Every one of the models pictured here is a work of art, perfect as to proportions and lines and embellished with hand-work, giving it that inimitable distinction for which the Parisian hats are famed.

Easter Coats for the Younger Set

When the "very youngest" promenade in new Spring togs, their small outfits can be just as smart as those worn by their older brothers and sisters and with equal claims to modishness. Scarf collars, circular flares, side plaits, and severe tailored effects characterize coats for the before-teen age, which choose the season's silks and woolens in the youthful colors.

Magic Pattern

The Fabric Flower
Inspiration, 1927

Fashionable for Spring—
It Is Easily and Quickly Made

Appearances indicate that more flowers will be seen on milady's frocks than in Spring gardens, for every dress, from the simplest sports costume to the most elaborate evening gown, is made more modish by a flower bouquet in a harmonizing or properly contrasting color. These blossoms differ in size, shape, and color but among the most favored are the soft, shaggy, raw-edge chrysanthemums originated in Paris by the house of Chanel. The softest and most feminine bits of fluff imaginable, as the illustration indicates, it is not surprising that, with present trend toward femininity in dress, they have acquired such a vogue.

Made of chiffon, georgette, triple voile, or *mousseline de soie*, their delicacy on the one hand and their simplicity on the other make them suitable for widely different types of costumes. One of their most desirable features is that they are easily made with results that are as attractive as in the more expensive or imported flowers.

To develop one of these chrysanthemums, circular sections of the material are cut in varying sizes, slashed to form the petals, and joined with the sizes graduated toward the top. The ends of the petals may be rounded, as the diagram shows, but in sheer material, they are just as pretty left square, as in the photo (shown top right) of the finished flower. From 1/2 to 3/4 yard of 40-inch material is required for a full, fluffy effect.

 See Notes, page 232, for modern tips and techniques.

First cut a paper pattern for each different-sized circle. Use a compass to mark the circular outline or improvise one by tying a thin cord to a pencil and holding your left forefinger at a point half the width, or diameter, of the proposed circle. The largest circle should be 5-1/2 inches and the smallest 3, with those between respectively 5, 4-1/2, 4, and 3-1/2. With these patterns, cut from the material four circles 5-1/2 inches in diameter, three 5 inches, two 4-1/2 inches, two 4 inches, two 3-1/2 inches, and nine 3 inches.

Beginning with the largest circle, fold each in half through the center and press or pin the crease, then fold over again in quarters and crease. Place pins at the corners and at intervals along the edges at right angles to it in order to

hold the four layers thus formed in place. Also, place a pin about 3/4 inch to the right of the corner, as at *a* in the diagram, and another 1-3/4 inches above the corner, as in *b*. Holding the material firmly with the corner to the left, cut the petals about 3/8-inch wide, running the first, third, fifth, etc., down almost to *a* and making the alternate ones about 1 inch shorter. This makes the base firmer and avoids the possibility of having the petals fall off because of their narrowness at

the inner end. In cutting, make no attempt to keep the width of each petal the same from top to bottom, for as the width of the circle itself becomes less, the petals will become narrower. A plain oval section remains at the center. Cut all layers in this manner. In the smaller sizes, cut the petals, of which there will be fewer, nearer to the center.

With the 22 layers cut, lay them out flat on a table for joining. Place one of the 5-1/2-inch layers with the long axis of the oval running from right to left; then lay the second 5-1/2-inch layer over this, with the long axis of the oval running from top to bottom. Continue in this way with all but the 3-inch circles, laying one circle on top of another with the long and short lengths of the foundation alternating, and graduating the circles in size toward the top. Then pin smoothly together and make a tiny slash not quite 1/2-inch in length through the center of them all.

Next, place the 3-inch circles one on top of the other, fold the entire set at the same time in half and then in quarters, and pin securely. Pull the corner of the set through the slash of the other group and fasten securely to the back of the flower. Overhand a fold about 1-inch long at the center back in line with the slash to be used as a stem.

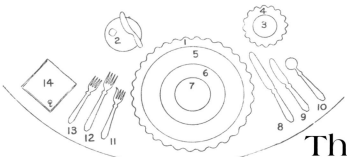

Section of a Table Correctly Set for a Formal Luncheon

1. Plate Doily.
2. Bread and Butter Plate with Butter and Spreader.
3. Tumbler.
4. Tumbler Doily.
5. Plate.
6. Bouillon Saucer.
7. Bouillon Cup.
8. Meat Knife.
9. Fish Knife.
10. Bouillon Spoon.
11. Salad Fork.
12. Meat Fork.
13. Fish Fork.
14. Napkin.

The Well-Dressed Table

by Mary Gilgallon,
Fashion Service, 1929

*B*eautiful silver permeates a meal with an air of elegance and refinement that no other table accessory can supply. The exquisite hand-wrought pieces of former days have given way to more utilitarian designs and shapes. So now the housewife can find in the shops silver that will lend dignity and refinement to her table settings yet will be easy to keep in perfect condition.

There are now on the market so many variations of very good, heavily plated ware with lifetime guarantees and attractive designs that every one may be in possession of a set of flatware for a nominal sum.

Table Settings and Service

The placing of silverware on the table is the next matter to consider. Each piece should be placed so that the end is one inch from the edge of the table, and all pieces must be parallel to each other. The knives and spoons are placed to the right of the plate, and the forks at the left. The knives are placed with the cutting edge toward the plate, the spoons with the inside of the bowl turned up; and the fork with the tines up. Place the silver in the order in which it is to be used, with the exception of the knife and fork for the main course. They are placed beside the plate—the knife at the right and the fork to the left. The article first used, aside from these, is placed farthest from the plate. At a meal where no knife is required, as is often the case at a Sunday night tea or a chafing-dish spread, place the fork at the right hand; if only one other piece of silver is required—as dessert spoons or forks—set this, also, at the right, the one first used farthest from the plate.

The napkin is placed on the left with the fold on the upper side. The napkin must be placed on a line with the silverware and plate. The bread and butter spreader is placed across the upper right-hand side of the bread and butter plate with the handle toward the right. Salt and pepper receptacles are set between each two covers or at the corners or sides, where they may be used by several people.

Just Among Ourselves

"If a woman wants her own money badly enough, she'll find a way to earn it," said a woman to whom I was talking the other day. And I believe she's right, for I can recall one instance after another of women who have set out with nothing much but their own determination and have made their own opportunities—just the usual home women with the usual home tasks or the average school girl with a school girl hunger for pretty clothes and good times. But nothing thrills me like the success of our own readers. Very brief are the letters from some of them, for scarcity of time prevents them from giving but the barest statement of what they have done, but inspiration to ambitious home women lies in just these few lines.

—*Alice H. Stone, Editor*

"I have been having a steady income for the last five months, for I accepted a position at the Federal Reserve Bank to serve lunches to their employees every month. Then, with the other catering I have done, I have cleared close to $200 every month. One month I cleared $235."

—*Mrs. B. R. B., Washington*

Mrs. L. W., of Texas, writes that she is sewing at home. She made $85 last month. And Miss L. K. S., of North Carolina, recently bought a car with money she made sewing. "Some months," she writes, "I make $100 and over and some months, less. But altogether I earn as much as a graduate teacher and I like the work better."

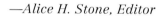

The pinch of hard times may come and money may be scarce, but "Billy Boy," an Illinois lad, will be able to hold up his head among his school fellows so long as his mother's fingers retain their cunning. With justifiable pride, she writes:

"I have made my little boy a nice overcoat. They are asking from $7 to $12 in the shops for them and I can't see that he doesn't look a trifle better than the other boys of his age. All the cost would be covered by $1 easily, I think. I made myself four house dresses, nice ones that you could not buy for less than $10, and they averaged about $1. Three are of fast-color prints and one of gingham. The prints were short cuts at 25 cents. I could go on page after page and tell how I saved on Billy Boy's play clothes, etc. By just this one season's sewing, I have saved enough to buy my new Singer Electric."

—*Mrs. R. M. H., Illinois*

Modern Notions

May is the month to celebrate our mothers and the mother figures in our lives. My own mother, Donna, has everything to do with my love of the creative arts, and my grandmother, Mildred, was a gifted painter whose vintage art collection has been a mainstay of my own archives. Clearly, the creative spirit is strong in the women in my family, and I know my ability to nurture that same spirit in my own children comes from the tradition these amazing women started.

As young people, it means the world to have a trusted adult nudge us along on the path of imagination. This is where we first learn what Mary Brooks Picken calls in this month's opening essay "child faith"—trust in the world around us that our needs, and even some of our wants, will be fulfilled. Also, you never know how that time you spend patiently assisting the small ones in your life can influence them. You may be passing the creative torch along by making the old new again for a younger generation, or even planting the seed for a lifelong relationship with the arts.

Speaking of seeds, as the weather heats up, the flowers you planted months ago with the utmost care and hope finally make themselves known. I can think of nothing more delightful than the view of my back garden as it gives its show of vibrant color, and where I first see the roses make their Summer debut. The early 1900s brought a hotbed of pamphlets and magazines catering to the garden enthusiast. Floral games and pressing flowers became popularized, and for the first time flowers crossed geographical borders in a frenzy of exchange and curiosity. This season carry on timeless traditions by exchanging a homegrown seedling with a friend, or refer to our *Department of Sewing* to pass on something just as lasting—a bit of your inspired handwork.

And if a hat doesn't appear over the hillside, as it does in Mary Brooks Picken's essay, simply make your own by referring to this month's *Department of Millinery*. After all, part of a child's faith is having "faith in your own two hands," as a student so beautifully puts it in a letter featured in this month's *Testimonials*. I am so grateful for my mother and grandmother who gave me faith in my own two hands.

Yours,

Amy B.

MAY

*Every day is Mother's Day.
Mother's Day has come and gone,
but the memories it has
awakened and the tenderness it
has created will do much toward
keeping us on the safe road.*

—Gustave L. Weinss, *Inspiration*, 1921

A Thimbleful of Faith

Child Faith

by Mary Brooks Picken,
Excerpted from *Thimblefuls of Friendliness*, 1924

May Day celebrations held in the little village near my childhood home were eventful affairs, at least for little girls. Well do I remember one time when May Day was coming nearer and nearer and my sisters and I had no new hats for the occasion. My mother had been ill and we could not go to the May-pole party without them. But the enthusiasm of our faith came to our aid and we prayed eagerly and earnestly for new hats.

We dreamed about them, we talked among ourselves about them, and we even pretended as we went about our household duties—and we thought then that the entire management of the household depended upon us—that we were wearing beautiful new hats, that we were at the May-pole party. We did all the imaginable pretending and dreaming of little girls and—we prayed. Our every thought was a prayer for those hats. And, besides, we kept our faith, never once questioning that the hats would arrive in ample time for the celebration.

On the night before May Day, we prayed most earnestly and with full assurance; and on the morning of the first of May, while we were out helping pull away straw from around some strawberry plants and the time was growing closer to May-party time, we again decided to pray for the hats we so much desired; so, in perfect confidence, we bowed our little heads. Our prayers were humble and sincere and as earnest and as fervent as our little lips could make them.

I shall never forget the unspeakable joy that came to us later when we looked up, for, coming over the hill, we saw our good father carrying a real, "sure enough" hat box. We had to wash our hands before we could touch the three hats it contained; and, oh, such haste with the washing! There was our prayer answered right before us!

The hats had been sent all the way from Illinois by a dear auntie, and they were truly the most beautiful hats we had ever owned. And coming as they did—we knew that we had not mentioned our great desire to any other than our three selves and that our prayers and our dreams were in secret—we adored them . . .

As grown-ups, we haven't the child faith in miracles, but we know the supreme power of right. We enjoy the confidence of earnest effort rewarded, a confidence that urges us on and on to individual victories. Emerson says: "Him we count the fortunate man whose determination to his aim is sufficiently strong to leave him no doubt."

. . . I do not believe in supplication, in begging that we may be granted that for which we pray, but I believe in recognizing the power of God to help man face clearly his actual needs and then to express openly an earnest desire for them. To seek good for the sake of good is virtuous, and worthy reverence is always present in sincere prayer, which, even when unspoken, is an expression of faith and kindliness. Such prayers are always answered and often more fully than is anticipated. Learning to eliminate all but the totally essential from one's wishes helps greatly in the sincerity and efficacy of prayer.

Always there is a quiet sweetness that comes into my heart when it is prayer time in church or when I hear little folks' goodnight prayers, or whenever I realize that I am in the presence of the Spirit of Prayer. Little folks taught to kneel in humble quietness start aright, for through the stillness that surrounds them all else can be excluded but the recognition of the Great Good that guides, guards, and encourages them to believe.

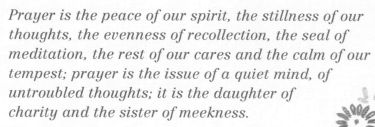

Prayer is the peace of our spirit, the stillness of our thoughts, the evenness of recollection, the seal of meditation, the rest of our cares and the calm of our tempest; prayer is the issue of a quiet mind, of untroubled thoughts; it is the daughter of charity and the sister of meekness.

—*Inspiration, 1924*

Mother: Queen o' the World

Inspiration, May 1926

"No girl can ever truly appreciate her mother until she has children of her own and finds herself loving, planning, sacrificing for them. Then she can understand how her mother felt and will be grateful and humble and appreciative in proportion."

—Mary Brooks Picken

Maytime is a *happy* time of the year. For isn't it the time of kite flying? And flower and garden planting? And May-pole dancing? And May-basket giving? And June-wedding planning? And sweet-girl graduating?

Maytime is a *beautiful* time of the year, too. For isn't it blossom time, when the apple and the cherry and the peach trees fill our yards and our hillsides with their fragrance and their delicate blooms? And there's balmy air, and gay wild flowers, and much bright sunshine.

Besides all this happiness and beauty, May-time sets apart a far more significant event—Mother's Day. The day when we pause in the midst of our busy lives to pay honor to our Mother. For she it is, who develops for us an affection that has never been equaled nor even approached. An affection so big and so flexible that she can appreciate and enjoy with us our greatest triumphs and can understand and help us to bear our deepest sorrows. It's fitting, then, that in this blossom time of the year, we show our gratitude for mother love—love that surpasses every human deed and word and thought in its all-encompassing nature.

Cooking with Cold

Mary Gilgallon, *Fashion Service*, 1932

In the manner of the stage magician producing rabbits out of hats before your astonished eyes, you may present to your family the dainty desserts, the appealing appetizers, and the novel salads made possible by the aid of mechanical refrigeration. And this with so much little trouble that those fortunate enough to be served by you will feel that you are, perhaps, using his magic methods.

In this case, it is his own cleverness that intrigues his audience, while in yours, it will be the magic of "cooking with cold" that makes possible so many interesting variations in your family as well as party meals. For without a doubt, there is no other form of food preparation that produces such excellent results so simply.

Many of us are familiar with the variety of attractive dishes whose making is simplified by this means, but not all of us appreciate how much of the usual preparation for a meal can be done hours beforehand. Muffins, hot biscuits, or rolls may be gotten ready early in the morning, placed in the pans ready for baking, covered with wax paper, and stored away until 20 minutes before dinner. Remember, however, to use a double action baking powder when this is done . . . Vegetables and greens for salads or desserts can also be cleaned and assembled hours before needed. Fruit cocktails are much improved in taste by early preparation . . . Frozen appetizers, entrees, and salads of all types are becoming more popular. And desserts! Their ease of preparation and their utter deliciousness make them irresistible.

Very light and appetizing desserts can be made using ladyfingers. These can all be prepared ahead of time and stored in the refrigerator for later use.

Fruit Compote

1 cup slightly sweetened
   whipped cream
1 cup crushed pineapples
1 cup raspberries
1 cup strawberries
Ladyfingers

Place this mixture in a bowl and mix lightly to coat fruit. Line the serving dish with ladyfingers or small wafers and then pile the chilled fruit mixture on top. This can be made ahead and placed in the icebox for one hour before serving.

 **Instructions for whipped cream are on page 117.**

Lemon Ice Box Cake

1 tbl. gelatin
1/4-cup cold water
4 egg yolks
2 lemons
1 tsp. grated lemon rind
1/2-cup sugar
1/4 tsp. salt
4 egg whites
1/2-cup sugar
Ladyfingers

Soak gelatin in the cold water. Cook the egg yolks, lemon juice, and the rind, 1/2 cupful of sugar, and salt together until of custard-like consistency, stirring constantly. Add the softened gelatin and stir thoroughly. Cool, and when beginning to thicken, fold in the egg whites, which have been beaten with 1/2 cupful of sugar. Rinse a large round or square pan with cold water. Pour in lemon mixture to depth of one inch. Arrange a layer of ladyfingers on the custard. Then alternate cakes and custard until pan is filled, having custard on top. Place in refrigerator for 12 hours. Serve garnished with whipped cream.

Ice-Box Pudding

2 squares chocolate
8 tbls. confectioner's sugar
2 tbls. water
4 eggs
1 tsp. vanilla
1/2 lb. ladyfingers

Put the chocolate, sugar, and water in a double boiler and heat, stirring constantly. Separate the eggs, beat the yolks, add to the chocolate mixture, and cook until thick. Set aside to cool. Beat the egg whites stiff, fold into the mixture, and add the vanilla.

Separate the ladyfingers, line a mould or baking dish with wax paper, and cover the sides and bottom with a layer of ladyfingers. Cover with the chocolate mixture, add another layer of ladyfingers, and so on until the mixture is used. Use ladyfingers on top to indicate rows for cutting. Set in the refrigerator for 24 hours. To serve, remove from the mould, pull off the wax paper, and place on a glass or other flat dish. Serve with whipped cream.

Every Woman's House—Her Castle

by Mary Brooks Picken, *Inspiration*, 1921

Recently, I heard a young woman say, "I start out thinking I am going to do everything as I should and not harbor ugly thoughts, but I haven't reached business in the morning before I am finding fault with someone. I keep it up all day usually, and by night I am totally miserable. I cannot settle myself even to read."

As I heard this, I could not help thinking what the day means to me. It is always like a new piece of cloth to use in the best way that I know. Material means so much to me—its texture, color, width, and purpose—that even if it is only a kitchen curtain or cloth for dish toweling, it has its use and should be cut and made the best way I know so that it may give the greatest satisfaction and

comfort. And our lives are as a day. We must make them fruitful. How? By total unselfishness. Selfish people often have comforts that the unselfish do not have, but they never possess the same quantity of richness and happiness.

The other night I read Robert Herrick's "The Master of the Inn," and I felt, were it possible, I should like to write a book and call it "The Woman of the Home," where I should place the woman of every household on the same pedestal of unselfish devotion as Herrick put this great master.

A woman, according to her love and energy, has a great responsibility in making her home an abode of peace, a place of protection from the winds of the world, a castle for her love, and a shrine to womanliness.

A LITTLE WORLD OF PEACE

By W. Dayton Wegeforth

Mould yourself a little world of peace
   To live upon in blissful, sweet content;
And place it in a cloud of silver fleece
   Amid the blue of your own firmament.

Build around your hope a golden fence
   To bar out care—to keep your joy within;
From radiant sunlight glean your confidence,
   And with its shimmering beams your future spin.

Place your faith in God, and tread the way
   Through flowered years, with some twin-hearted soul;
Let no dark sorrow dim your perfect day,
   But seek the myriad joys that make life whole.

SEWING DEPARTMENT

Clothing the Wee Ones O' the World

by Alice H. Stone, *Fashion Service*, May 1926

"**M**y two most important reasons for wishing to learn to sew," writes a student whose picture shows her with a youngster on each knee. . ."Children's clothes are so high, and you know you do love to have your child look as nice as your neighbor's," writes another student. Most mothers are human enough to recognize such a feeling—not that they wish to outdo their neighbors in any vainglorious way, but out of the love they bear their children there comes the desire to see that the little ones have every chance to appear at advantage among other children. . . .

Because they have once been children themselves, mothers realize the acute discomfiture of childish hearts over being obliged to wear unbecoming clothes, and out of the greater wisdom of their years they realize, too, the subtle danger to a child's self-esteem through his habitual subjection to such discomfiture. . . But they have seen the reverse side of the picture, too. . . they have experienced the joy of creating for such beauty-loving youngsters attractive garments that have made them proud and happy way down to the bottom of their stout little hearts.

"So many women want to learn how to sew—not for themselves, but for the sake of certain little babies whose smiles bring hope and happiness . . . they want to be able to give to their little Blossoms the 'pretties' that they themselves did not have."

97

Magic Pattern

A Magic Scarf for Every Mood

Fashion Service, 1928

The scarf continues to hold its magic touch of smartness to our newest costumes. It may be a sports triangle, a large draped affair for afternoon, taking on almost the proportions of a cape, or it may be only a graceful wisp that adds its own flattering touch of softness to a chiffon gown. Into whatever category it falls, it is no longer just a piece of material, cut square or oblong. It shows interesting variation in cut, and is so carefully planned as part of the costume as to remove any hint of the haphazard in its choice.

The printed crepe-de-Chine triangle at the far left (A) has a clever touch in the three smaller triangles of plain Georgette that flutter gaily at the corners. Such a scarf

 See Notes on page 232 for modern tips and techniques

is a fitting accessory to a sports dress that consists of plaited, printed skirt and plain blouse. Diagram A gives the sizes of the triangles. Finish all edges with picoting or rolled hems, overlap the small triangles, as shown, and attach them with stitching or machine hemstitching.

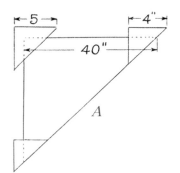

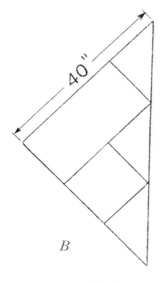

B

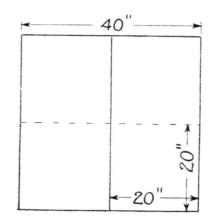

The modernistic triangular scarf on the previous page (B) combines any three harmonizing colors, being particularly attractive in three new summer colors— minuet, a pale orchid, rhapsody, a pale greenish blue, and serenade, a soft cream yellow. Diagram B shows the arrangement of the sections. The three small triangles are of one color, and the other two sections, of the second and third colors. Join the sections with machine hemstitching, turning one edge under 1/4 inch and lapping and basting over the edge to which it is joined. After hemstitching, trim the edges away.

The large scarf (C) on the previous page combines black and tan satin to form an interesting accessory to a black satin dress. The Diagrams C at right show the method of cutting it from a 40-inch square of the tan and a 24-inch length of the black satin. Cut the tan squares on the heavy lengthwise center line, and fold on the dotted crosswise center line, for the two double end sections. From the black section, cut two 20-inch squares and two strips 20 inches long and 4 inches wide for the double collar. Gather one edge of each black square and insert between the two collar thicknesses at the ends. Insert the opposite ungathered edges between the two edges of the tan sections, and finish the free edges with narrow handmade hems.

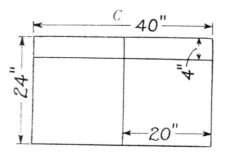

To the right (D) is a simple and graceful scarf of chiffon. The diagram shows how it is cut from 3/4 yard of 40-inch material. The collar section is 40 inches long and 7 inches wide. After this is removed, cut the remaining material on the center line to produce two 20-inch squares. Finish these and the long edges of the single-thickness collar with tiny handmade hems. Lap the corners of the squares over the collar, trim away surplus material, and finish the joining with tiny hand-felled seams.

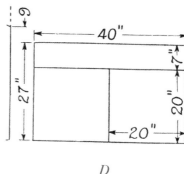

D

Summer Skin Care

by Barbara Ellison, *Fashion Service*, May 1928

*S*ummer is a time of rejuvenation. Our skin, which has become pinched and dry in resisting the wintry blasts, basks in the genial warmth. We perspire freely and thus our complexions are cleared in Nature's own way. Our diet becomes lighter with plenty of fresh green vegetables and these are excellent for the skin.

But with all its friendliness, one must observe certain precautions in summer lest the skin become dust dried or the direct rays of the sun work irreparable damage. We shall have something to say about protecting the skin from direct sunlight, but let's begin at the beginning, for there are two general classes of skins, the oily and the dry, and each must be treated differently. . . If your skin is oily, avoid fattening foods—cream and butter, fat meats, rich cakes, and sauces. These are for the woman with a dry skin. . . .

In general, creams, cold creams and cleansing creams should be light and melty, for a soft, melting cream penetrates the pores, more easily dissolves the dirt, lubricates, and does not stretch the skin in the process. Plain olive oil is good, especially for a dry skin. Daily cleansing with some fatty preparation is good for dry skins and helps to keep them soft and supple. . . .

Massage is cleansing, too, and therefore helpful to oily skin. A novel method of stirring up the circulation, which is likely to be sluggish in skin of this type, is by means of cupping . . . Simply place a small glass cup on the face, holding it there for a few moments til the suction draws the blood to the surface. Then, move it to a new spot, continuing in this way until the face has been covered and the blood made to circulate freely.

Sports Hats Are Smartly Ornate

Fashion Service, 1928

Individuality knows no limits this season so long as good taste is preserved. Expressing this new spirit, these practical, stylish, and becoming models, supplemented by matching bags, present typical fashions for sports wear.

Brimmed body straws in entirely new weaves and varied sizes are distinguished by simplicity of outline and ornate trims. Dusty colors, giving an old and sun-faded effect, are the newest note in the sports realm, which also favors exquisite handwork.

The most pronounced novelty of this season is found in the crocheted body hats of visca and hemp. Because of their exquisite workmanship and suppleness, which make them adaptable to all forms of millinery work, former favorites are being discarded ruthlessly to make way for them, regardless of their high cost.

—Mary Mahon,
Fashion Service, May 1926

DEPARTMENT OF HOUSEKEEPING

A Smiling Garden

Fashion Service, 1926

Suggested Flower Groupings

Annual delphinium
Pink poppies
Ageratum
Calendula
Red and yellow celosia
   (Feathered cockscomb)

*   *   *

Pink geraniums
White and lavender petunias

*   *   *

African marigolds
Purple petunias

*   *   *

Deep blue sweet sultans
Calendula

*   *   *

Salvia (scarlet sage)
Red and yellow zinnias

*   *   *

Rose zinnias
Flesh pink candytuft
Rose lavender candytuft

*   *   *

  For a sweet-smelling bed
Mignonette
Tube roses
Pansies

*N*ot only because the raising of flowers is a pleasure, but because beautifying the setting of one's home should be quite as much the concern of the homemaker as the care of the interior, do I urge you to plant just a few seeds this year if you never have done so before. An amount as small as fifty cents makes it possible to have a plot of flowers that will delight you in three ways—first, through your sense of sight; secondly, through your sense of smell; and thirdly, through that joy of all flower lovers, the luxury of giving away.

Just Take a Walk

Just take a walk in the morning,
Don't say you haven't the time.
Climb out of bed twenty minutes ahead
Of the hour you're expected to climb.
Quit riding down to the office,
Walk at least part of the way—
Walk for a mile for a change for awhile,
And see what it does to the day!

—Douglas Malloch

102

Making the Lights Friendly

by Clarice Carpenter, *Fashion Service*, 1932

The art of homemaking includes many branches. The members of the household look to its guiding spirit, not only for physical comfort, but also, in part, for that more subtle joy, the satisfaction of the almost universal striving for beauty, which can be expressed in the adornment of the home.

Of the forms of handwork directly related to the home, the making of lamp shades is one of the most interesting. It is profitable, too, in the sense that the savings effected in constructing rather than purchasing lamp shades is decidedly worthwhile. The materials required for this work are not difficult to procure, and the rules of making are simple and easy to follow, the shades being built on two foundation principles—neatness and accuracy. It is essential that each detail be accomplished with the utmost care so that the shades may occupy a conspicuous position in the room and admit of close examination.

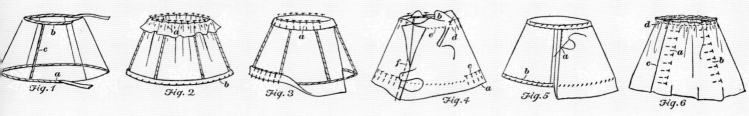

Fig. 1   Fig. 2   Fig. 3   Fig. 4   Fig. 5   Fig. 6

Materials and Trimmings

The amount of material required for each shade may be calculated by measuring the depth of the frame and allowing twice this amount plus generous seam allowances, top and bottom. If the shade is wider at the bottom than at the top, allow beyond this at least 3 inches to allow for the fitting required, provided, of course, the material is to be applied plain. If there is to be fullness at the top, or at both top and bottom, the excess need not be considered. When plaiting is to be used, remember that it takes three times the space to be covered.

The average lampshade requires a finish of some kind for the edge. Gold braid is frequently employed, as are plaited or gathered frills of the fabric of which the shade is made. Ribbon in the proper width and color may be substituted for fabric, too. The bottom may also be finished with fringe, either silk or metallic or a combination of both. Appliqued fabric flowers are frequently seen on boudoir shades and on those for the living room, too.

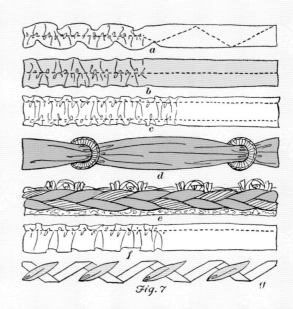

Fig. 7

Just Among Ourselves

Notes in appreciation of Spring *Fashion Service* have been coming thick and fast to Mrs. Picken. Many of these notes are prompted by different points of view, coming, as they do, from a wide range of trades people and professionals in the sewing world.
—*Alice H. Stone, Editor*

Miss Jane Martin, probably the best known woman in advertising circles, writes:
"It is the most explicit, yet comprehensive, the most complete, yet conservative, and alto-gether the most helpful *Fashion Service* I have ever known."

Miss Marion L. Tucker, of the Massachusetts Agricultural College in Amherst, writes:
"I find the fashion newsletter very helpful in my work as a clothing specialist. I think it has in it more practical and valuable suggestions for the woman who sews than most fashion magazines."

In a letter to Mrs. Picken, one of our students writes of *Inspiration* in this manner:
"*Inspiration* gives me a real thrill every time I see it in the mail box. We all have to use self-restraint when it comes. It is mine, but of course I let mother read it first, then I get it, and after that my daughter has it."

And my favorite one, from Mrs. C. D. McK., California:
"My Woman's Institute Course has meant a savings of much actual cash and of infinite worry. It has proved the most profitable investment my husband and I ever made. It has given me the ability to express my own personality in clothes that are mine and not to be duplicated. And it has given me something that is more than all of these—*Faith in my own two hands.*"

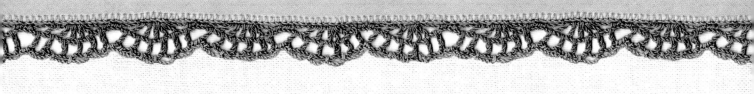

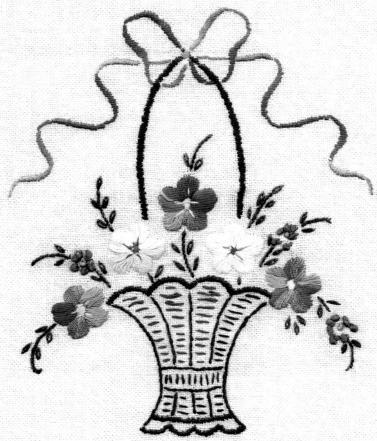

Summer

Modern Notions

My porch is my front row seat to life. When my husband and I were building our house, a friend urged me to include a spacious, covered front porch in the design, and I am so grateful for the suggestion!

My favorite afternoons are ones spent reclining on this porch with a bowl of fresh raspberries, a magazine, and a big iced tea, while my children and their friends turn cartwheels or play ball in the front yard. I remember how much I loved my grandparents' screened-in back porch with its white wicker furniture that was identical to the images in this chapter. What a nice place it was to gather family and friends in the fresh air. You can also use your deck, driveway or front steps as your porch. Just be sure to take the time to enjoy your outdoor sanctuary wherever you create it.

Chitchatting is easy from a front porch and over the short span of the lawn! Your whole neighborhood will benefit from the relationships you build with those who live beside you. In my experience, sometimes making friends is as easy as getting our dogs together to play or meeting a neighbor's child along with my own at the corner school crosswalk. I live on a cul-de-sac, which was not the usual design for neighborhoods in Mary Brooks Picken's day, but I certainly recommend it. And fortunately, I am blessed with a friend like Mary's who cooks an extra helping of dinner or batch of cookies when she knows I've had a hectic work schedule or am working late.

My front porch has become everything I hoped for—the space where my schedules and structure fall away and I can actually feel the simple joy of being part of the greater world of life. And with the beauty of the natural world all around me, I often pause to think how grateful I am to have the best seat in the house!

Best,

Amy B.

JUNE

*Days are too precious
to let drift by without the touch
of a friendly heartstring
some place, some where.*

—Mary Brooks Picken

A Thimbleful of Friendship

What Kind of Neighbor Are You?

by Mary Brooks Picken,
Excerpted from *Thimblefuls of Friendliness*, 1924

Out West there is that delightful custom of borrowing something from the new neighbor—an egg, a cup of sugar, a spoonful of tea, or a handful of matches—evidencing that you want to be neighborly, that you welcome the newcomer. Your borrowing invites your neighbor to borrow from you, to drop in informally, and that is the only kind of neighbor worthwhile. We seldom take time to call next door, though we would make a special effort to call on someone three blocks away.

I had a "Little Gray Home in the West" for a few years, and of the definitely happy memories that come again and again, those of my neighbors stand out clearest.

I remember once a neighbor's furnace was out of kilter. 'Twas cold—a Kansas January. The husband and wife brought their wee baby and visited us for two days. We sewed, cooked, kept house, and at night read aloud, played, sang, and visited as we had never had the time to do before.

Once, when an economical streak struck me and I decided to dye my wedding dress, white to tan, a neighbor across the street, the wife of a police officer, saw me coming from the drugstore with a dye package and volunteered to help. She had had much experience and real success with dyeing. I learned more from her that morning than I ever could have learned in a half-dozen attempts alone. She took her time; we had a good visit. I only thanked her, yet the information she gave me has been valuable these fifteen years.

Days when I was sewing, my neighbors would bring pie, baked beans, scalloped potatoes, soup, always something for dinner so that I could stay at my work longer. One neighbor whose husband came home for lunch would often send a delicious plate lunch to me. All I could ever do for her was help her get her sleeves in right, miter square yokes, hang hems, and lend her my dress form. But she did a lot for me, for now as the years go by I can look back with treasured happiness to the days when I had the joy of being home and of having real honest-to-goodness neighbors.

If folks obey the golden rule on both sides, there is sure to be a happy neighborhood—one that will provide all with an enviable store of memories.

Life is too short to be stingy with; days are too precious to let drift by without the touch of a friendly heartstring some place, somewhere. And the surest ways to make the best of the days is to try to be good friends with your neighbors. They may not think as you do nor have the same standards, but this is a sure rule—you can help them or they can help you, and a give-and-take spirit is a wonderful thing.

As Douglas Malloch says:

"So much is bought, so much is sold,
We miss the value of
The things that are not sold or bought,
The gifts that only loving brought,
The words of honest praise,
The friendly smile, the friendly thought—
The things of happy days."

DEPARTMENT OF INSPIRATION

Meeting Summer Halfway

by Laura MacFarlane, *Fashion Service*, June 1928

Have you ever tried walking a narrow plank bridge over a little stream? You start out real bravely and take a very few confident steps. Then, as you come to the middle, you find yourself looking down, you see the water below, you falter, and who has preceded you over, shouts, "Here, take my hand!" My, what a relief! Like a flash you regain all your courage, grasp the offered hand, and take the rest of the plank in one or two strides. Some one has met you half-way.

Then there's that girl down at the silk counter at the department store. You always wait for her even though some of the others aren't busy. She can make suggestions if they don't have just what you want. And she always knows how much material you need for a dress. She meets you half-way. I'll wager her sales just about double those of the other clerks.

At church, Mrs. Brown came the same Sunday that Mrs. Black did. But have you noticed how many people Mrs. Black seems to know already and how often she is mentioned in connection with the various church affairs? Wondering about it, I watched them one Sunday, and soon found that Mrs. Black met everyone half-way, while Mrs. Brown waited for others to make all the advances.

Will you meet Summer and her engaging friend half-way? Make cute little suits and dresses for brother and sister's playtime hours. Pack the young camper's bags full of sturdy, warm camp clothes. Sew up becoming frocks and fashion smart hats for yourself so that you'll be ready for all the happy times at home that come in summertime. Help your teen-age daughter with her clothes, but let her enjoy the satisfaction and pride of making most of them herself.

Spend your spare hours on the cool porch, making colorful new linens. These moments will be doubly pleasurable if some gay zinnias brighten that north corner and the sweet pea bed over in the side yard has been well tended. Met half-way, in this delightful manner, Summer will be a long-remembered one.

❋ Amy B.'s Favorite Vintage Advice ❋
FROM THE QUIRKY TO THE CONVENTIONAL

Summer Hospitality
by Laura MacFarlane, *Inspiration*, June/July 1921

Too often the inviting of guests is accompanied with so much preparation for their comfort and entertainment that the true meaning of the occasion is practically lost. Nothing is more disappointing to the guests than for the hostess to absent herself during the greater part of time. It would be better for her to omit some of her social duties than to entertain in this way. But this is not really necessary. The solution is a simple, inauspicious method of entertainment. It has been very truly said, "There is majesty in simplicity." And, you know, the weightiest of household problems are often solved over a social cup of tea.

The ingenious housewife usually has in her refrigerator tea of double strength that has been poured from the grounds as soon as it is made, fruit juices of various kinds, and plenty of ice. It is the little touches that make the most essential element of true hospitality. Thin wafers, small-sized cookies, attractive little cakes, dainty sandwiches, crisp toast, cheese crackers—all are splendid accompaniments for tea.

So, during the summer months, when there is a little relaxation in the general routine of household cares and more inclination toward companionship, why not urge your friends and neighbors to drop in informally with their sewing or knitting or darning and spend an hour or two in a social way? With this in view, make your outdoor spaces as comfortable and attractive as possible, for it is always more pleasant to sit in the open than indoors when "the year is at its highest beauty."

Summer, with its pleasant mornings, invites us to take as much of our work outdoors as possible. In the afternoons, with the front porch shaded, there are long hours to chat with old friends who pass by. And so the delightful days of summer bring new friends and the leisure to renew old friendships.

Porch Settings for Summer

by Margaret Murrin,
Inspiration, June/July 1925

*a*s you ring in the summer, when the family living room is transferred out-of-doors, it means a great deal to have the outside so furnished that it is a pleasant place to spend one's leisure hours. By furnished, I mean not so much the chairs, settees, or tables, but the accessories that go so far toward creating out-of-doors an atmosphere of sunny welcome both to the members of your family and to the guests who by chance come to visit your home.

Because color is so much a part of summer, it may be used more freely on porches and decks than would be possible indoors. Once you decide on a color scheme, be sure it is carried out in the rug as well as the materials used for cushions or chair upholstery. These materials should always be durable and sun-fast, if possible; so you will find cretonne, gingham, chambray, and cotton duck cloth fabrics best not only for their color choices, but also for the ease with which they can be laundered.

To carry out your plan of beautifying your outdoor living room, you must consider the furniture, too. The work of painting a chair is not all that difficult, so even if you have not had any previous experience, do not delay your first step for you will find this branch of reclaiming furniture truly fascinating. A miscellaneous collection of chairs, when painted all one color, are surprisingly improved, and when finished with cushions of harmonizing colors, they will fully repay you by their appearance for the time you have spent on them. The list on this page provides ideas for colors to be used for your furniture as well as for rugs, cushions, and upholstery. Select a scheme that is harmonious with the color of your house if it is possible to do so.

Color Schemes for Porch Furnishings

Rug	Furniture	Upholstery	Cushions
1. Green	Gray or Natural	Cretonne with violet predominating	Rose Blue
2. Rag	Black	Yellow-and-white check gingham	Yellow Blue
3. Gray	Grass-green	Gray poplin	Orange Violet
4. Tan	Deep écru	Cretonne with rose predominating	Rose Violet

INSTRUCTION DEPARTMENT

Simple Embroideries for the Porch

by Clarice Carpenter
Fashion Service, 1929

Living outside is one of the greatest assets to family happiness in summer. Impromptu parties, family picnics, neighborly chats, and happy afternoons with a bit of needlework are fostered in its hospitable atmosphere. And out of these very afternoons with the needle grow some of the most effective means of making the porch inviting. The chair protectors, luncheon sets, and cushions, shown here, are decorated with simple stitches that require no concentration and only a limited amount of time for their development which may be accomplished while one chats with neighborly callers.

Model 7-7—This very simple chair-back protector of lavender Indian Head is made like a small pillow slip, to fit snugly over the upper half of the chair back. It is appropriately decorated with a simple morning-glory motif which may be developed in outline-stitch with three strands of six-stranded embroidery cotton in morning-glory colors. The open edges are finished with purple or violet bias bindings.

Model 7A-7—In keeping with the informality of porch parties is this luncheon set with its colorful decoration of Japanese lanterns. The cloth and napkins are of pale yellow cotton crepe and the lanterns are of the same crepe in jade green, orange, lavender, and blue. Black thread is used for outlining the lantern handle, tassels, and the dashes on the appliqué sections which are whipped on invisibly. The cherry blossoms are white, and the leaves, jade green. All edges are finished with tiny hems, held by black blanket-stitches that are graduated in Oriental

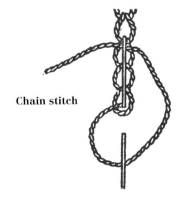

Chain stitch

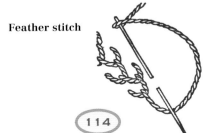

Feather stitch

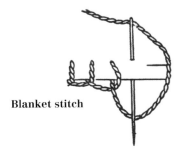

Blanket stitch

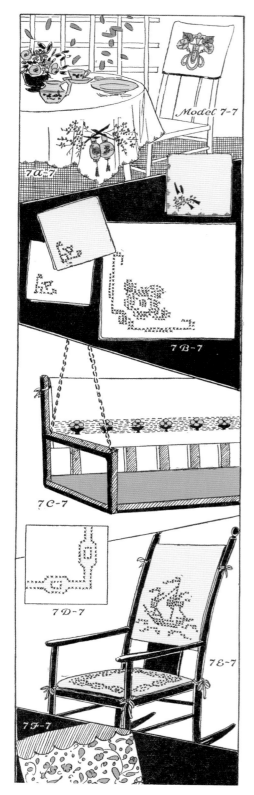

manner. The design, which is used on the napkins, is shown at left. This is done in black, white, and jade green.

Model 7B-7—Heavy, oyster-white linen or cotton is used for this luncheon set which achieves a Russian effect by means of the colors used for the cross-stitch embroidery, a light navy blue for the outer lines and flower center and dull red for the flower and leaves. The edges are finished with very narrow whipped hems.

Model 7C-7—The protector for the porch swing may be made of linen crash, Indian Head, or unbleached muslin decorated with a simple border design in appliqué and running-stitch. An effective color scheme is yellow for the flowers and green for the urns and flower centers. Patterns for cutting the appliqué patches may be obtained by cutting up some of the border motifs in the embroidery pattern and allowing 3/16" on all edges for turning under. Whip the patches in place invisibly with matching sewing thread. Use green mercerized embroidery cotton, No. 5, for the running stitches.

Model 7D-7—A thin seat cushion that can be tied at the corners to the porch chair protects light summer clothes and adds a decorative note to the porch furnishings. As shown, it can be made of natural-colored linen or any heavy cotton, with cross-stitched border in green to match the paint on the chair. This shows the enlarged detail of the embroidery design. The cushion, in place on the chair seat, is shown at the left below. Since the stitches are fairly large, use either heavy, single-strand cotton or the full six strands of the six-strand cotton.

Model 7E-7—A cross-stitched ship, with its suggestion of cool breezes, is the motif chosen for the chair-back protector that is used with the cross-stitched pad. The chair protector should be made with the same material as the seat pad and cross-stitched in the same color. Toweling is very satisfactory for this kind of protector, as the selvage edges may be used as a finish along the sides and thus only narrow hems at the end are required. Tapes are used to tie the protector near the top of the chair back.

 Twill tape or bias tape are good choices.

Model 7F-7—Plain and figured glazed chintzes are combined in this attractive cushion. The plain color may be rose, yellow, green, or any color that harmonizes with the figured material and with the furniture and other porch furnishings. Make the back and front of the cushion alike, stitching the scalloped borders close to the edge of the scallops. If you like, you can insert a covered cord or piping of a second plain color under the edge of the scallops.

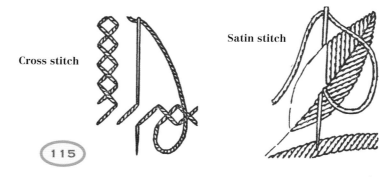

Cross stitch

Satin stitch

Dainty Summer Refreshments

Inspiration, June/July 1924

When the mercury mounts high and spirits drop correspondingly, the summer hostess will find her hospitality greatly appreciated if she serves cooling drinks and dainty refreshments. And it will be all the more delightful if she sets her iced tea or refreshment table in a cool, shady spot out-of-doors.

Tinkling iced drinks, attractively garnished and served during the warm days of summer, add much to the joy of living. Less food is needed in summer than in the cooler months, and especially to be taken in moderation are the foods that produce body heat. The diet should consist largely of fruits and vegetables.

The refreshments should be light and delicious, the beverages cold and tangy, the china and glassware gaily colorful, and the linen fresh and snowy. And if a few flowers, beautifully arranged, give a lovely decorative note, the setting will, in truth, be one that is quite pleasing. Set a side table with a dainty pitcher of sparkling fruit punch, sandwiches of white and brown bread, little cakes with icing in pastel colors, bonbons, and nuts, supplemented with graceful footed tumblers, and long, slender iced teaspoons.

To make tiny, rolled sandwiches, fill them with cream cheese and crushed pineapple; some with orange marmalade and the others with raspberry jam. The simplest sandwich, from the standpoint of the materials used, is the bread-and-butter sandwich, which can be made in fancy shapes by using cookie cutters. Color may be added also to the butter—watercress may be used to produce green butter, pimientos for red butter.

When an especially attractive and yet simple form of entertainment is desired, just cake and a refreshing drink may be served. Serve the cake along with fruit drinks.

An excellent way to make fruit drinks is to cook together one part sugar to one to two parts water, add fruit juice, and keep in the refrigerator until needed. When a cold drink is desired, iced chocolate will be much appreciated. In making it, a shaker, which may be procured from a kitchen supply house, may be put to good use.

Mint Julep

1-1/2 cups sugar
2 cups water
A few sprigs of mint
1 quart ginger ale
4 lemons
2 oranges

Boil the sugar and water and cool. Add the juice of the lemons, strained, the mint leaves, crushed, and the ginger ale. Half-fill glasses with ice, pour in the julep, and add the oranges in half-slices. A sprig of mint may garnish each glass.

Lemon syrup is another "first aid" to have on hand and it is easy to make and keep.

Lemon Syrup

2 cups sugar
Juice of 5 lemons
1 cup water
Grated rind
of 3 lemons

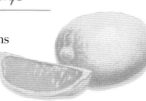

Make a thin syrup of the sugar and water, boiling it to about 215°F, add the juice and grated rinds of the lemons, bottle the mixture, and put in a cool place. To serve, fill a glass with finely chopped ice, add 2 or 3 tablespoons of the syrup, and as much cold water as the glass will hold.

Iced Chocolate

3 tbls. crushed ice
1/4 cup milk
3 tbls. chocolate
  sauce *(below)*
Few grains salt

Put all into a shaker and shake vigorously. Pour into a tall glass and garnish with whipped cream.

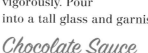

Chocolate Sauce

1/4 lb. chocolate	Pinch of salt
1-1/2 cups sugar	1-1/2 cups boiling water
1/3 cup corn syrup	

Melt the chocolate. Add the other ingredients. To prevent it from congealing, stir constantly or whisk while adding water; and allow to boil for 5 minutes. Cool and place in a covered jar in the refrigerator to be used as needed.

Successful Whipped Cream

A precaution that must always be taken with regard to whipped cream is that it must be fresh and ice cold. Be sure to keep it on ice until you are ready to use it, and then, if possible, whip it in a cold place. If it seems very slow in stiffening, set the bowl containing it directly on the ice and continue whipping.

 Place the bowl and beater in the freezer before beating.

A delightful new washable fabric, rayon alpaca, is used very simply in *Model 14a*, the plain trimming bands accenting a tone of the stripes that are used across the figure.

Model 14

The new plaid ginghams are very tempting. In *Model 14*, the black that runs in tiny lines through the rose and white, is played up in the simple blanket-stitch and outline embroidery.

14 α

14 B

"It is such a delight to slip into a cool, dainty summer frock, for the fashions for summer are delightfully simple and summer materials are so easy to work with."

—Alice Stone, Membership Department

Dresses for Home and Garden

Fashion Service, Summer 1926

Summertime, with its outside pleasures, its balmy evenings, and its golden days, is made much more enjoyable if the gayness and freshness of its mood are matched by the frocks we wear. Fabrics may be dainty or sturdy, depending on one's activities, and fashions may be equally versatile, as the models pictured on these pages offer considerable variation in choice.

The most pleasant part of a summer day at home comes when you don a fresh, cool becoming frock, take your book or your sewing, and select a comfortable chair on the deck or screened porch. It's a delightful time for entertaining friends, too, and they will enjoy looking at your frock quite as much as partaking of your hospitality, if it is as attractive as the models shown here.

English print in a pattern suggestive of sunlight and gay flowers is fashioned into *Model 14B*, an appealing frock for morning or garden wear, with Picoted ruffles.

Field flowers bloom in their own natural colorings, against a backdrop of black and white in the chiffon that makes *Model 5*. Black silk lace, sheer as a cobweb, outlines the simulated surplice closing, edges the scalloped front of the skirt, and winds itself into spiral medallions for the waist line.

Cut on lines that flatter the youthful figure, the blouse is close-fitting, and the skirt with the graceful circular swing so lovely in chiffon, *Model 5a* chooses as its trimming cream lace and a ribbon bow in orange to repeat a color in the chiffon.

5a

5b

5c

Model 5

SHEER COLORFUL FROCKS

The flippant little shoulder cape of *Model 5B* draws much attention to itself, yet one notices that this tan crepe Elizabeth dress has also a finely plaited apron and long sleeves, smartly full at the cuffs. The tie that fastens the collar to the dress has the effect of a very narrow and very erect collar.

A slip of Brittany blue crepe de Chine, then a demurely simple little dress of Brittany blue chiffon with a deep band of gossamer-sheer white lace at the bottom of its full skirt and narrower bands of the same lace for its short sleeves, and we have *Model 5C*. Satin or velvet ribbon in a darker tone of old blue makes the sash.

Magic Pattern

Making a Summer Purse

Fashion Service, 1929

*A*ccessories increase the smartness of new ensembles of cotton or linen. This smart purse may be made of cotton, linen, or printed silk. As shown, it is of printed cotton suiting over a foundation of buckram. It is lined and the edges are piped in plain yellow cotton. A yellow wooden bead or novelty button and a knotted loop of yellow bias tubing effect the closing. A simple handle is attached to the back.

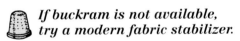

If buckram is not available, try a modern fabric stabilizer.

Cut a paper pattern, having the flap and one side of the pocket in one piece and the other side separate. Cut the larger pattern piece, shown in views A and B of the group of illustrations, 11-1/2 inches by 8-1/4 inches, and round off the corners as shown. Cut a buckram section from this and fold crosswise 6-1/4 inches from one end and again 3/16 inch nearer the shorter end which will be the front flap. These folds are shown in view B.

For the other side of the purse, make a pattern like the first section with the flap omitted. It will be shaped like that in view C, being 6-1/4 inches from top to bottom and 8-1/4 inches wide. Cut this from buckram. Cut plain cotton in bias strips 3/4 inch wide and baste these around the edges of both pieces of buckram as shown in view A, without turning in the edges.

Cut the covering for the outside and the lining of each section, allowing 1/16 inch on all edges. Turn in all edges of the outside material 1/4 inch and pin over the foundation, as in view B, so that 1/16 inch of the plain binding shows. Prepare the fastening loop of plain bias tubing, making it just large enough to slip snugly over the wooden bead or button. Insert the ends between the buckram and the covering of the edge of the flap, as shown in view B. Cover the smaller piece of buckram in the same way, as in view C. Replace the pins in both sections with bastings. Sew the bead or button 1 inch above the curved edge of the short side, as in view C. If a bead is used, sew it on with heavy embroidery thread, making a knot between it and the material.

To give roominess, a fitted gusset-like insert is necessary between the purse sections. Make a pattern for this from the shorter-purse section pattern by cutting away the inner part to leave a horse-shoe-shaped section 1-3/4 inches wide, as shown in view D. Cut two such sections of the outer material and join them with a plain 3/8" seam along their

inner curves. Cut two more of the lining material and join them in the same way. Trim these seams to a depth of 1/8 inch and clip them at the curves. Join the straight edges (at the top of the U-shape), as shown in view D, so that all seams turn inside and baste the curved seams right sides together, turn and press. Also, baste the outer edges so that the gusset may be handled as one piece. Press thoroughly.

Prepare the lining for the larger sections by stitching to it a strip of the material to form a pocket 2-3/4 inches deep, divided at the center for mirror and coin purse, as in view E. Baste one edge of the gusset to this lining, turn in the edges of both together, and pin and baste to the foundation. Replace basting with machine-stitching around all edges, and stitch on the flap crease, as shown. Make the covered buckram handle, shown in view F, 1 inch wide, with plain binding on all edges applied as on the purse. Stitch in a vertical position on the back of the purse, securing the ends only.

Baste the lining to the smaller buckram section across the straight edge and stitch. Then place this section over the rest of the purse, baste

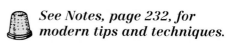

See Notes, page 232, for modern tips and techniques.

the free gusset and lining edges together, turn them in, pin, baste, and finally stitch to the buckram.

Coin Purse

Use a buckram foundation, 3-3/8 inches by 7 inches, for the coin purse. Cover this with figured material and line with plain fabric, using no edge binding. The lining side is shown in view G with bastings replaced by stitching at one end. Fold as shown in view H, sew on the part of the snap fastener that comes on the pocket, and stitch around both sides and the flap end. Here sew on the remaining half of the fastener.

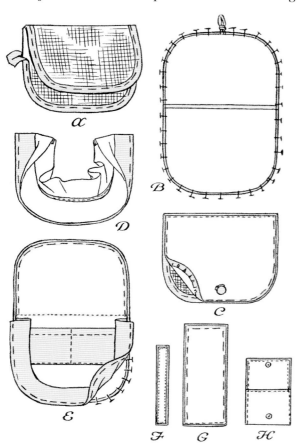

Constructive Play for Summer Days

by Hilarion Doyle, *Inspiration*, June 1926

The long, lazy summer vacation stretches forth delightfully in the imagination of school children during midwinter and spring, but after a week or two of perfect idleness, their active minds become a little bored and long for "something to do." Then it is that the wise mother will propose searching through the old trunks in the attic or through the scrap bag for odds and ends of cloth and paper that can be transformed into dainty articles for home use or gifts.

Embroidery work suggests itself immediately as a summer pastime, for almost every little girl has an aptitude for sewing. Designs, involving only the simplest stitches, should be used, for they are most easily and accurately done. Cross-stitch designs are very satisfactory, especially when they come stamped in colors and offer such gay motifs as the familiar dancing sunbonnet maids.

"Stamped" describes a design transferred to fabric.

A towel with a pocket for a wash cloth is a novel idea that even a very young child can carry out when the pocket is simply shaped and secured with blanket-stitching. The patch should be basted on to hold it in position and care taken to catch only the stitches at the sides and bottom through the towel. The washcloth itself has a blanket-stitched edge. This idea can be carried out on either a hand or bath towel, using color-fast scraps for the pocket.

Just Among Ourselves

And so the delightful days of Summer bring new friends and the leisure to renew old friendships. And when these friends come to your porch, they will no doubt find some of your Woman's Institute Instruction Books on your reading table or on the arm of your chair. Every day the mail brings to us hundreds of names from students and friends and messages that show how satisfied they are with the benefits that come from membership in the Woman's Institute.

—*Mrs. Alice H. Stone, Editorial Department*

Summer Work Covered Entire Expense of Course

"Would it interest you to know that this summer alone I have made enough to cover the expense of the entire course," writes a Michigan student. "This includes postage, samplers, yes, and all the supplies I've needed, with some left. I can't tell you how much I've enjoyed it. It has been easy and yet I've worked hard, too, for I've done all of my own housework and sewing and kept up my music, which I am still studying. Yes, and I go to church and club affairs sometimes, too."

—*Mrs. Stella Bristol, Michigan*

Even the First Lesson Useful

The other day, we received a picture of Mrs. Alice Nelmes French and her two children, her two most important reasons for learning to sew.

"Since starting the course, I have made my small daughter two bloomer dresses and embroidered another one using blanket stitching, so even that first lesson on blanket stitching has been of much help to me. I love to sew and am surprised at the quickness and ease with which the little garments go together."

—*Mrs. Alice Nelmes French*

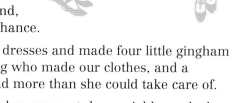

Quick Benefits from Study

"When I decided to take up the Woman's Institute Course, we were in very poor circumstances. I have been very ill for months and we had spent all of our savings on doctor bills, and my husband had just started in a new line of business and had to begin at the very bottom. I saw the advertisement in a magazine, and when I talked it over with my husband, he said he didn't see how we could afford it, but we decided to take a chance.

"Well, after I completed my fifth lesson, I had remodeled two of my old dresses and made four little gingham dresses for my seven-year-old daughter and the neighbors began asking who made our clothes, and a dressmaker two doors from us began sending work to me when she had more than she could take care of.

"Soon we moved to a strange town and we were there only two weeks when my next-door neighbor asked me if I could make a dress for her little girl like the one I had just completed for mine, which, by the way, was made of two remnants costing 30 cents. From then on I had all the work I could do, and in three months I earned over $200."

—*Mrs. Ethel P. Crawford, Illinois*

Modern Notions

Ah, summertime—the barefoot days spent with neighborhood children, the twilight games of hide-and-go-seek or capture the flag, and for me, the memory of summers spent eating ice cream at Higgins General Store in Alden, Michigan, where I now take my kids for huge scoops during our summer retreat to Torch Lake.

After all, ice cream is serious business. We all have a favorite flavor, and we all have summer memories that include the sharing of a scoop or two with our family and friends. This month's *Department of Cookery* is an all-out celebration of the old-fashioned ice cream that, at the turn of a crank, has power enough to turn back the hands of time. Whether waiting at the curbside for the ice cream truck, or helping mom crank the ice in the backyard, ice cream is a favorite summer tradition. And worrying about my waistline doesn't seem so important when I consider the benefits of a summer evening spent on the back porch with my family, listening to the laughter of my children in their dessert appreciation.

Speaking of waistlines, how our appearance is perceived by others is always a timely subject for women. The cosmetics industry brings in billions annually, so it's nice to be reminded in this month's *Department of Good Looks* that our unique personalities and kind actions are the true dictates of how beautiful we are. We are also reminded that, in so many words, small details in carriage and presentation can make more of an impression than a designer outfit. I translate this to mean I probably shouldn't wear my pajamas out to run errands, although this month's *Department of Instruction* feature "Profiting from the Pajama Mode" may have changed my mind about that!

Most importantly, enjoy those little moments with your loved ones this summer season. Think about what makes you beautiful, both inside and out. And remember, a few crow's feet are a fair trade for a lifetime of smiles.

Yours,

Amy B.

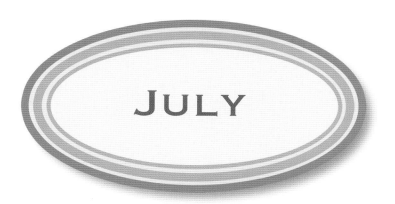

JULY

*There is no cosmetic
for beauty like happiness.*

—Lady Blessington

A Thimbleful of Beauty

Beauty Spots

by Mary Brooks Picken
Excerpted from *Thimblefuls of Friendliness*, 1924

*W*alking down the street the other day, I saw a little doll sitting on some steps and a little girl five or six years of age with a broom, energetically sweeping the ground. I watched her as I came near and I remarked, "My but you are a good sweeper." She lifted her little face and said, "I'm making a clean place for my dolly and me to play."

This is a beautiful thought, expressing one of the most essential threads in our garment of life—"a clean place for my dolly and me." The woman who tidies herself up for her family's home coming, who provides a clean table and attractive food, if possible, for her family to eat, who happily keeps her floor swept clean, is building for herself in the hearts of her people tender memories and appreciation, which, though not expressed, will reflect in their lives over and over again and will help them in being kind and lovingly considerate of someone else. And, after all, that is the way rewards should be expressed. They should travel down through the years to serve as good examples.

Some women say that they haven't anything "to do with," but the only people that I have ever known who didn't have anything "to do with" were those who did not have the "desire to do." There are people living now who can tell of the dugouts out in Kansas before there was lumber or money there to build houses. These dugouts were caves in the ground with dirt floors, but many a time I have heard folks tell how cozy they were and how very clean and smooth the earth floors were kept. The women had no conveniences, yet they built happy hearthstones and gave a good start to their children. Kansas is a great state, and much of its greatness today is due to the love and unselfishness of its far-visioned pioneers.

I once visited a woman who lived in a box car on a railroad siding. A new piece of railroad was being built, and her husband was supervising engineer.

A cleaner little place I have never seen, a soft cream color inside with white curtains on the four windows that had been cut in the sides of the car. The furniture, except the bed, table, and stove, were made from boxes painted in cream color and finished by means of white scarves and curtains. Blue denim covered two trunks and several boxes, which served as seats. A box of pink geraniums was in each window, having been carefully packed and carried from the city. I asked if it was difficult to keep the scarves, curtains, table cloths, and bedding white, and the answer was: "Yes, quite a problem, but not so difficult as to do without them."

The husband of this little woman is going forward to a splendid success. They no longer live in the isolated region nor in the box car. I have often thought, as I have heard from these people, that this treasure woman is a true example of the old quotation: "Many women are like candles, finding their brightest moments serving others. 'Tis they who joyfully consume themselves in lighting the way for their loved ones."

"Give that ye may receive," is instruction that we hear, forget, and fail to heed; yet application of it can mean literally picking up a life of happiness instead of misery. Give smiles if you have nothing else. Give encouragement, good cheer. Make beauty come to you through your desire to express it. Your thoughts, deeds, motives, acts, industries, and desires—all can express beauty if beauty is in the heart; all can give happiness if love is the carrying vehicle.

Sweep a clean place for you and your loved ones to "play." Learn to love people and their little ways—odd, queer, or lovely. Love folks and your work, and you will be doing a big part of what God wants you to do.

Though we travel the world over to find the beautiful, we must carry it with us or we find it not.
—Ralph Waldo Emerson

INSPIRATION DEPARTMENT

Looking One's Best

by Mary Brooks Picken
Excerpted from *Thimblefuls of Friendliness*, 1924

When we lose interest in pleasing people, we have lost the greatest incentive for making ourselves attractive. That is what I thought not long ago while waiting for a friend to join me for luncheon.

As I watched the throngs of women passing by, I wondered what was the incentive that prompted each of them to strive to attain or retain their attractiveness. Pondering this question, I thought of the motives that govern a great majority of women, making them exert themselves to the utmost to look their best. Is it not the hope of winning the attention, admiration, and love of those they hold most dear? And after their love and respect have been won, is it not the desire to retain what has been gained, that makes a woman care to keep herself attractive?

A beautiful woman is rarely, if ever, as gracious as her homely sister, for she feels that her beauty gives her the right of way. But her plainer sister knows that kindness, a pleasing consideration for every one she meets, will help her to make friends, and if she applies to this an intelligent, persistent desire for attractiveness, she is sure to be loved and appreciated.

Wives can help their husbands by keeping their attractiveness; mothers can win the admiration of their children and keep them nearer by being always pretty to see; and grandmothers, who have in a delightfully dignified way kept the spirit—the incentive for pleasing—may be such a very real inspiration that their memory will live in the hearts of their loved ones like exquisite music.

DEPARTMENT OF COOKERY

Frozen Dessert for Warm Weather

by Laura MacFarlane and Mary Gilgallon
Inspiration, July 1926

No other variety of food appears to retain its popularity throughout the year with old and young alike as ice cream and its closely related desserts. But there is no time or season when these delicacies are so much appreciated nor so nearly "touch the spot" as when the mer-

 This method from 1921 uses a hand-cranked ice cream maker.

cury is creeping perilously near 100 degrees. Reinforced with a heaping dish of fresh-fruit ice cream, you will be prepared to baffle even the cruelest plans that Old Sol will take such delight in perpetrating during the next month or so.

There is scarcely a town of any size but has its "Sweet Shop" where ice cream may be procured; but the wise, careful housewife, who has the welfare of her family at heart, will try to superintend the making of their frozen desserts herself. The two things necessary for freezing desserts are ice and salt. While the mixture that is to be frozen is cooling, the ice may be gotten ready for use. With the ice broken into small pieces, empty it into a large pan. The finer the ice pieces, the quicker it freezes. Mix thoroughly with the chipped ice, salt (coarse crushed rock salt is best), in the proportion of three parts of ice to one part salt. If preferred, instead of mixing the ice and salt together, put a layer of ice in the freezer tub, then a layer of salt, and so on, until it reaches the top.

Then, fill the tub of freezer with this mixture to the very top and keep it full during freezing. Place the ice cream mixture in the can, cover securely, and set in the outside container. Then pack the salt-and-ice mixture down into the space between the can and the container into which it fits. Pack as tightly as possible so that the ice comes higher than

the surface of the mixture inside the can. After finishing the packing, attach the top securely, when everything is ready to begin the final work of freezing.

If you wish to mould ice cream or serve it in forms, have the mould ready at the time you remove the dasher from the can, and also have a tub or bucket containing a mixture of coarse ice and salt. Moisten the mould with cold water, then fill it quickly with ice cream, pressing it down with a spoon to fill every part of the mould. Lay a piece of wax paper or strong manilla paper, over the cream, large enough to project beyond the edges when the lid is on, put on the lid and imbed the mould in the tub of ice and salt. Cover with a piece of carpet and set aside for two hours. When ready to use, lift the mould from the ice, wipe it carefully, plunge into a pan of warm water, remove the lid and paper, and turn the mould carefully on a napkin placed on a pretty dish. If it should stick, wait a moment, as the heat of the room will, as a rule, loosen it in a few moments.

Vanilla Del Monica Ice Cream

1-1/2 pints of cream
1 vanilla bean
Yolks of six eggs
1/2 pound of sugar

Put the cream into a double boiler, with the vanilla bean split into halves. Beat the yolks of the eggs and the sugar together until light, add them to the hot cream, stir until the eggs begin to thicken, strain through a sieve, and when cold, freeze. Serve in small blocks.

Philadelphia Chocolate Ice Cream

1 quart of cream
4 ounces of sweet chocolate or 2 ounces of Baker's chocolate
1/4 teaspoon of powdered cinnamon
1 tbls. vanilla
1/2 pound of sugar

Put one-half of the cream, the chocolate, sugar and cinnamon on to boil, stir and beat until smooth; strain while hot, through a fine muslin, add the remainder of the cream and the vanilla. Let cool and freeze.

Fresh Fruit Ice Cream

1-1/2 cups fruit and juice
1 cup sugar
1 quart cream

Add the sugar to the fruit, crush, and allow to stand until the sugar is dissolved. Scald one-half of the cream, cool, and combine all the ingredients. Freeze. Milk may take the place of part of the cream if desired.

By substituting water for the cream, and adding 2 tablespoonfuls of lemon juice, this recipe may be used for fruit-flavored ice water. In this case, the best results are obtained when the water and sugar are cooked to form a thin syrup, allowed to cool, and the fruit and juice then added.

Profiting from the Pajama Mode

Fashion Service, July 1929

"Those of us who are going down to the beach this summer may have beach pajamas to match our moods . . ."

Whether they be so romantic as to demand a pirate's garb or so nautical as to long for sailor's togs . . . this quality of vesting us with new personalities may partly explain the lure of pajamas, but their quite general becomingness, as well as their very practical aspects, are also points in their favor. Materials range from sturdy cottons to luxurious silks, while colors are usually those bright, clear shades that appear best under direct sunlight, surrounded by wide, out-of-door spaces.

All feminine America seems suddenly to have realized that the wearing of trousers is conducive to greater freedom, and so to greater joy. This discovery has started a new vogue, and now pajamas are worn on every possible occasion. They appear in the boudoir, made of washable silks and cottons for sleeping and of more elaborate fabrics for lounging. The beaches are teeming with bright-colored, picturesque types, charmingly individual in design and worn by those who prefer the sands to the surf. And college girls like nothing better than smart, colorful pajamas for lounging, study hours, and the social gatherings that mean so much in campus life.

This new, but already firmly established, vogue offers an opportunity to the woman who is alert for new things to make for sale. Of course pajamas will not sell with equal rapidity in all places. The most advantageous locations are those near enough to the beaches to permit people to go every day, or at least for the weekends and places where there are a great many college girls. Such places need not be college towns but any towns that send many of their daughters to college.

Watch all the fashion magazines, the advertisements, and the newspapers that carry fashion features, and clip and mount all the pajama illustrations you find. You will be surprised at the variety and versatility of the designs. The descriptions will give you many ideas for materials and colors, and you will find that the pattern companies

Model 6

offer patterns that can be used as foundations and varied in countless ways.

Make up a few sample suits and show them, together with your collection of clippings, to your prospective customers. Take orders for any style or color that appeal to the individual, allowing her to furnish her material. It is advisable to charge by the hour for your work.

Summer Beauty

by Barbara Ellison, *Fashion Service*, 1931

Summer is so short! I want you to have an abundance of outdoor life and enough exposure to the sun to give you a summer look of wind and sun and health, but not enough to coarsen and darken your skin irreparably. We feel as if we could not absorb enough of it and as if it could do us only good. But, as a matter of fact, it can do our skin a great deal of harm unless we protect it.

The thing that gives color to your skin is the tissue of blood vessels underneath the epidermis. As long as this remains thin, silken transparent, the bright natural color shows through. But when, after repeated exposure to wind and sun, the texture of this outer skin is coarsened and thickened, it is very difficult to restore the natural, youthful tints. And so, either shade your face or protect it with a foundation cream and a powder when you are to be much exposed to sun or wind.

You do not need heavy nourishing creams in summer unless you have a very dry skin, in which case it needs nourishment the year round. You do need, however, to use a generous amount of the lighter creams to replace the natural oils of which the dry winds and parching dust tend to rob the skin. Don't ever let your skin grow flaky and rough. It should be soft and supple at all times, and your creams and nourishing oils will help to keep it so.

We have proved that we do look better when we take care of ourselves! We have finer teeth, glossier hair, and lovelier skin than we used to have, and youth lingers a great deal longer than it did in our grandmother's day.

DEPARTMENT OF GOOD LOOKS

Beauty Versus Personality

by Barbara Ellison, *Inspiration*, 1925

"Nothing in the world has ever been beautiful merely on the surface. Beautiful women hold their preeminence through a single unchanging possession— an inexhaustible, rich store of vitality."

If being attractive were merely a matter of good looks, one might with justice feel that the cards had been stacked and a few fortunate persons had drawn all the trump. But, the appeal of beauty is transient. Having no roots, it quickly dies, and one turns for refreshment either to a newer type or back to a personality that interests or stimulates or that has in some way grown grateful.

There are two or three women who always have, or always will, stand out in my mind, as being singularly attractive. I recall one, in particular. I remember most distinctly the lovely line of her head in profile as it was revealed by the simple arrangement of her hair. Nor shall I forget the whole graceful picture she made in her invariable costume of dark blue, so plainly made that it stood out among the costumes of the day. She understood the art of making herself beautiful in a distinctly individual manner. But suppose she had been only a beautiful picture. You can imagine the disappointment one would have felt if, behind an exterior of so much promise, there had been only an empty head and heart.

We talk a lot about the subtle and indefinable charm of personality. Every one admits that it is more powerful than beauty or than intelligence. You often see a woman of fascinating personality who is not beautiful, but did you ever see such a woman who was not at all intelligent? I am positive that you never did, for personality is primarily a quality of the mind. It is the result of a warm, alive, dynamic intelligence—a combination of heart and brain, of feeling and thinking.

Let no woman feel that because the gods have seen unfit to endow her with beauty, she must take her place among the unattractive. She may have had a better opportunity than her fairer sister to cultivate the rarer graces of mind and heart. And no woman who is alert, intelligent, and always warmly and sincerely responsive can long be unattractive.

Model 3

3 a

3 B

DEPARTMENT OF FASHION

Around the Clock with the Summer Girl

Fashion Service, Summer 1926

She is a light-hearted creature, the summer girl, so a happy choice of apparel means much to her, whether she goes away for a change of scenery and air, or to business and merely spends half-holidays and evenings in lighter pursuits.

Wherever she is or whatever her activities, good taste dictates an appropriate type of costume with fitting accessories for every hour of the day. For informal morning wear indoors, simply made cotton dresses, such as the white-dotted blue Normandy voile of Model 3 with its plain voile trimmings, are so satisfactory. If she goes to business, or spends the morning hours pursuing her favorite sport, she'll enjoy simply tailored dresses of washable silk, such as Model 3A, a striped silk, cut in one-piece style with plaits for ease and plain white silk for the long tab. Her smart, low shoes are decorated with snake skin. Scarves for sportswear come in squares or oblongs.

Good taste demands that the traveler be inconspicuously and simply but appropriately attired. The tailored suit, shown in a new interpretation in Model 3B, is ideal for the purpose. From the

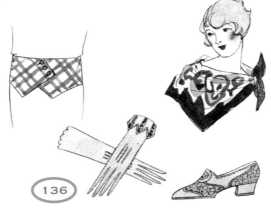

136

twills, tweeds, and novelty flannels, she may choose a navy, black or her favorite lighter color, and follow her fancy in selecting over-blouses, or tuck-ins with little vest-like belts in novelty silk or leather. A simple pouch or envelope bag, decorated with a silver monogram only, and plain, washable suede, or ribbon-trimmed silk gloves are correct accessories.

There are the beloved printed chiffons, silk crepes, voiles, and silk-and-cotton crepes. Finely plaited ruffles of self-material are effective as trimmings for these, as pictured in Model 3F. One Paris house is adding a matching parasol to each gown.

The wrap for afternoon and evening is of silk, satin, or moiré, or of chiffon or Georgette, if for evening only. Model 3G illustrates a single wrap tastefully combining the two sides of crepe satin, a straight length of satin making the cape.

The more tailored type of dress is softened for afternoons by collars, gilets, cuffs, and boutonniere. An interesting lace and net set has its scalloped edges bound with colored silk. The new oxfords for afternoon have high heels and combine leathers.

Then comes evening! The simple morning costumes and the more ornate afternoon ones lead up quite naturally to the fluttering, diaphanous beauty of those designed for that climax to a full day—evening! Chiffon and lace are favorites, sometimes alone, often together, and always in flattering pastel colors. Model 3H is of pink chiffon and white lace. With such dresses, one wears satin or kid strap or opera pumps, chains, wide bracelets, and necklaces inspired by the Russian crown jewels.

Magic Pattern

Magic Bias Slip for Summer Frocks

Fashion Service, 1931

Falling into the lines of each individual figure as if by magic, this slip (shown on opposite page), ultra modern because of its bias cut, is a perfect foundation under fitted frocks. And it's as fascinating to work out as a picture puzzle, built up, as it is, from squares and triangles of fabric. For the average figure, you will need 2½ yards of material, such as flat crepe or radium in silk or rayon. The measurements given are for the average size, but they may be readily adapted to smaller or larger types.

 See Notes, page 232, for modern tips and techniques.

Cutting Your Pattern – For the skirt sections, provide a piece of paper 27 inches square. Tie a string 27 inches long to your pencil, and, holding the free end on the corner *a*, as in Fig. 1, draw an arc, as shown. From *a*, measure toward you 15 inches and place point *b*. From the corner *c*, measure along the curve 8 inches and place point *d*. Connect *b* and *d*. From the opposite corner *e*, measure along the straight edge 3 inches, place *f*, indicate *g* halfway between *e* and *c*, and draw in a new curve from *f* to *g*.

 To draw the second curve (f to g), try a flexible ruler.

Cut from *a* to *b* to *d* to *g* to *f*. Cut four paper patterns like this. For the remainder of the slip, four 15-inch squares of paper are necessary. Number the pattern sections, place as shown in the diagram, and cut. Mark each fabric section like its pattern.

Making the Slip – Turn under all edges of front and back squares a seam's width and baste. Baste remaining sections to these, matching the numbers. Make the shoulder straps, slip the garment on for fitting and pin on shoulder straps. Trim off the corners of the under-arm squares, as shown in the small figure, and keep them for filling in the front and back at the top. Deepen the seams that join the four squares enough to produce a snug fit through the bust line. Lessen this seam depth gradually toward the hip.

Turn under all straight edges of the two tri-angles removed at the under-arm and place at the center-front and center-back, the points of the triangles meeting the points of the squares, as shown on the garment.

Remove the slip, stitch the center-front and center-back skirt sections in the plain seams, then stitch the edges of the front and back squares and the small triangles. Face the top edge, holding in the bias edge to the straight facing. Attach the shoulder straps. Finish the lower edge with a 1-inch hem. Trim off excess seam allowances and press.

Variations For Size – When the figure is short and slender, lessen all measurements. When tall and slender, make the squares smaller, but make the skirt sections the length suggested or longer. Make the line *a* to *b* the same length as the edge of the square. For the tall, large figure, increase all measurements. For the short, large type, increase the size of the squares but not of the skirt sections, making line *a* to *b* the same length as the square.

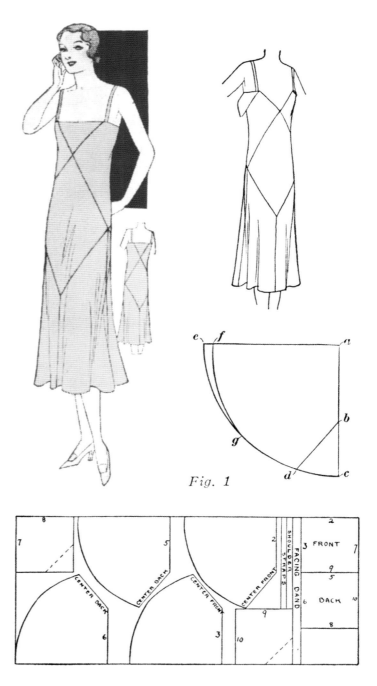

Fig. 1

DEPARTMENT OF HOUSEKEEPING

"This Is the Way We Wash Our Clothes"

by Margaret Murrin, *Inspiration*, 1924

A special time should be given to the washing of one's clothes, because of the careful handling required by fabrics of delicate color. At the very first, the articles to be washed should be examined carefully so that fancy buttons or, in fact, any trimming that would be harmed by water may be removed. Stitches holding draper or linings should be loosened to simplify cleaning and ironing. If there is any doubt in the mind as to the "fastness" of color, take the precaution of soaking the dress for about 2 hours in a salt solution consisting of 1 cupful of common salt to 1 gallon of water. The garment should be dried before washing.

Authorities differ as to the proper method of hanging dresses and blouses on the clothesline. If there is plenty of room, garments may be hung lengthwise; that is, held to the line by clothes pins at the shoulder, the waistline, and the hem. A garment will dry more quickly, however, if hung by the hem, and if the position on the line is changed at least once, there will not be much danger of stretching. Circular shirts, or flared effects, will sag if that is done, but most wash frocks are cut on comparatively straight lines so this need not be considered.

Very sheer dresses may be placed over a hanger that has first been wound and padded with a strip of clean old muslin or Turkish toweling. The hanger may be hung over the line and held fast by a clothes pin. Always dry delicate materials in the shade, and if no shade is available, hang the garment inside where there is a free circulation of air.

It is essential that the entire work of cleaning garments be undertaken in a spirit of interest and joy in the task. There is a certain grace about the accomplishment of most household duties that makes for good results, and especially in the process by which the attractiveness of the clothes is restored and their true beauty born again.

Laundry and Stain Removal from Clothing
Quick action, care, and knowledge in using the correct chemical for the stain are all the requisites of stain removing, which becomes a simple process instead of a bugbear to housewives.

To Remove Tea and Coffee Stains
Stretch the stained place over a bowl and pour boiling water through the stain.

To Remove Wine or Fruit Stains
Put a layer of salt on the stain as soon as it is made and treat with boiling water the same as tea stains.

To Remove Machine Oil Stains
They should be rubbed with soap and cold water. Hot water may make these stains permanent.

Just Among Ourselves

This is a glorious morning and I've had the best time reading your letters. Everyone says I've been at my desk the entire forenoon, but I haven't. I've been miles and miles away, over in the Orient, down in languourous South America, and out in our own bustling Middle West. And if you've been responsible for carrying my imagination to such physical distances, you've been no less responsible for showing me life in its contrasts. That's the idea that comes up oftenest when I read your letters—how widely many of you are separated by distance and by environment and by circumstances. Yet I believe you get together here on an unusual plane of sympathy and understanding and that you draw inspiration from one another.

—*Mary Brooks Picken*

Opportunity took a turn with one of our Iowa readers, who was able to earn extra money and not upset the family domestic machinery.

"Last winter," she writes, "after being asked many times to give sewing lessons, I decided to launch out even though I did feel some inexperience. However, I gave no hint of my doubtfulness to my friends. I began with one class a week of seven members, for that was about all I could have in a class. Another group insisted that I take them, and in a short time still a third group besieged me. I gave ten lessons to each class at fifty cents a lesson per member, taking about 2½ hours to a lesson. Everyone seemed to feel they had spent their money well, and my husband and I were delighted to see how easily the money was earned in so short a time."

—*Mrs. F. O., Iowa*

Another modern mother, dreaming of the avenues to beauty that she will open up to her children, writes:

"I wish you could see my sewing room. It is full of sewing for the coming weeks, and the best part is I have not lost a single customer since I started sewing. I am sending for the boy's violin today. A family of six children, yet they can have their violins, too."

—*Mrs. Me. E. C., Michigan*

And from out West, a college student writes:

"This spring I made over a green crepe de Chine dress and received numerous compliments on it. I also made pajamas, which are a very important item in the life of this campus, for we do most of our studying in them, and wear them to our fireside parties, and I am so pleased with mine as I am with the ones the other girls have. My friend is an instructor here, and I am confident, when I am with him and his friends, that I am dressed as well as they, for he is proud to introduce me to them and to take me with him on all occasions."

—*Miss V. R. C., Oregon*

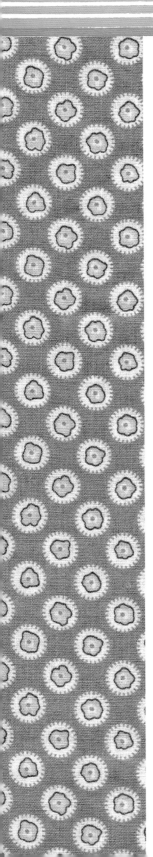

Modern Notions

While I adore a break from my life's familiar landscape, I've also found that a change in scenery makes everything left behind seem more vibrant and cherished upon return. This month is all about the globetrotter and the gift of a new perspective, both at home and away. We've consulted our trusty vintage sources for fresh ideas for all of your modern travel needs this month, down to the smallest details, so you can be sure to take in the sights in high style.

Travel became a major source of excitement for people with the introduction of the railway, when daytrips to the coastal seaside became popular. A whole culture emerged around this new leisure, with seaside clothing and accessories becoming must-haves for the fashionable woman. To pack for your summer vacation, consult the *Department of Good Looks*, which has nothing short of the definitive checklist of wardrobe and beauty necessities for the traveling gal. The woman who traveled by automobile surely needed the perfect scarf to hold her hair in place, and the brave sea voyager absolutely required a darling and functional hat for the windy deck (see *Department of Millinery* to make your own). And staying cool and looking stylish don't have to be mutually exclusive—see this month's *Magic Pattern* for some simple tricks of the needle and thread to fill out your summer wardrobe.

Something to remember is that the vacation attitude can be practiced throughout the year—taking time to smell the flowers can mean a chat with a neighbor or a jaunt through the local park. As I sit overwhelmed by my full plate of projects and my recent commitments that required traveling three weeks in a row, I realize that what I am missing in my life right now is play. This chapter reminds us how important down time really is—and how unhealthy it is not to make space for what should be high on our priority lists.

This month's departments encourage us to get ready on the spur of the moment for an impromptu picnic with friends and family, a time to relax and enjoy each other— suggesting that we linger over an evening bonfire where we can roast marshmallows. Even if you only get as far as your own backyard this summer, make it a getaway worth writing home about and one that rekindles your creative spirit and reenergizes your body for the busy days ahead.

Yours,

Amy B.

August

*Play makes for better work and easier work, for in
reality, healthy playing is cooperating with oneself
toward a better expression of life and love.*

—Mary Brooks Picken

A Thimbleful
of Fun

A Little Recreation Now and Then

by Mary Brooks Picken
Inspiration, July/August 1924

The days in summer, when even the lanes, let alone the asphalt, send up their rays of heat, make us all feel that we would like to be lazy. And, after all, why should we let our whole plans of living be upset just because of a few hot days? It is poor management that keeps one in the kitchen the whole of a hot afternoon. It is poor management that keeps one two hours getting dinner. It is poor management that prevents one from having happy afternoons outside and outings now and then. And poor management comes chiefly from lack of foresight.

Some folks go, year in and year out, on a routine schedule, taking the days as they come and using all the time they have in just "doing the work." Summer time is a good time to get out of such a rut. Put a little novelty in the day, find a way to have appetizing foods without spending the whole day in the kitchen, and plan to have smart and attractive clothes without taking weeks to make them and hours to launder them. Every woman should complement herself by being her own efficiency expert and should plan her days so that she can have a little recreation now and then.

There is no tonic so good as to forget the habitual plan and hurry for a trifling cause, such as, for instance, getting ready on the spur of the moment for a careless little jaunt or picnic with the children. Try it sometime and see for yourself how happily comfortable your heart will be when, after a day in the open, you pull your tired muscles into bed and declare that you really enjoyed yourself better than you thought you would.

So long as we are interested in other folks, we can have a good time ourselves, for they will be glad to join with us in planning joyful, innocent fun that helps in keeping us well and happy. In the Winter, we have books, pictures, concerts, and indoor visits to keep us alert and interested, but all of these things seem rather like canned vegetables in garden time when in Summer we have the mountains, the forest, the streams, and even the stars bid us visit them. It's a good thing to feel, once in a while, as did Eugene Field when he wrote:

It seems to me I'd like to go
Where bells don't ring nor whistles blow;
Where clocks don't strike and gongs don't sound
And I'd have stillness all around—
Not real still stillness, but just the trees'
Low whisperings, or the hum of bees,
Or brooks' faint babbling over stones
In strangely, softly tangled tones.
Or maybe a cricket or a katydid,
Or the songs of birds in the hedges hid,
Or just some such sweet sounds as these
To fill a tired heart with ease.

The Importance of Play

by Barbara Ellison, *Inspiration*, 1926

Beauty is born of health, and health depends, among other things, on rest, recreation, and relaxation. Life is so highly organized these days that many of us suffer unconsciously from over-organization. What we need is now and then to set our faces obstinately against the duties, real and imaginary, that crowd us and give ourselves over with the glorious abandonment of children to the spirit of the small boy who, with delightful inconsequence, goes off fishing when he ought to be doing something else.

A loosening of tension is one result of such practice and this puts us in a receptive condition to all the benign forces that rebuild and revitalize. But it must be more than a gesture—this declaration of independence of ours. It may mean, if we wish, a running away from our desks or our pots and pans for a day in the country, or even for a walk within sight and smell of fields and woods and flowers, for quite as much as we need the fresh air and exercise, we need the sights and sounds and smells of the country, particularly at this time of the year.

We need play, too. Doctors say that a large part of weariness comes from denial of the play instinct and encourage its release through swimming, dancing, walking, tennis, the theater, congenial friends—in short, through whatever forms of recreation give us most pleasure. Time spent in such a way is not wasted when it adds to one's store of health and happiness by driving away boredom and worry. And don't forget that you need a vacation at least once a year, to get completely away for awhile from the usual routine, to see new scenes and new faces, and to have your thoughts directed into new channels. Live in the sunshine and out of doors till your house-bound or office-bound body loses its weariness and apathy and your blood runs as warm as your country cousin's.

The Picnic Lunch
Home Arts and Entertainment, 1922

It is wise to have picnic foods prepared as far ahead as possible, leaving comparatively little work for the time of the party. Sandwiches make for labor, however, and some hostesses prefer to take with them cold meat, eggs, cheese, or whatever fillings they intend using and then they let the guests help themselves.

Salads are good foods for picnic consumption, when used in sandwiches, but they entail the use of silverware and plates, if served separately, and are therefore taboo in that form. Relishes should be added to the sandwich plates, chopped or ground. Pickles and olives may be carried along in paper containers and should be well wrapped or there is danger of the liquid moistening the remainder of the lunch.

Fruits are sometimes the only means of making the luncheon moist and raw tomatoes are excellent thirst quenchers. Never take soft, creamy cakes to a picnic. They will mush into pulp before half the journey is completed.

Crabmeat Salad Sandwiches

1 can crabmeat
2 small stalks celery
2 hard boiled eggs
1 green pepper

1/2 cup nut meats
1 cup mayonnaise
1 tbls. cream

Flake the crabmeat, removing all skin and tough particles. Chop the celery into quarter-inch pieces, and the pepper into fine shreds. Add the nuts, chopped, and the eggs, cut into small pieces. Mix the dressing with the cream and moisten the salad with it. Spread between pieces of buttered bread, placing a small piece of lettuce on each sandwich.

Raisin Sticks

1/2 cup sugar
2 tbls. melted butter
1 egg, beaten
1 square melted chocolate
4 tbls. flour

Speck of salt
Few drops of vanilla
3 tbls. raisins
2 tbls. chopped walnuts

Mix the melted butter and sugar; then add the beaten egg, the melted chocolate, flour mixed and sifted with the salt, the flavoring, raisins, and chopped nuts. Line a square pan with waxed paper, put in the mixture, spread evenly and bake in a slow oven (300°F) for 30 minutes. Remove from the pan, take off the paper, and cut at once into bars.

The Bonfire Picnic

No picnic is half so much fun as the bonfire picnic in the woods, with food cooked on twigs or on old iron grills, and toasted to just the proper turn. Armed with rolls and buns, buttered and spread with mustard, salt, pepper, butter, Frankfurt sausages, bacon or steak, pickles,

Among the delights of summer
Were picnics in the woods.

—George Brandes

potatoes, marshmallows and fruit, the party needs no implements except a little paper with which to start a fire, a box of matches, a knife and a damp towel. The knife should be handy in order to sharpen twigs upon which to cook the meat and the marshmallows. A fork is sometimes needed to remove the meat from the twig onto the bread. Otherwise, the carefree spirit is preserved by dependence on nature's supplies.

It is not always easy to find the right kind of twigs. The wood must be dried and not likely to burn quickly. For this reason, fresh green twigs are not particularly good. Twigs, when sharpened and cleaned by rubbing with a damp towel, are left in lengths that allow the holders enough distance from the fire to prevent undue warmth. Marshmallows may be toasted by holding them some distance from the hot part of the fire and letting them get golden-brown. There is constant danger of burning or melting, so they should be watched. Just a few moments should brown them sufficiently.

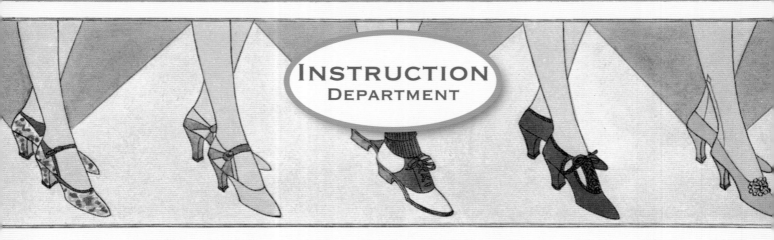

Putting Beauty on a Better Footing

Fashion Service, 1928

A woman should have, if possible, at least three pairs of shoes, a stout pair for hard usage, a pair for everyday wear, and one for dress occasions. It pays, also, to change the shoes once or twice a day. This rests and strengthens the feet and is a means of prolonging the life of your shoes.

We often jump suddenly, too, from very high to very low heels, and because they didn't feel comfortable just at first, we flew to the conclusion that we needed arch support. You should never go suddenly from a very high to a very low heel. Just drop off a lift or two at a time. And be sure that you are well-advised before you use arch supports. They are like a crutch to your foot, and are better left alone than used ill-advisedly.

And what might we do for our corns and calluses? Change your shoes often to avoid continued pressure on any spot. Then, after the bath, rub any hardened spots with a Turkish towel or a nail file and massage with castor oil.

When the feet are tired and ache, try soaking them for 10 or 15 minutes in hot water and ordinary washing soda, about 2 tablespoonfuls of baking soda to a foot tub of water. This will loosen calluses and corns. Follow this with a massage of the feet for five minutes with a good cold cream, working it especially into dry places, and you will often be able to cure quite stubborn calluses. If your feet are inclined to become soft and tender from the use of hot water, use cold water afterward. This tends to harden and toughen them, especially if a little salt is added.

If you are troubled with ingrown toe nails, do not round them at the corners. Instead, cut them straight across, and in the center cut a V-shaped notch. If persisted in, this will eventually cure an ingrown nail.

Beauty Care for the Traveler

Fashion Service, 1931

Vacation time finds us all atingle. For aren't we all going somewhere, even if it's only for a day or so? Most summers I'll warrant you've planned for your vacation weeks ahead, and then, at the last minute, as an afterthought, you tucked a jar of cold cream in your bag and forgot to take it out until a night or two before you came home. And, instead of arriving home a dazzling vision of health, your nose was red and peeling, and you had an unbecoming half-burn, half-tan that took months to wear off. Skin must be cared for on long trips by motor, train or boat, and beauty care must be continued consistently just as at home.

Experienced travelers "travel light," for too much baggage is a vexation. Therefore, preparation is key when it comes to packing. For skin care, I recommend assembling a beauty kit with all of the essential items of skin care. In addition to your cold creams and lotions, you'll very likely need extra cleansing tissues, too, and a roll of absorbent cotton, the latter providing convenient powder puffs that can be used and thrown away. The small guest-size cakes of soap are very handy, especially for short trips. A holder for your toothbrush is also indispensable. Then, of course, you'll need toothpaste, a nailbrush, and a brush and comb, and you'll do well to include dental floss. Don't forget the care of your hands, either. You can secure complete manicure sets in flat, easy-to-pack boxes. And by all means, take along a lipstick.

In addition to the articles suggested, you should include in your traveling bag a small first-aid kit containing just the simplest emergency aids, such as gauze, bandage, adhesive tape, mercurochrome, etc.

Suppose, with these suggestions in mind, you list the most necessary articles for personal comfort and grooming, considering the sort of vacation you plan to take. Then there will be no last-minute confusion and you'll have a pleasanter and more successful trip.

Vacation Clothes

Fashion Service, 1931

To get the greatest amount of pleasure from a vacation, one must have clothes specially planned for the activities involved. Even though your vacation consists only of short weekend trips, or occasional picnics, vacation clothes of the right kind will double the fun by making you comfortable and putting you in a care-free out-of-door mood. The most perfect outing clothes are made of cotton because you feel so free in them and they require so little in the way of care.

In planning a vacation, there is not only the question of "Where shall I go?" but also "What shall I take with me?" to be answered, for although mere clothes should not be allowed to spoil one's enjoyment of any occasion, still it must be admitted that the right sort will help to make any event more successful.

Certain essentials, however, must be provided for any trip, and it is not too early now to plan for the summer holiday. If you must add a garment, make it a sports dress, and if you must add two garments, make the second a summer wrap, a shawl, or a cape in a lovely color that will add just the right touch to your evening outfit.

Certain toilet articles are necessary to keep the skin and hair in best condition. In addition to your usual combs and brushes, include in your list: cold cream, witch hazel for insect bites, talcum, face powder, rouge, manicure outfit, soap, washcloths. And to care for your clothing, provide: a clothes brush, a spot remover, thread of the proper colors, Ivory soap for washing stockings and underwear, needles, scissors, a darning outfit.

For reading matter, bring the latest preferred fiction, a book of short stories, poetry to your liking, and a favorite magazine or two.

Hats for Vacation Needs

by Mary Mahon, *Fashion Service*, 1929

Summer days, crowded with social and sports activities, again emphasize the immediate need of smart hats and harmonious accessories. Though small things in themselves, the accessories spell the difference between a costume and mere clothes. With the new styles manifested in hats, there's an excellent opportunity to achieve novelty in resort millinery and accessories.

We are now in a season of personality clothes. Women are wearing individual things. They appreciate the necessity of being perfectly groomed for all occasions and have grown away from the practice of making one snug-fitting hat do for all purposes. In consequence, there is more variety than there has been for some time. The individual type hat is wanted and this demands variety in size as well as shape, all sizes being worn, small, medium, and large, according to the silhouette that the woman requires.

Not only are milliners accenting the correct hat for the personality and for each occasion, but they are emphasizing the matching of hats to the fabrics and colors of the frocks and coats, a woman's entire wardrobe today being built around the ensemble idea and every detail being in perfect harmony.

As the vacation season advances, the ensemble becomes linked more closely than ever with fashion, resulting in the problem of extra baggage. To overcome this difficulty, it is interesting to note the introduction of collapsible fabric hats, made of the fabrics used for the frocks, a group of such hats being shown here.

Chiffon and maline, self-draped in swathed turbans, are particularly effective for dancing and formal affairs while transparent-velvet and belting-ribbon berets are suggested for semi-dress and smart tailored occasions. Flat crepe, silk linen, and cotton prints are made into small-brimmed hats with fine quilting and stitching for sportswear. In addition to these brimmed models, the new bandeau turban has been introduced for active sports.

Magic Pattern

The Indispensable Kimono

Inspiration, 1925

It's a good plan to make ready now for the weekend visits and vacation trips that you are likely to enjoy this summer. Of course, you need a good-looking kimono anyway, but at such times a garment of this sort is especially useful. In fact, you can hardly get along without one. So if you do not have one that is entirely satisfactory, suppose you give us the opportunity to help you with the planning. Whatever your size, the kimono flatters, especially in handsome colors such as champagne, gray, Chanel red, or Copenhagen blue.

A robe is an interesting article of wear. Sometimes, if there is one that is particularly handy to get into and especially becoming, it is worn and worn until threadbare. Again, an ugly disheveled one is made to do because time for making a new one, patterns, and materials do not assemble themselves at the same time. Here you have two essentials to an attractive kimono and you will see for yourself how easy it is to get the third. The instructions require no pattern, and the time for making is of no consequence, two hours proving ample.

First, you take two lengths of 40-inch material, measuring from your shoulder at the neck to the floor, usually 3 yards, and fold this lengthwise, selvage edges together.

 We recommend using non-directional 44" wide fabric.

Then, a crosswise fold through the middle brings two lengthwise folds together, and four selvages together on the opposite side. Lay this on a table with the folds away from you, the selvages toward you, and the crosswise fold to your left. The rest of the simple task of cutting is indicated clearly in the accompanying diagram.

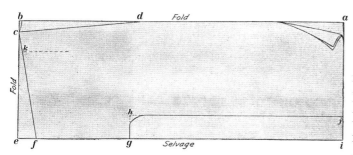

Slash the upper one of the two lengthwise folds from *a* to *b* for the full-length front opening. Measure and cut down the crosswise fold at the left from *b* to *c* 2-1/2 inches. From your shoulder, measure down the front to the low waistline you wish to emphasize. Locate *d* to the right of *b* at a distance equal to this measurement. Cut in a straight line, diagonally from *d* to *c*, cutting the two upper thicknesses that were slashed along the fold, but leaving the fold underneath undisturbed. Curve the back-neckline slightly, as indicated from *b* to *c*.

Now, to shape the shoulder, measure from *e* along the selvage 3-1/2 inches and locate *f*. Cut through the four thicknesses from *f* to *c*.

To the right of *f*, 10 inches, locate *g*. Straight up from *g*, 4-1/2 inches, locate point *h*. Measure up from the corner *i* 4-1/2 inches along the four cut edges and locate *j*. Begin at *j* and cut straight toward *h* through all four thicknesses. As you approach within 3 inches of *h*, cut in a gradual curve to *g*. This completes the cutting.

Join the shoulders with plain seams. The four pieces that were cut out from under the arms are joined end-to-end and used as a wide binding for the front opening and neckline.

In applying the binding to the neck line and front opening, use the full 4-1/2 inch width of the band, and lay it on the kimono, edges even and right sides together. Stitch 1/4-inch from the edge. Make a 1/4-inch turn on the free edge of the binding and fold it over to the wrong side so that the creased edge just covers the row of

 See Notes, page 232, for modern tips and techniques.

stitching. Baste this down and hem the edge by hand if an invisible finish is desired.

At a becoming point on the shoulder, as at *k*, fold a tuck 1-inch deep, letting it extend down to the bustline in front, and just below the low waistline in the back. Catch the ends of the soft satin ribbon that forms the belt in the stitching that holds the tucks in the back.

Only one thing remains to be done. Put in the hem, preferably by hand, but with machine stitching if time is limited. Then slip into the kimono, and admire your handiwork.

Just Among Ourselves

All work and no play makes Jill a dull girl, but all play and no work is quite as unhealthy for developing young minds and hands. And so we recognize the wisdom of the mother who encouraged her young daughter in a self-appointed vacation task. She might have found it easier to do the work herself, but that, of course, wasn't the point. She writes: "At the beginning of the summer vacation, my daughter of twelve decided she would make a dress for herself. Though I became discouraged several times, she made it and had wonderful success."

—*Alice H. Stone, Editor*

Vacation plans must have been running riot in this young teacher's mind when she wrote:

"I have made at least a half-dozen sports dresses for myself besides two silk ones and two sports coats. All of them have an air such as ready-made dresses have, being just as smart and more distinctive."

—*Mrs. L. O., New Jersey*

A woman from Kansas writes of her recovery in the hospital:

"When I know I look fairly well, I can accomplish much more and with a much better spirit than otherwise. Last summer before going into the hospital, I made several dresses, slips, a kimono, and gown. Shoes, hat and everything cost less than $25 and I just can't tell you what a comfort and satisfaction they were to me while there. A person looks unattractive enough at best when ill, but I knew I looked my best all the time and it helped wonderfully."

—*Mrs. M. B. A., Kansas*

A woman in Colorado wrote that she had an opportunity to take a trip East:

"I have no idea what your policy is or what your requirements are, but if you can help me, I'll certainly appreciate it," she said, sending a description of herself and her measurements. Such confidence was well rewarded, for we sent her dress and hat materials, samples of others, made her a member of our student body, and hurried her first lessons along.

And so it goes from day to day. A trousseau for one, traveling clothes for another, remodeling for a home, a layette for the lovingly expected little one, a party dress for a happy-hearted girl—*a real service to women*. And only a small share of the credit can we take ourselves. For it's only as women come to us with their problems, their desires, their ambitions, that we can put our service to its real test.

—*Alice H. Stone, Editor*

Modern Notions

It's back to school time, and as the featured *Testimonials* consistently illustrate, the domestic arts were more than mere ways to pass idle time—they granted women access to unexplored avenues of education and empowerment. As women learned new and better modes of handiwork and artistic production, they passed their newfound knowledge on to other women who also wanted to learn. A vast exchange of ideas and information was happening right there in the back pages of women's magazines like *Inspiration* and *Fashion Service*.

Around the time that The Woman's Institute was gaining steam, women were entering the work force as teachers. In the early 1900s, young female teachers were similar to the working girls of the 1980s—smart, forward-thinking, and intimidating to the established social order. They had strict dress codes and face powder was banned, but nonetheless, they were also experiencing an unprecedented freedom.

While I left my school days behind a while ago, the school season is as special to me now as it was then. School is also a rite of passage for the student, the first chance children have to show their independence and self-sufficiency. I can still remember how, as a child, I anticipated the beginning of the school year so much that I had trouble sleeping the week before the first day. The only difference is that now I'm busy sending my little ones to school, getting their backpacks ready, helping them organize their pencil boxes, and encouraging them when that homework assignment gets tough. Sometimes it's little things like these that force us to slow down and see the gift in the ordinary. As Mary Brooks Picken says in this month's *A Thimbleful of Knowledge*, "We women hurry all too rapidly through the days, forgetting how big they are and how many times we could touch hands with real happiness if we would but appreciate the opportunity."

This month is full of inspiration, reminding me that we should strive to be lifelong learners, in school and out of school, and that even our mistakes offer new learning opportunities. Something I've learned as an entrepreneur who specializes in crafts and sewing is that sometimes a mistake leads me into surprising creative territory, with an exciting and fresh result. For a more traditional, fail-proof excursion into the D-I-Y realm, simply consult this month's goof-proof *Magic Pattern*, which tells you all you need to know in order to make your own apron. Even if you're not the cooking type, you can sport this little number while fixing school lunches, packing backpacks, and making preserves from this season's bounty to store for the coming cooler days ahead.

Yours,

Amy B.

September

Cultivate a sense of appreciation. Love your work, trust your work, keep in touch with today. Teach yourself to be practical, up-to-date and sensible. You cannot fail.

—Henry van Dyke

A Thimbleful of Knowledge

Appreciation Is
The Key to Knowledge

by Mary Brooks Picken

Excerpted from *Thimblefuls of Friendliness*, 1924

Appreciation is the key to knowledge, the key to art, to literature, to good work. Without it, beauty is not seen nor understood and perfection is never acquired. The woman who does not understand the texture, beauty, and service of a piece of cloth will have the most difficult time in making a beautiful garment out of it. The woman who does not appreciate her home and her responsibilities there will never make hers a happy home.

It may be that I am denied the privilege of much time at home that the thought of it is so bright to me. Perhaps if I had all of the crosses that come with each day in the home, I should fail to appreciate the opportunities that are prevalent there and I should see the opportunities not as diamond dollars, but as leaden crosses. But I believe that with the sense of appreciation I have acquired, I should recognize the opportunity that the home actually affords for keeping spirits gay, hearts together, and bodies well nourished. I believe I should practice the little economies that would result in bigger things and set examples that would serve to build character and hold secure that which makes life permanent.

We women hurry all too rapidly through the days, forgetting how big they are and how many times we could touch hands with real happiness if we would but appreciate the opportunity. A few weeks ago when I was traveling, a woman from across the aisle of the car in which I was riding came over and sat with me. She was a deep-souled person who had lived and thought and who had a delightful sense of appreciation for humorous, as well as for serious, things. She had been a pioneer in the extreme West. She told me of accomplishments out there—of the women, of church and school difficulties, of community sewing classes, of the inability to procure adequate materials, how one magazine traveled the rounds of all the homes, and how recipes are exchanged and bits of sewing and housekeeping knowledge passed on to the neighbors.

I realized that the charm of the woman was her ability to appreciate life, situations, and opportunities, and to use them all to good effect. She found beauty in the most obscure places, saw good in people, discovered skill in fingers, and evidenced actual delight in every possible service.

My little lady of the train demonstrated that she knew the virtue of perseverance and the value of vision, for her every act, her every word, was for happiness and cheer. She was unselfish, thoughtful in a most intelligent way, and I am sure the brightness of that visit with her will remain with me always.

For those of us who wish to make progress, no matter what our aims may be, there is no better teacher than a child. If a child wants to know about something, he asks a lot of questions. If something happens with which he is unfamiliar, he demands an explanation. Of course, the child looks to his parents for answers. But what a fine example he is to all who want to learn. "If you don't know, ask!" Ask somebody else, or ask yourself and then answer yourself by consulting the proper authority, be it a person or a book. But ask! Don't stifle your desire to learn. Be as a little child, and ask.

—Gustave L. Weinss,
Inspiration, 1923

INSPIRATION
DEPARTMENT

When the School Bell Rings

by Laura MacFarlane, *Inspiration*, 1923

With the first tinkle of the school bell, each year comes back as if it were yesterday, the thrill of my first day of school. I remember how eager I was to get there, for I had gotten big ideas about it from my older cousins, who were very learned in the ways of the school world, and from my mother, whose preparations for my going cast a real glamour around the event. And fortunate for me that I was not disappointed. A charming teacher made life glow and sparkle and taught us at the same time—a happy combination.

Year after year went by, each one bringing for me a new teacher, new experiences, new sorrows, new joys. But for my mother what? Responsibilities as to my getting the most out of my school life. Responsibilities as to the companions I chose. Responsibilities as to my clothes, my health, my happiness. All necessary. All important. But then, as now, none more vital in a child's life than the last—happiness. In fact, some one has gone so far as to say "The first duty to children is to make them happy."

And just what constitutes happiness for children? Well, as we all know, that depends largely on the child, each one finding joy in a different source. The problem is to study each little nature until we understand it and then work to give the greatest pleasure.

They need training, encouragement, often praise, and always friendship, if they would have their share of happiness. So, as they answer the call of the school bell some day very soon, an added responsibility devolves upon all parents. They must be careful to prevent the things that "hurt" young folks, to guide them in their work and their play, to help them at self-expression. By meeting the task thus squarely and whole heartedly, parents can render a most valuable service to their children and to society. And if, in addition, they make companions of the children as they go along, they will enjoy the experience and renew their own youth.

DEPARTMENT OF INSTRUCTION

Perfecting the Woman's Own Workshop—The Kitchen

"Every woman who must manage a home, be it large or small, owes it to herself to have a well-planned kitchen or workshop, one that is good to look upon and easy to work in."

We have been hearing a great deal about efficiency during the last ten years. And what has been the result? A marked improvement in the running of business concerns, in the working of farms, in the making of automobiles—in fact, every line of endeavor has shown an upward tendency. But can we say the same thing of the running of the home—the domain over which the housewife presides? Much has been accomplished by the home economics departments of schools, colleges, and magazines, but there is no business today that has been so backward in adopting up-to-date methods and the findings of science as that of housekeeping. How many kitchens do you see that are equipped with the same devices that the housewife's mother and grandmother used? A great many, I'll wager.

Instead of making so brave an attempt to furnish living rooms, reception halls, and bedrooms so that they will be admired by your friends, why not resolve to expend the same energy and money on the kitchen with the thought that this room—your workshop—must be your most interesting room, since it is here that you carry on the engineering of your home? Then it will become a pleasant spot and the usual drudgery of housework will lose its sting. And the best part of the plan is that your vitality will be saved for the more aesthetic aspects of life, which are conducive not only to growth and development but to happiness and contentment as well.

If the home is wired for electricity, you may take advantage of the numerous electrical devices for cooking that the market boasts. The electric toaster, grill, waffle iron, griddle, percolater, all permit cooking at the table and naturally encourage conversation and good feeling. And the mere mention of electricity brings to our minds numberless household devices for eliminating fatigue in housework—the vacuum cleaner, the electric washer, the electric iron, the motor dish washer, the electric ice-cream freezer, to say nothing of mayonnaise mixers and related utensils. Yes, "chained lightning" has already overcome much of the drudgery of housework and is constantly exploring new fields.

The sink with the double drain board is the most efficient kind. Then the soiled dishes can be piled on one drain board—the right usually—washed, and placed on the other, thus overcoming wasted motion and the breakage that often results if the dishes are piled in the sink. The mixing faucet makes it possible to have water at whatever temperature is desired.

The electric ranges now on the market have been brought to a degree of perfection just short of marvelous. Now you may set the thermostat control at the oven temperature that is required to cook a certain dish or a whole meal, place the food in the oven, set the electric timer properly, and then banish all thought of it from your mind, or spend the afternoon calling, or shopping, or what not, while your cooking goes efficiently on. Ovens, too, may be purchased, choosing whichever type gives the best results both as to good lighting and step-savings.

Preserved Fruits Give Pleasure

by Laura MacFarlane and Mary Gilgallon,
Fashion Service, July/August 1932

The other day I read a charming little poem in which the jars of jellies and preserves stored away on shelves were compared to jewels, bright and sparkling. I thought how nice it would be if the housewife, when preserving and pickling, could think of currants as rubies, peaches as amber, grapes as sapphires, and pears as pearls! There is indeed poetry in the everyday things around us, for a well-made jar of conserve or relish, distinctive in flavor, glowing with color, and fragrant with fruit or spices, is an artistic as well as a culinary achievement.

When properly made and attractively packaged, the excellence of these products finds for them a ready sale, a worthwhile thought just now, it becoming increasingly apparent that the high-quality product has the best market. An offer to "put up" the fruits of a neighbor's trees might be the means of starting such a business, with a comfortable income as the result.

In fact, I know a woman who offered to preserve a bushel of peaches purchased by a neighbor unexpectedly called away. Putting into her work all of her skill and originality, she laid the foundation for a business that now brings her in about one thousand dollars during each canning season. So the wise homemaker or the woman who wishes to increase the family income by selling her products should stock her jam closet while the fruits are cheap in the market and plentiful in the garden.

Whether you are doing the work for yourself or for others, use good equipment, such as preserving kettles that are large enough and that will not scorch readily, jars and glasses of the proper sizes with perfect-fitting tops, and spoons, both wooden and metal, for stirring. Also, strive for utter cleanliness. When to care for detail, imagination is added, the results will be captured sunbeams, the gems of summer's garden and orchard to brighten winter days.

All preserves and relishes are bottled while hot. Protect the sweet thick products, such as jams, conserves, and preserves, immediately with a thin coating of melted paraffin, and add a little more when the product is cool. Pickled fruits and vegetables do not require these precautions. In every case, close-fitting covers are necessities.

To make jelly, you must combine sugar in the proper proportions to a fruit juice that contains a certain amount of acid and a sufficient amount of pectin. Pectin is the jelly-making property of fruits and berries. The preparation of the fruit depends on the kind selected. Remove all stems, clean the fruit thoroughly, and cut it up into small pieces. From these basics, you can follow the individual recipes below.

 We suggest adjusting the proportion of sugar to desired sweetness.

There is a certain subtle quality in the flavor of pineapple which seems to intensify the individuality of the fruits with which it is combined, thus explaining its frequent use. In the recipe below, it enhances the cherry flavor.

Cherry Conserve

3 cups white cherries
(measured after pitting)
1 pineapple
Sugar
1 lemon, juiced
2 oranges, juice and rind

Add to the cherries the pineapple chopped fine or run through the food grinder. Measure, add an equal amount of sugar, the lemon juice, and the grated rind and juice of the oranges. Bring to a boil, then simmer until thick, stirring frequently.

Orange & Peach Jam

4 oranges   3 lbs. peaches   Sugar

Cut the oranges in half from blossom to stem end, and slice thin, leaving on the skins. Cover with boiling water and allow to stand overnight. Wash the peaches, nearly cover with boiling water, and allow to stand overnight. In the morning, remove skins and pits. Put the oranges and peaches with liquor from both in the preserving kettle and cook for 30 minutes. Measure, add the same quantity of heated sugar, and boil until thick, stirring frequently.

❊ *Amy B.'s Favorite* ❊ *Vintage Advice*

FROM THE QUIRKY TO THE CONVENTIONAL

Nourishing Lunches

As you wistfully watch the school-age member of your family hurrying off on these September mornings, turning at the corner to wave you goodbye, there's a catch in your throat and a mist in your eyes as they trudge off to be gone from you all day long. But these are quickly dispelled by the thoughts that they'll be in good hands and that their bodies will be properly nourished. For haven't you packed them appetizing, nourishing lunches which they are proud to take and delighted to eat?

If there is any doubt in your mind as to the type of food your children are likely to select, or if the school does not have a lunchroom, never fail to prepare a lunch for them. And make sure that you select the foods properly and that you pack them well, as the right sort of lunch will help to form proper food habits, particularly in your littlest tots.

First of all, there is the equipment, which, though simple, should be right. A metal box is best, because it can be readily cleaned. Then, there should be a thermos bottle that will fit into the box, paper napkins, inexpensive spoons, knives, and forks are other requirements.

Next, and of greatest importance, is the contents of the box. Thinking of the food requirements of children and the relation of this meal to the other meals of the day, you will be wise not to take this matter lightly but to consider the preparation of their school lunch to be met with all the resources at your command. The food should be appealing, varied, and occasionally it should contain surprises. All of these things must be done with foods that will pack well, and as the lunch must be prepared attractively each day that the child will want to eat it, you can see that the school lunch is something that requires thought, time, and ingenuity.

Looking Our Charming Best

by Laura MacFarlane, *Fashion Service*, 1931

There's the big subject of color. This Fall, there'll be every opportunity for us color-loving folks to indulge ourselves, but we must do it wisely. The safest, most conservative combination is the two-color scheme with dark costume and light accessories. These tones of color are easy to handle, too. Harmonizing shades of different colors call for more planning, yet many combinations suggest themselves, such as a tan jacket costume, an orange blouse, and brown hat, bag and shoes. Combinations of contrasting shades of more than two colors are less simple but are being worked out charmingly by means of such novel combinations as red with turquoise, delft blue with raspberry, and ocean green with violet, the search being for combinations of an interesting and original flavor.

With hats assuming so many tilts and angles, there's an art in the way we wear them. Unless we would ruin their effect, we must wear them well back on the head, exposing the forehead, not after the fashion of the last few years. Yet we need not sacrifice our looks on the altar of fashion, for we can now show a little hair in front for a softening effect.

The main problem, after all, in any costume, is the way we assemble and wear it. Colors smartly combined. Textures in harmony with each other and with the occasion for which they are selected. Even hem lines for the office. Tweeds or tailored rough silks for sports events. Conservative prints for daytime, large ones for evening. Long skirts for dressy frocks. Everything in the proper feeling, and then worn with that subtle something which gives even the simplest outfit the air of chic.

Color Contrasts

Two-Color Combinations
Brown, white
Blue, white
Powder pink, violet
Dove gray, apple green
Green, brown

Three-Color Combinations
Black, emerald, flame red
Black, topaz, garnet
Navy, white, chartreuse
Beige, capucine, turquoise
Gray, chartreuse, capucine

Cross-Stitch

by Clarice Carpenter, *Inspiration*, 1927

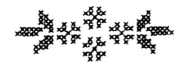

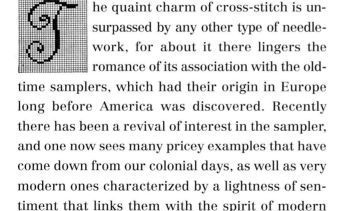

The quaint charm of cross-stitch is unsurpassed by any other type of needlework, for about it there lingers the romance of its association with the old-time samplers, which had their origin in Europe long before America was discovered. Recently there has been a revival of interest in the sampler, and one now sees many pricey examples that have come down from our colonial days, as well as very modern ones characterized by a lightness of sentiment that links them with the spirit of modern interior decoration both in color and in motif.

But cross-stitch is by no means confined to samplers. In simple motifs and borders, it makes the most delightful decoration imaginable for children's clothes, underwear, blouses, handkerchiefs, and innumerable household linens. By varying the color, the size of the stitches, and the kind and size of thread, a great number of different effects may be obtained from a single pattern.

Perhaps the simplest way to learn is to follow a pattern stamped on the material, although the method has certain drawbacks. It is almost impossible to transfer the pattern so accurately that it follows threads of the material exactly and the blue lines of the transfer may show through the stitches after the work is completed.

The original method is probably the one of counting the threads of the fabric and working over the same number of threads in both directions for each stitch. And undoubtedly it is the most accurate one.

The most used method is that of working the design over cross-stitch canvas basted to the material, afterwards removing the canvas by pulling it out, thread by thread, thus leaving the cross-stitching on the fabric underneath. Designs to be used in this way are of two kinds, printed on cross-barred paper. One has the design printed in colors, each square in the color is intended for the cross-stitch

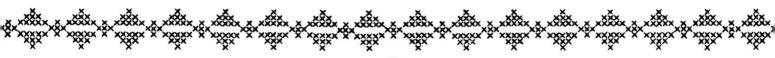

that it represents. The other is a black-and-white diagram with each square marked by a color symbol. A chart explaining the color represented by each symbol accompanies such a diagram.

Cross-stitch canvas is a stiff material, resembling scrim and woven with the threads far enough apart to block it off into definite squares. They come in a variety of sizes, ranging from 6, 8, or 10 squares to the inch for very coarse work and 12, 16 or even more squares for fine work.

Having determined the size of the design, cut the canvas 1 inch wider each way and locate the square that comes to the exact center. Place this over the center point of the space to be decorated, and when you are very sure the threads of the material and of the canvas run exactly parallel, baste them together around the edges, and, if the space is large, at intervals across the canvas.

You are now ready for the embroidery. Select the thread to fill the squares of the canvas, and choose a long-eyed embroidery needle. It is well to start near the center of the design as there is less danger of making a mistake in counting and it is simpler to work the large masses of color first.

To make the cross-stitch, bring the needle up from the wrong side through both the material and the canvas, running it through the center of a large square of the canvas, as at *a*, Fig. 1, at the left end of a row of stitches to be the same color. Leave an inch of the thread on the wrong side and work over it instead of knotting the thread.

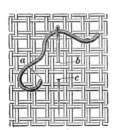

FIG. 1

Next, bring the needle a block to the right and a block above *a*, insert it at *b*, and bring it out at *c*. Continue in this way until the right end of the row is reached. This leaves diagonal stitches on

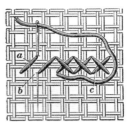

FIG. 2

the right side, as at *a*, Fig. 2, and vertical ones on the wrong side. Complete the stitches by returning to the starting place, working from right to left and being careful to bring out the needle for each stitch in exactly the point where a stitch of the first row was made, as at *b*. The completed stitches appear as at *c*. Take care to have each top stitch cross the lower one in the same direction so that the result is uniform. Only isolated stitches should be completed separately.

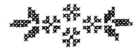

Magic Pattern
A Comfortable, Economical Apron
Fashion Service, 1926

Such a stylish and economical apron may be cut from 1 to 1-1/2 yards of material, depending on one's size (1 yard for average size), and with very little effort because of the small amount of shaping needed. The fact that the belt is made to fit securely either at the waistline or just above the hips, takes away the strain that is likely to occur when the weight of an apron hangs from a strap about the neck.

Straighten the cut edges, and then trim off a strip 6 inches wide from selvage to selvage to form the belt, bib strap, and pocket, which is made 5-1/2 inches wide and 6 inches deep. The part of the 6-inch strip remaining after the pocket has been cut is then cut through the center to form two bands, one for the bib strap and the other for the waistband.

See Notes, on page 232, for modern tips and techniques.

Now fold the apron material through the center lengthwise and place it on a table with the fold nearest you, as shown in the diagram at the right of the page. Consider the corner at the lower right, a, and from this point measure away from you a distance equal to one-half the width of the bib, and locate b. For the average figure, the bib may be about 8 inches wide, finished, so make the distance from a to b 4-1/2 inches, the extra 1/2 inch being allowed for seams. Now from point a to your left, measure the depth of the bib, about 10 inches, and place point c. From point c, and at right angles to the fold ac, place a line of pins extending out to the open edges of the material, as at d. Measure along this line a distance equal to that from a to b plus 1/2 inch, and consider this point e, providing in this way a bib that is slightly wider at the bottom than at the top. With these points indicated, cut from b to e and from e along the guideline of pins to d.

Gather the sides by hand or by machine, allowing a reasonable amount of fullness, and then prepare to baste the bands in place. Cut into two equal parts the strip set aside for the waistband, and trim off from the pieces whatever is neces-

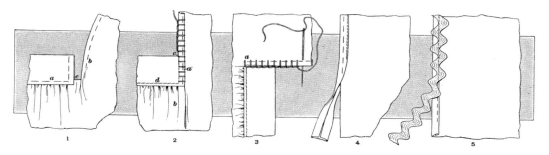

sary to make them the correct length, remembering to add the width of the bib in determining their finished length. For wearing over one-piece dresses, it is best to have the belt long enough to fit around a low waistline.

Including the ends, turn in the raw edges of the bands 1/4 inch and press the turns in place. Fold the bands through the center lengthwise, with the raw edges inside, and crease on the fold. Then place the turned edges over the gathered portion of the apron on each side of the bib, and baste in place, as at a, Fig. 1. Now turn the raw edges of the bib over in a 1/4-inch hem and baste this in place also, as at b, clipping across the end c, as shown. Bring this hem over on top of the end of the band, placing it so that the inner edge of the hem coincides with the edge of the band, as at a, Fig. 2, which shows the wrong side. Notice the small plait formed below the band, as at b.

Begin to stitch the band to the bib at point c on the right side, stitching as near the edge of the hem that finishes the bib as possible and continuing around the edge of the band, as shown at d. Before finishing the hem of the bib, make the strap that holds the bib in place by folding through the center, lengthwise, then stitching and turning it. Baste this band in place at the upper corners of the bib, trying the apron on to make sure of the correct length of the band and turning in the raw edge carefully.

Start the blanket-stitching, which should be done in mercerized thread of a contrasting color, at point a, Fig. 3, bringing the threaded needle up from the wrong side just beyond the turned edge of the hem. Take the stitches over all thicknesses of material, so they will hold the ends of the neckband and waistline band, as well as the hem that finishes the bib, smooth and flat, as shown in the view of the wrong side, Fig. 2.

Use the same finish for the top of the pocket, first turning this in a 1/4-inch hem. Shape the lower part of the pocket, or leave the edges straight, turning them in once before stitching. Finish the lower edge of the apron with a 3-inch hem. Place a buttonhole and button on the belt in the proper position to have the apron fit easily at the low or normal waistline.

The use of binding, as in Fig. 4, or rickrack, as in Fig. 5, as a finish for the edges of the bib and the top of the pocket, offers interesting variation. As the stitching of these trimmings should be continuous with that which holds the waistband in place, make sure that they are properly basted before permanently attaching the bands that finish the waistline. If you use rickrack, place it over a hem turned to the right side.

Return to School

Fashion Service, August 1929

*"There is no day when a new dress means more to a little girl
than on this opening day of the fall term."*

Any school house in September, eight-thirty of the first day of the term! A brightly colored, excitedly chattering crowd of children fills the yard and halls. Here and there teachers dart hurriedly about, and suddenly a bell sounds. More or less order prevails now, as the small throng breaks up, little ones going one way and bigger ones another, always with glances of interest at the costumes of small neighbors, and then with satisfaction at their own, for there is no day when a new dress means more to a little girl than on this opening day of the fall term.

Just Among Ourselves

In this letter, the daughters made school clothes while mother earns.

One of our busiest mothers dropped in at the Institute not long ago. She came to shop for school-girl dresses in the Merchandise Department, and we had a delightful chat. At the time she began her course, Mrs. Haggerty was ill in bed with a slow recovery in view. Meanwhile, the doctor and hospital bills were growing bigger and bigger and since she could manage to use her hands—well, it just seemed that sewing was the one thing she could learn that would be a big enough help. So with a little money borrowed to begin the lessons, she enrolled. Most of her lessons were completed right there in bed . . . that was in the early months of 1921; now the hospital and doctor are paid. Still our student is going right on with her outside sewing because it adds so much to the family income and one can't have too many sources when there are five children . . . Now the older girls, 12 and 15, are learning to make their school clothes. All this and more Mrs. Haggerty told me while we selected materials together. "I promised to come back with an "Institute dress" for each of my oldest three girls." They were ready to prepare for school, so we chose practical girlish things . . . then we talked about finishing touches, something simple to give each dress a prettiness all its own. I like to imagine that first day of school, the children starting off with gay touches of appliqué or simple embroidery in harmonious yet contrasting colors. But I like still more to imagine our little dressmaker-mother happily sewing away with the satisfaction of a back debt cleared up and the security of a profitable profession ahead.

—Alice H. Stone, editor

Canning Pays Off

"I have been busy canning meats, vegetables, fruits, and chicken, and have canned about 625 cans since the first of February. Have also made and sold about 200 pounds of candy. I live in a farm community and it seemed money was so short; however, I earned something by sewing, too, and there isn't anything now that I wouldn't attempt to make and be sure it would be a success. Every few days some 4H girl comes to me for help."

—Mrs. C. M. M., Indiana

Modern Notions

Halloween, at its core, is about the thrill of being someone (or *some-thing*) else for a day. No one understands this transformation more than children, who spend a great deal of their time playing they are someone other than themselves. And how seriously they take the task of becoming another! Think of the way trick-or-treaters arrive at your doorstep, hands outstretched for candy, truly believing they are whatever costume they have on. I love their willingness to believe in a world they themselves have created.

This month it's all about our attitude and what we make of our world—everything from how we parent to how we carry our burdens is directly influenced by our attitude (read the *Department of Inspiration* for an enlightening story). Even how we carry ourselves and how high we hold our heads is a result of our attitude (see *Amy B's Favorite Vintage Advice* for info on posture). How much fun we have at any given moment is primarily dictated by our attitude, and October is a month where fun belongs to both children and adults. As the *Department of Housekeeping* declares, Halloween is "fun time pure and simple."

It's not hard for me to subscribe to that motto. It's always been my favorite time of year—for cool nights that call for a blanket while enjoying a warm fire outside, for the joy that comes from creating costumes, and for the looks on the kids' faces when the jack-o-lantern lights up the room for the first time. At heart, it's just that I love being part of my children's lives, from the big moments down to the smallest. When it comes to Halloween this means taking their costume ideas seriously, helping them execute their vision by sewing or gluing (hint: the costumes in this month's *Department of Fashion* are frighteningly adorable), and attending the school's parade of costumes before we set off on a night of trick-or-treating fun. Little people learn to feel proud of themselves with the loving guidance of the adults around them, as Mary Brooks Picken explores in *A Thimbleful of Character,* and it's so rewarding when children feel safe and secure enough to let their imaginations take over.

And when the long evening is over, and all of the candy spread out and admired and traded and tasted, and the teeth are brushed—I'm going to slip into the nightgown I made with the help of the *Magic Pattern*. Truly, nothing feels more magical than a comfortable nightgown at the end of a busy day and a long night. Seeing them asleep, the costumes off and back to their child selves, I feel overwhelmed with gratitude—I'm thinking next year may find me costumed as Lady Luck.

Yours,

Amy B.

OCTOBER

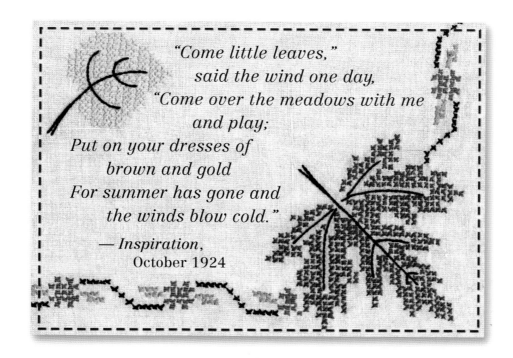

"Come little leaves,"
said the wind one day,
"Come over the meadows with me
and play;
Put on your dresses of
brown and gold
For summer has gone and
the winds blow cold."

— *Inspiration,*
October 1924

A Thimbleful of Character

"Roof Trees" Building Soundly

by Mary Brooks Picken
Excerpted from *Thimblefuls of Friendliness*, 1924

I have read John Burroughs's essay, "The Roof Trees," many times. It tells us how to build happy homes—the kind that invite us to live connected lives. Every person who is helping a child to a healthy, happy grown-up-ness should read it. It reveals so clearly the importance of careful building, whether the structure be a house or a human soul.

Just as each foundation stone and joist and rafter and door and window and bit of siding and roof is selected with care as to quality of material, and shaped and placed with a thought always of its part in making the finished house beautiful, substantial, and comfortable, so should we strive to choose and shape the principles, desires, motives, and purposes that go into the forming of character of the developing young life.

Burroughs says, "I notice how eager all men are in building their houses, how they linger about them, or even about their proposed sites. It is a favorite pastime to go there for a Sunday afternoon and linger fondly about; they take their friends or their neighbors and climb the skeleton stairs and look out of the vacant windows, and pass in and out of just sketched doorways. The heart moves in long before the workers move out."

The young life should interest us more than the skeleton house. We should keep close enough to see the new joists go up, the windows in, and new supports take their places in the child mind. If we watch close to the building of their characters, the forming of their ideals, the development of courage and poise within them, they will mean more to us when they are grown up. We will love them more unselfishly, understand their motives better, just as we would appreciate more the houses we helped to build.

Mothers and fathers should make time for their children. Mothers, especially, should be kind, fair, and happy.

The constant "Don't do that" is not healthy, for it cripples the individuality of a child inclined to obey and makes for discredit and disrespect with those who are not so inclined.

A mother's power is very great. A mother can build soundly and give her children a heritage of good health and the still greater heritage of a good moral background, which means a substantial heart and a permanently forward heart. In the divine scheme of harmony, the mother, who knows her children, holds the magic key that locks the door against squabbles, misunderstood feelings, or corroding resentments. A mother who knows her children directs and guides them, lives with their questions, but avoids every semblance of criticism.

If mothers would only realize that it is the minds and hands of humans that make the wheels of commerce go around, controlling all material strength, they would be inspired to help their children to a healthy, happy maturity, rather than to accept them as burdens of responsibility. No mother knows but that her child could come to be a Lincoln or an Edison.

In these pages, I wish I might encourage every mother to picture an ideal building of the characters of her children, using for the foundation stones, cleanliness; the joists, industry; the siding, kindness; the floor, truth; the windows, individuality; the doors, generosity; the roof, love; and nailing all securely together with courage and sentiment. Then she could know definitely that their Roof Tree would shelter them through every storm of life and find itself set always in that garden of flowers that blooms wherever there be happy hearts.

Character is higher than intellect.
A great soul will be strong to live, as
well as strong to think.

—**Ralph Waldo Emerson**

INSPIRATION
DEPARTMENT

Carrying Your Problems Cheerfully

Inspiration, October 1924

When I was in New York the other day, a boy, perhaps sixteen years of age and small at that, offered to carry two large bags for me. I remarked that I thought them too heavy for him, but he insisted, and with a boy's "braggy proud" smile he picked them up and walked right off with them. He chatted happily all the way to the Hudson Tube.

I asked if he was not young for that kind of work, but he insisted that he was not, that the job paid well, if he hustled, and that was what he liked. The boy was happy and bubbly with talk and he said one very true thing, "Folks won't pay you big unless you smile and act like you really want to carry their truck." And I thought, sure enough, success is for those who can smile and be cheerful about any load they have to carry, especially when the load belongs to someone else.

We speak often so casually that we wish we could be happy and have good times like other folks. We wish that we could cook delicious foods like some one whom we know, or make beautiful clothes. But we spend days and weeks just wishing instead of picking up smilingly the idea and buckling right down to the hard work of it and achieving the right thing we wish for. The golden pot of accomplishment is at the end of every wish rainbow if we reach out and grasp it while the rainbow lingers in our hearts.

The little fellow carrying the bags seemed, at first, not equal to the job, but when he got a good hold and started, he wasn't thinking over and over about how heavy the bags were, but that soon he would be at his destination. As a result, he had only the bags to carry and not even a tiny bit of his own self-pity, which is indeed the heaviest known thing. We can find joy in carrying every burden, if, while we bear it, we think not of the load, but of the happiness that awaits us at the end when we lay it down with the satisfaction of work well done.

Walking Like a Princess

by Marilyn Madison, *Inspiration*, October 1925

Funny how people walk—some people I mean just slump along as if they were carrying the weekly wash or else "getting there" on roller skates. Some move like lumber wagons, and others flit like sparrows. Or maybe someone you have in mind walks as if swimming while in the river, trying to walk and swim at the same time.

These women may have beautiful complexions, glossy hair, glistening teeth, snow-white hands, and polished nails, but all these points are discounted 50 percent, instead of enhanced, with poor carriage. Every woman can take on a new beauty, a new charm, if she will practice lightness on her feet, will wear her clothes rightly, and will carry her accessories as well as her arms and head in a graceful and smart manner. As for me, I am practicing, and one of these days I am going to hear someone say, to my back, of course, "Isn't she charming? She has the carriage of royalty, the poise of a princess." Do I have any accomplices? If so, here we start.

Now, *obey orders!* Your mirror is your boss, you know, so face it carefully and obey the commands diligently.

Stand as tall as possible with: Heels 4 to 6 inches apart, unless you are the small type. One foot slightly forward. Head poised with dignity, not arrogance or affectedness. Hands in front of you. Stand still five minutes. Remember, no shifting or wiggling.

What to do for the five minutes: Think beautiful thoughts. Resolve to write letters to your friends, to call Mrs. Jones and tell her how much you like her new hat. Carry on an imaginary conversation with a woman to whom you have just been introduced. Perhaps she is a writer whose books you haven't read. Plan what you will talk about. There are millions of things to think about in five little minutes. I know you are saying right now, "Why, five minutes—that's nothing. I can keep perfect posture for a quarter of an hour." But just try it.

What five minutes a day accomplishes: It reminds us of our ambition, of our determination to stand, walk, sit, and gesticulate gracefully. To keep up the good work, every time during the day that you catch yourself standing awkwardly, or sitting slumpily, or carrying your hands unbecomingly, or walking heavily, straighten up, put your whole body to rights, and remember that you have an aim, definite and sincere, to hear some one say about you, "Isn't her poise wonderful? Such grace and carriage, truly charming, truly charming."

(a) Using her arms like propellers.

(b) Picking her way on feet that hurt.

(c) Limp, weak-kneed, and ready to drop.

(d) Swinging violently on feet wide apart.

Charm Through Grace and Poise

by Marilyn Madison, *Inspiration*, October 1925

Poise is a word that greets us so often these days from the printed pages of beauty articles that even the most complacent of us have begun to ask ourselves whether we possess shortcomings of posture and carriage. In a beauty sense, a body, graceful and well-poised, is one of the greatest assets that a woman can have, and doubly fortunate is she who possesses this sort of charm.

Long ago a great French dancing master discovered what constituted the normal line of poise in the body and that complete relaxation, or ease of posture, is possible only when the line of poise is maintained. He learned that there is a point of conscious center in the body, the notch in the top of the breastbone just below the throat pit. Whether standing, sitting, or walking, one should, if in poise, be able to feel a line of weight down through the body from this point to the balls of the feet.

FIG. 1

It is preferable for the line of weight to fall upon the ball of the forward foot. Meanwhile, the whole body may relax except the muscles of this one limb. To relax, keep the shoulders erect but not stiff, the breastbone inclined forward over the forward foot, and the accompanying hip and thigh bent slightly out to the side in order to keep a straight line across the hips while standing. During walking, the line of weight is shifted gradually from one foot to the other, the heels falling lightly and each step following along an imaginary straight line. Meantime, hold the head up, throw back the shoulders and straighten the neck so the chin will be in. Never allow the head to sag.

In order to strengthen the muscles and acquire suppleness, there is a program of exercises in which the relaxation feature is especially stressed. With the weight over both feet, slowly bend the knees outward and lower the body to a squatting position, as in Fig. 1; keep the line of poise by inclining the chest well forward; then slowly rise. Think of the conscious center at the chest as rising up to the standing position. This expedient helps to relieve strain either while raising or lowering the body. Next, lower the body to a kneeling position, as in Fig. 2, keeping it poised over one foot with the other side relaxed. Slowly lower the body until the relaxed knee meets the floor and the foot is slipped backward until the instep lies flattened against the floor, then rise.

FIG. 2

The Costume's the Thing

Fashion Service, October 1927

When the Halloween moon casts its eerie light over all the land and sends weird shadows creeping through the trees, the stealthy spirits abroad often feel something more than moonlight creep along their not too courageous spines! For a sudden encounter with another ghost, goblin, witch, or preposterously large black cat produces real shivers even when one knows the evil thing is only a schoolmate in clever disguise. Yes, the costume's the thing that strikes terror to the heart and gives zest to the party, so make it original.

Model 5—The **Modern Witch** is truly bewitching in this costume of gray cambric in two shades made formidable by black cambric owls and bats tacked to her skirt. The kerchief, sleeve frills, and hat ruffles are of cheesecloth, and the bodice is laced with black velvet ribbon.

Model 5A—This **Charleston Belle** adds much to the gaiety with her trousers half orange and half gray and flared by the slanting lines of a pajama pattern. The fitted bodice is attached to a tunic that is decorated with jazzy black notes and trimmed with a gray band. White organdie frills edge the sleeves and neckline. The wig may be made of stocking-net covered with black yarn.

Model 5B—**Lady Luck** uses cambric for her full skirt and bodice, and voile for her blouse. Lucky stars of gold, black cats, wish-bones, green four-leaf clovers, and gold horseshoes are cut from paper and tacked to the dress.

Model 5C—The **Spanish Dancer** drapes her diagonally folded shawl by placing one corner under the left arm, drawing the edge straight across the front and up diagonally across the back to the left shoulder, where it is held with a large rose. A strand of beads forms a strap over the right shoulder.

Model 5D—This **Black Cat** is distinguished by a large ribbon bow and tiny bell. Teddy-bear cloth makes the costume realistic, but cotton flannel or cambric may be used. The hands are covered by mittens.

Model 5E— **The Straw Man** costume is a clown suit of cambric, with long shreds of crepe paper or cambric placed thickly over it and tacked at neck, wrists, and ankles, the ends forming frills. The frills around the hat are made from dried cornhusks.

Making Merry on Halloween

No other party time of all the year holds quite the possibilities of Halloween. It is "fun time" pure and simple. Decorations and games, weird and ghostly, and refreshments of an informal nature are a matter of tradition. Unexpected surprises always add to the fun of a Halloween party. We heard about a party where in the middle of dancing, the doorbell rang and in came a street cleaner, dressed in work clothes and flourishing a big broom. Talking a lot in mixed English and Italian he used the broom to sweep the company right and left. The hostess pretended to argue with him, but he kept right on, announcing that as long as you can't dance in peace, you might as well go to supper, sweeping them into the dining room.

Party Invitations

Write on yellow, orange, or plain white cards, this verse, then sign your name.

> **HALLOWEEN PARTY**
>
> If you want to be you and yet not you,
> Dress in a costume old or new.
> Many others I plan to ask
> So wear a wig or at least a mask.
> Come at (time) and don't be late.
> The rest of the time we'll leave to fate.

Games

FORTUNE TELLING is, perhaps, the most popular form of entertainment for Halloween, for no one seems yet to have reached the age when his or her "fate" is not altogether the most interesting feature of an evening's fun. Old customs, too, that have been handed down from time immemorial never fail to create merriment. The initial of one's future mate may be found by paring an apple in one long peel and then throwing it over the left shoulder. It must remain undisturbed until all agree upon the letter it looks most like. Frequently, the imagination of one's companions plays a most important role in deciding this, as the apple peel does not always form a perfect letter.

EYE GUESSING—Hang a sheet straight down to the floor—sufficiently high to conceal all of the child. Cut a slit in the sheet just large enough to reveal the eyes. Divide children into teams. Have all of one team behind the sheet, but only one pair of eyes showing at a time. Other team must guess identity by eyes. The teams guessing the largest number wins. (Note: An adult might need to help lift a child high enough to look through the eye slits, or taller children will need to bend slightly down to fit.)

185

Our Hallowe'en Party

Decorations and Table Arrangements

Make the house look as mysterious as possible with heaps of corn shocks, autumn leaves, and grinning pumpkin lanterns. You can stick a scarecrow in one corner, a ghost in another, and do not have too much light. Orange and black are the colors that seem most appropriate, but reds and browns and all of the warm autumn shades may be used in the decorations. Autumn leaves, pumpkins, and corn stalks all play their part in providing a fitting background for the evening's festivities. And there seems to be no end to the quaint, amusing crepe-paper novelties that may be called upon to liven the occasion. Flickering candles may be placed around the dining room so as to cast long, spooky shadows.

For a very informal party, the table may be covered in orange crepe paper, strips being sewed together lengthwise to form a covering of sufficient size. The centerpiece can be a large pumpkin with two faces—one on each side. And the place cards might be black cats, each with a fortune tied to its tail. Or, at each place, use real candied apples, a horn blower or noisemaker and a cat that can be made from orange and black gumdrops.

Hallowe'en
Greetings

MENU

SAND-WITCHES

HOT COCOA WITH
MARSHMALLOW FACES

DEVIL'S FOOD COOKIES

JACK-O-LANTERNS

WITCH'S BREW
CIDER PUNCH

Sand-Witches

Spread a mixture of cream cheese and chopped black olives between slices of dark rye for one style and white bread for the other. You could also top with two green olives with red pimiento eyes.

Hot Cocoa with Marshmallow Faces

Prepare hot cocoa according to directions. With a toothpick dipped in melted chocolate, make eyes, nose and mouth on top of marshmallows. Float on cocoa.

Devil's Food Cookies

3 tbls. of butter
1/2 cup sugar
1 egg
1-1/2 cups flour

1-1/2 tsp. of baking powder
1/8 tsp. salt
1-1/2 squares of unsweetened chocolate

Cream the sugar and butter together thoroughly and add well-beaten egg, then milk. Sift flour once before measuring together with baking powder and salt. Chill dough, then roll 1/4-inch thick and cut with a round cookie cutter. Bake cookies in a 350-degree oven for 10 to 15 minutes. When cool, ice with basic white icing and after firm, paint on the shape of a black cat or jack-o-lantern, using melted chocolate and a fine-hair paintbrush.

Plain White Icing

1 cup butter
4 cups powdered sugar
1 tsp. vanilla
2 tbls. milk

Cream butter until light and fluffy, about 3 minutes. Add in powdered sugar, 1 cup at a time. Add in vanilla and milk. Add additional milk or powdered sugar for desired consistency.

Witch's Brew Cider Punch

2 oranges
2 lemons
1 cup sugar
1 quart water
1 quart grape juice
1 quart cider

Add a little of the grated rind of the orange and lemon to the juices and stir in the cider, sugar, and water. Pour in a punch bowl, in which there is a block of ice, and serve in sherbet glasses.

Jack-O-Lanterns

Cut a slice from tops (save the tops) of sufficient number of oranges and scoop out all of the pulp. Cut faces in each and chill. Serve with chocolate ice cream (see page 131 for recipe), and top with the lids.

Magic Pattern

A Practical Nightgown

Inspiration, October 1925

A nightgown that has the advantages of rapidity of cutting, ease of making and distinction of style is shown on this page. It is practical, too, since it is planned in nainsook or long-cloth, either white or a pastel tint, and trimmed with bias-fold tape in a harmonizing color, this forming bindings and a smart appliqué motif. If a gift nightgown is being planned and one of silk seems desirable, this same plan may be followed in the more expensive materials.

To compute the amount of material needed, measure the figure down from the shoulder line to the floor and multiply the result by two. At this time, take the armhole and the hip measurements and note also the distance from the shoulder line to a point in line with the hip bone. Now fold your material through the center lengthwise, bringing the two selvage edges together; then fold again through the center crosswise, bringing the two lengthwise folds and four selvages together and the raw edges even.

 See Notes, page 232, for modern tips and techniques.

For cutting, place the material on a flat surface with the selvage edges toward you and the cut edges to your left as shown in the diagram on the next page; then from the lower right-hand corner, marked a, measure to the left a distance equal to one-half the armhole measure plus 1-1/2 inches and place b. Consider the upper right-hand corner c, and from this point measure along the double folds to the left 4 inches for the depth of the front neck opening and mark this point d. Then at a point 2-1/2 inches from c for the back neckline, mark point e. Place a second point to the left of c, a distance equal to the length taken from the shoulder line to the hip bone, and mark this f; halfway between c and f, place point g. If the armhole measure is large, drop point g down enough so it will not come opposite or above point b. From f measure

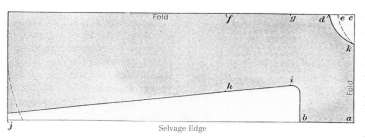

Fold | f | g | d | e c

Selvage Edge

toward you one-fourth the hip measure plus 3 inches and place point h; from g measure toward you one-fourth the hip measure plus 2 inches and place point i.

To form the underarm line, start at point b, and draw a line straight toward the folded edges until point i is approached, where you should curve the line down to i, and from there continue through h to the bottom of the garment as shown, making the slant such that the side seam will come to point j or above it, depending on the width you prefer the garment to be. A good width for the average figure is about 60 inches. Measure up from the cut off edges on the side seam 2 inches and trim a section from this point as shown by the dotted line.

An additional point is needed for a guide in marking the neckline. To place this, measure from c toward you along the crosswise fold about 3-1/2 inches and place a point k. From k, draw a curved line to d and a dotted curved line from k to e. Before trimming out the neck opening, trace with your tracing wheel on line ek through to the underneath section of material. Trim out the section, starting at d on a single fold, and then to k and from k to e on the traced line underneath. You may cut on these lines; or if you prefer, mark them with pins or tailors' chalk first for safety.

Apply the scallop trim before sewing the side seams. Using a saucer or similar size object mark the scallops with either chalk or basting thread using the image at the right as your placement guide. Baste the bias tape to the gown along the marks. To form the points between scallops, make a tiny dart in the bias and stitch it down with small stitches. To join the two ends, stitch the bias, press open and then baste finished seam to gown. Stitch down the bias.

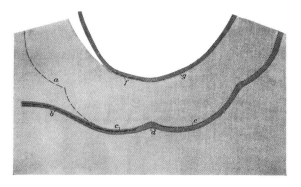

Apply the scallop trim around the sleeve in the same manner, beginning and ending at the seam instead of joining the two ends together.

Use French seams for joining the sides, making them very narrow so the curve at the underarm will lie flat. Finish the neckline and sleeves with the bias tape. Slip the nightgown on at this time and decide on the length you wish it. Finish the lower edge with a hem 2-1/2 inches deep.

189

Colorful Effects from Bias Tape

by Clarice Carpenter, *Inspiration*, 1926

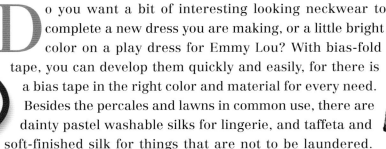

Do you want a bit of interesting looking neckwear to complete a new dress you are making, or a little bright color on a play dress for Emmy Lou? With bias-fold tape, you can develop them quickly and easily, for there is a bias tape in the right color and material for every need. Besides the percales and lawns in common use, there are dainty pastel washable silks for lingerie, and taffeta and soft-finished silk for things that are not to be laundered. Taffeta is used for a flat-edge finish, and the soft-finished silks for round, unpressed effects and for covering cords.

The sketches on this page show some of the new ways of using this decorative sewing help which goes on so easily. In some of these, we suggest that choosing certain colors will give the trimming its chief charm. This is true of the one at the upper left, using jade green and bright red on white collar and cuffs and knotting the ends of the tubes of the same color for a tie. Beside it, try pale yellow and green to form the interlaced corner trim, shown in detail at the upper right, and orange could bind the edges of the gray linen. Black and orange embroidery stitches could be added for accent. For the Georgette jabot at the left, try shaded tan colors. The palest could be peach, the next orange, and the last brown, with brown thread for the fagoting.

Novel Trims That Save Time

An answer to the question, "What shall I use as a short cut to finishing edges and at the same time add a touch of color or trimming?" is bias tape or one of the many allied trimmings that can be purchased in a range of colors and widths. Displayed here are a group of these novelty edgings and bindings, capable of supplying many needs in the development of gifts, wearing apparel or distinctive household furnishings. Though much used on small articles, their cost is low enough to permit their use as finishes on such large surfaces as bedspreads, curtains, and table covers, for both the edgings and the trimming details.

Testimonials

Just Sixteen—But Planning for the Future

"I have made many things for friends and relatives, and so far as I know they are always pleased, for they keep coming back to me. Being in school, I have not been able to devote much of my time to sewing, but I expect to do a great deal during the summer months. All the money I make I put in the bank. I have quite an account already—the proceeds of my sewing—and if it keeps up, I shall be able to realize my ambition to go to Paris for a year or so to study art!"

—*Miss D. R., New Jersey*

Before the Baby Arrives—A Young Mother Writes

"Before my baby came, I made myself three morning dresses, a négligée, several comfortable and dainty teddies, and a navy blue crepe afternoon dress. They were so comfortable and I felt so happy in them that they lightened some of the burden of my discomfort. I also made all of my baby's layette. Each garment was pretty and dainty and I enjoyed making them. On these articles alone, I realized a savings of nearly enough to pay the doctor's bill."

—*Mrs. A. H. M., Florida*

Saving for Her First Home

"*Fashion Service* has helped me immensely in selecting fashions for myself, the kiddies, and my little cottage home. We are only renting now, but some day very soon we hope to have a home all our own. And what pleases me most is that my husband says time and again it is due to my saving nature plus my ability to make so many things for myself, the kiddies, and the home. My husband was getting only $25 per week when we were first married. Since then he has gotten a better job with a few raises but still makes not more than $40 a week, so you see, with four in the family, I've got to help or we wouldn't be able to save for our little home. We did not spend much for our furniture; that is, actual money, but I spent a lot of time with paint, cushions, handmade bedspreads, curtains and rag rugs, and my present home is quite cozy."

—*Mrs. P. B., Illinois*

Sending a Child to College

"I have done all of the sewing for my four girls and three men folks. Limited finances would not have permitted my eldest daughter to spend two years at the University if home sewing could not have helped. She is taking Domestic Science, specializing in design."

—*Mrs. B. F. Morris, Indiana*

Modern Notions

Often it's only long after the Thanksgiving dishes are soaking in the sink, the leftovers have been put away, and the children are asleep that I have time to pause and reflect on the holiday season and what it means to me. I'm so busy just trying to survive the holiday that I forget to enjoy it—not afterward but while it's actually happening. But with the help of The Woman's Institute and the timeless wisdom of Mary Brooks Picken, that's starting to change. In these women's words I've found new ways to do "holiday." These days, I'm working my hardest at trying to slow down, savor the moment (and the food), and share in the joy.

At heart, the Thanksgiving tradition is about the importance of community, and if anyone knows a thing or two about community, it's the teachers and students of The Woman's Institute. As we've discovered throughout these pages, these women practically wrote the book on what it means for women to communicate and connect, no matter the distances. So, if they can manage to support, encourage, and appreciate each other, often without even leaving their living rooms, I think we can agree to make some extra effort this November to reach out to our neighbors.

And while Thanksgiving is a highly traditional holiday of food, family, and gratitude, that doesn't mean you have to do it the same way every year. Play around this season, expand on a classic, be brave! Of course, I must make Jack's and Emma's favorite Pumpkin Bars—our personal family favorite. But this year, I might also take the *Department of Cookery*'s lead and expand on a favorite classic—cranberry sauce. Try a cranberry jam, a salad, even a meringue pie. The *Magic Pattern* page has a great apron pattern to keep you looking smart while you whip up your tasty treats, and instead of crowding the mall on the most popular shopping day of the year, refer to the *Department of Sewing* for ideas for darling homemade gifts. Doesn't a round of hot cocoa with friends or family members while you whip up one-of-a-kind Christmas cookies sound far preferable to the high stress experience so many Americans have come to equate with the holiday?

If you do decide to go for it, one caveat: Make sure to read the tips in *Department of Good Looks* for "Calming Your Nerves During the Holiday Season." Trust me, I've utilized these tips many a day (not just the holiday season!), and they come with my tried and true guarantee.

Yours,

Amy B.

November

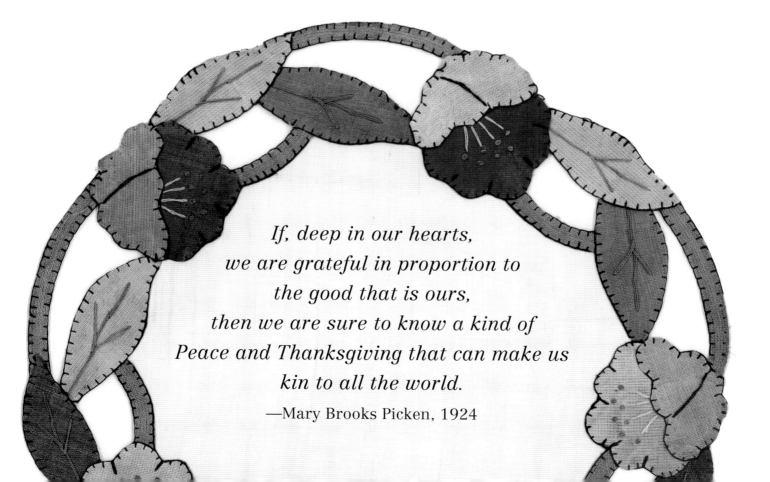

*If, deep in our hearts,
we are grateful in proportion to
the good that is ours,
then we are sure to know a kind of
Peace and Thanksgiving that can make us
kin to all the world.*
—Mary Brooks Picken, 1924

A Thimbleful of Gratitude

Be Grateful

by Mary Brooks Picken

Excerpted from *Thimblefuls of Friendliness*, 1924

About the only time we ever stop to realize how glorious it is to be well enough to go and come as we will is when we are indisposed for a day and have to stay at home. Funny thing the way we accept good health as a matter of course, just like good drinking water or hot coffee for breakfast! We never think how seemingly unnecessary it is until we are deprived of it.

It's a pity we take so much for granted—our food, our clothes, a bed to sleep in—why, of course, we have all of them. But go roughing it some time and sleep on a sparse, ill-equipped bed for a night or two. You will then appreciate, as you never did before, your own good bed at home.

We all grow so used to having things done for us—this is taken care of, that is looked after—that we get out of the habit of doing them for ourselves. But let the paper boy forget to leave the paper just one evening, and we are lost completely. We would insistently help to get him "fired" from his route; yet day after day, sun or rain, he brings the paper, and we are conscious of its importance only when we miss getting it just once.

Habit causes us to accept family, friends, comforts, and pleasures as a matter of course. Every now and then we should find ourselves without them all, just to learn to appreciate them the more.

I told a little nephew the other day to say a good-night prayer for a friend who was ill. The little boy, who was once very ill himself, lifted his bright, happy face and said, "Aunt Mary, there must have been a lot of prayers said for me, 'cause see how well I am. I know mother's prayers helped doctor because he knew what to do without anybody telling him." It was wonderful to see the appreciation in the child's eyes, a kind of appreciation that is even more than gratitude.

I have always felt I could be grateful for charity, but I could appreciate love and kindness. And that is what we need, it seems to me, more than anything else—to be kind . . . to help, to encourage, and comfort those who need us, to say a happy word when a happy word is wanted, but never to be guilty of doling out kindness as we would plant beans, never more than the specified amounts.

Not long ago I was in Philadelphia, and I visited Independence Hall, Betsy Ross's House, Congress Hall, and other landmarks of our great independence. Everything there reminded me of the sacrifices that were made for our freedom, comfort, and well-being, and I wondered a dozen times and more whether we appreciated it all as we should or whether we were in the habit of accepting it as we do the daily paper, forgetting how much real effort had gone before to give us our many great privileges.

Service to Others...

We pursue the rainbow and either never reach the end or, if we do, there is no bag of gold; in other words, life is a pursuit of something which can never be found in the acquisition of money, the acquirement of position, or the consummation of some large enterprise. When you reach this it is nothing, except as it gives us reasonable physical comforts. The secret is to be found in the knowledge that service for others is the one thing which brings constant pleasure and reacts upon the person rendering the service as helpfully as upon the one to whom the service is rendered. We are happy when we learn to feel from the heart that it is better to give than to receive.

And there you have it—service to others. Mine to you; yours to me and others; and so on without end. That is the secret of success.

INSPIRATION DEPARTMENT

It Is Thanksgiving!

by Laura MacFarlane, *Inspiration*, November, 1927

"As we gather round our glowing hearths and our tables of November bounty...
right from the heart, let all of us busy and needed folks give
thanks that we are indispensable in this place, our own particular home spot."

Work to do and the strength to do it. A place where we belong and a necessity that holds us there. How deeply we should return thanks at this Thanksgiving season for the blessedness of toil and the happiness of being needed!

However enviously we may look at those who have leisure and the means to lead a life of ease and change, and however pleasant a taste of it may be when we have earned the right to it, let us thank a goodly Providence that our feet are of necessity deeply rooted in some home spot where we may have a chance to use the humble talents that have been placed in our keeping.

Are we not as a nation too ambitious—a bit too intent on some future distant goal when we shall be rich or famous or envied, and do we not often miss the best things of life by refusing to surrender to life as we find it? . . . As you look about you this Thanksgiving season, are not the most contented people those who have found usefulness rather than fame or riches—who are content to take their places, in some humble and quiet corner, though it may be, and be used?

As we pause quietly on this, our own American anniversary, let us give thanks that this spirit of co-operation and service is spreading abroad in the land and that housewives are awakening more and more to the beauty of an occupation that permits them to be needed—to bring into their homes greater comfort and beauty, better food and surroundings, and better training for their young folks.

In Cranberry Season

Inspiration, November, 1926

*The mellow tints of the summer fruits give way to the warm orange
and russet of the pumpkin and the glowing red of the cranberry.*

In truth, the cranberry comes at a most opportune time, for during the early winter months we are beginning to include in our menus those heavier meats which are so much more palatable when accompanied by a relish. And no accompaniment to the meal offers greater appeal than the cranberry, with its lusty color and appetizing tang.

So much has the cranberry been used this time of year that it has become almost symbolic of the season. Looking back across the years to other fall and winter holidays, we may not remember whether the pièce de résistance of the feast was turkey or goose or even a crown roast of pork, but standing out clearly in our memories is the glowing ruby cranberry sauce, deliciously tart, which gave such zest and color to the meal. The woman who looks carefully to the seasons and the fruits thereof, will plan to serve cranberries not only in her special menus but also in her every-day meals while they are still plentiful and the price is not too high. And she need not be restricted to the proverbial cranberry sauce that was formerly the only way in which the fruit was prepared. There are all sorts of unusual ways to cook and serve cranberries, as the recipes here indicate, so no one need be at a loss for suggestions as to how to vary their preparation. The chief thing to remember is that berries that are firm and of even size should be selected.

Cranberry Sauce

2 cups berries
1 cup sugar
1 cup water

Pick over and wash the berries carefully, meanwhile boiling the sugar and water until a thin syrup forms. Add the cranberries and cook them in the syrup until they become transparent. They should burst during this process or they will not be sweet, but they should not entirely lose their shape.

This recipe may be multiplied two to four times if a greater amount of sauce is desired, but it is well not to cook too large a quantity at one time, for this will mean longer cooking, which will darken the berries and cause them to become bitter.

Cranberry Salad

2 cups water
1 pound cranberries
1-1/2 cups sugar
1 box lemon Jello
1 cup chopped celery
1 cup chopped
  sweet apple
1 cup chopped nuts

Pour the water over the cranberries and cook until at least half of the berries have burst. Strain, add the sugar, and boil for three minutes. Then dissolve the

 Cook until about half of them make a popping sound.

Jello in the hot cranberry juice, of which there should be about 2-1/2 cupfuls. Set this mixture aside until it begins to thicken; then add the celery, apples, and nuts. Mold this salad in any desired shape and serve with mayonnaise for a dressing.

Cranberry Meringue Pie

1-1/2 cups sugar
1/2 cup cold water
2 cups cranberries
1 tbls. flour
2 eggs
1 tbls. butter
1/2 tsp. vanilla extract
2 tbls. powdered sugar

Cook sugar and water over medium heat to a syrup, add the cranberries, and cook until they pop; then allow them to cool a little. Mix smoothly in a bowl the flour and yolks of the eggs only. Add 3 tablespoons of the juice of the cooked cranberries, then add to the berries and simmer for 3 minutes. Stir in the butter and vanilla and set aside to cool. Turn into a deep pie crust that has been previously baked. Cover with meringue that is made by stiffly beating the egg whites and powdered sugar. Brown the meringue in the oven for a few minutes.

For perfect meringue directions, see page 45.

A Running Start on Christmas

Inspiration, November, 1925

Christmas giving is something more than a lovely custom. It is an art—a fine art which you have mastered when your gifts are individual and thoughtful and fitted to the needs of those to whom they are given. The gifts shown here serve to illustrate the point. On Christmas morning, no box is opened with greater pleasure than the one that contains a handmade gift, evidencing loving thoughtfulness in its making. A simple, useful gift, neatly made and fitted to the needs of the one to whom it goes, will be cherished for the thoughtfulness that prompts it.

Smart Bags

Harmony and smartness should dictate which bags to carry or for sewing. A variety of them shown here are suggestions—material harmonizing with the costume with which the bag is to be used is the first and foremost consideration. Beads, embroidery, ribbon and luxuriant materials may be combined or used singly for bags this season. See a bag and then improve on it is the best way to get a truly individual one that will ever delight the recipient of these special hand-made gifts.

Child's Toy Bag

The habits of neatness cannot be inculcated in a child too early. This toy bag hangs on the door of the nursery and furnishes the nucleus for a game the child can play with the toys that must be "put to bed" at night. The red bindings combined with brightly colored appliqués make it a serviceable and useful gift.

SEWING DEPARTMENT

Handkerchiefs

Handkerchiefs are not only more decorative than they once were, but are more useful as well, for now the decoration is planned to conceal that very useful thing, a tiny powder puff. These three such handkerchiefs show that, with the first one having for its diminutive pocket an embroidered square, the second a tiny parasol, and the third a lace-edged circle. A tiny button and loop or a snap fastens the pocket so that these hidden powder puffs remain secure.

Laundry Bag

When each child in the family receives a laundry bag in his or her favorite color, the general interest in the neat disposal of soiled garments is markedly increased. If the bag is made with a slashed-and-bound opening on the side, as shown here, the child need not open it at the top each time a garment is inserted. Grown-ups like these convenient bags, too.

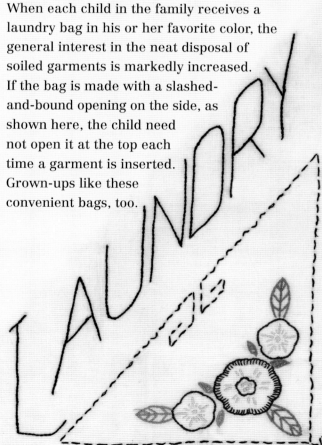

Little Gifts for Little Fingers

by Hilarion Doyle, *Fashion Service*, November 1925

When the November winds blow cold and keen, there are few of us who do not realize that it is high time to plan Christmas gifts. Peggy, who feels quite grown-up since reaching sixth grade, confides in Mother that she wants to make every one of her gifts herself. Mother suggests that she make a list and decide just what would please everybody most. Here is a project that she could put on her list.

A gift that would please Mother consists of a half-dozen embroidered tea towels, which would appear to even better advantage when tied together as shown here. For these, buy 5 yards of toweling, and, after dividing the strip into six pieces, outline a cup and saucer on each, using a transfer pattern if needed. Work the pattern in outline stitch in a color to match the border of the toweling. If desired, variety may be secured by using a different design on each towel, keeping each very simple.

For more embroidery instructions, see page 114.

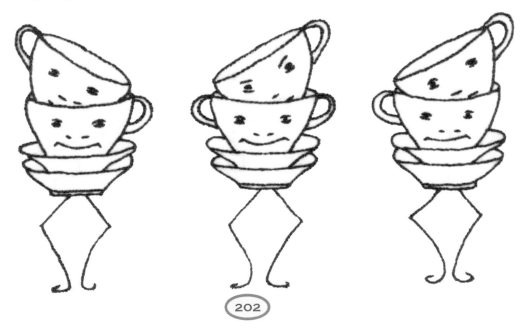

The Road to Beauty

by Marilyn Madison, *Inspiration*, 1924

I just read a book called *The Road to Beauty* by Mabelle Burbridge, and found what promises to be an interesting path leading to the castle of good looks. In the book, the author prescribes for two of her friends, Rose, fat and forty, and Nona, thin and nearly forty, who have been careless in their diet and indifferent to the need of physical attractiveness, forgetting that a glossy head of healthy hair is much more attractive than polished silver, and a clear, clean complexion more essential than smiling linens. To obtain a clear complexion and to accomplish the desired change in weight at the same time, she gives them the following prescription:

Take the juice of one-half lemon in a glass of hot water and always drink two full glasses before breakfast each morning. This has a three-fold effect—cleanses, tones, and fills enough so that one piece of toast suffices for two. Also, when you feel hungry (if you are working for less weight) drink water with fruit juice, or eat an orange or an apple instead of the tempting bit of candy, cake, or bread and jam.

. . . But for the stout ones, the following is suggested: *Upon arising, lemon and hot water and exercises, with special emphasis on ten minutes of morning exercises.*

. . . I wish I could give you all of the good tips in this book, for there are prescriptions for creams, lotions, and shampoos, that *sound wholesome and efficacious*. And there are exercises and other health-giving prescriptions, all so delightfully simple and presented in such an appealing way.

Tips for Calming Your Nerves During the Holiday Season

by Barbara Elllison, *Fashion Service*, November 1927

If you believe that you are overworking, lie down for at least fifteen minutes after every meal. Or get home in the afternoon in time to lie down for an hour before dinner.

Lie flat on your back and withdraw every bit of resistance and strain from your body. Relax your arms and legs and let down your back till you lie all soft and fluid, melting into the mattress or couch.

If you can drop off to sleep, so much the better. But don't fuss if sleep refuses to come.

If you find your mind working overtime, pick up a magazine and read a story that has a wholesome bit of humor or pathos, the entertaining sort that is light but agreeable reading.

Nerves are best relieved by vigorous, stimulating exercise that transfers the activity to your muscles. Plan to be out-of-doors two to three hours every day if you can.

If you play golf or tennis, play to win.

If you swim, pretend yourself that you are training for a championship.

Drink a glass of milk in the mid-afternoon and at bedtime. Have the bedtime glass warmed if you can drink it that way. It will help you rest better.

toque (tŏk; toke). 1. Small, close-fitting, brimless hat. See HATS.

cloche (klōsh or F. klôsh; closhe). Close-fitting hat, the basic hat fashion for more than ten years, beginning early 1920. See HATS. French word for bell.

Department of MILLINERY

Dress-Up Hats for the Holidays

Fashion Service, November 1927

Now that we have emerged from the dominating influence of the felt cloche into the realm of the flattering, close-fitting conceptions, the toque again comes into its own with its ever-delightful charm. So many new designs, however, are presented that nothing remains of the traditional turban of past seasons.

All sorts of liberties are taken with tiara drapes and self-trims, posed artfully to accent the eyebrow line and raised in a point at one side, completely captivating the smart woman. One thing they have in common is crowns that invariably hug the head. Gone are the high effects of last year. Crowns are low, rounded and molded very snugly, but tiaras, drapes, or trimmings attain extra breadth at one side or at both. Also, the ear-lap effect is continued in many new forms, not so much an actual ear-lap as before, but the simulated ear-lap produced by a drape or fold of the fabric.

cloche (klōsh or F. klôsh; closhe). Close-fitting hat, the basic hat fashion for more than ten years, beginning early 1920. See HATS. French word for bell.

cloche (klōsh or F. klôsh; closhe). Close-fitting hat, the basic hat fashion for more than ten years, beginning early 1920. See HATS. French word for bell.

toque (tŏk; toke). 1. Small, close-fitting, brimless hat. See HATS.

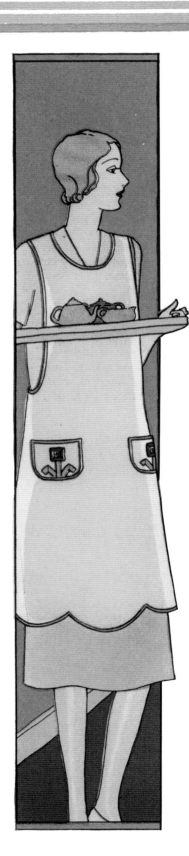

Magic Pattern

A Hostess Gift for the Holidays

Fashion Service, 1928

There are two things that some folks consider a sin to make—unbecoming boudoir caps and aprons that won't launder. To go into the kitchen in a best dress and know that there is in the drawer an apron that will be comfortable and attractive is a real satisfaction.

A few straight pieces of fabric, a few yards of bias tape, an hour or so of time, and presto! a cover-all apron that will make housekeeping a joy! It's attractive, practical, and economical of material—1-7/8 yards of fabric and 11 to 12 yards of 1/4-inch bias tape being all that's needed to create the apron above at right. A print design, with trimming matching the dominant color is smart; but, if desired, a combination of the plain material and the sides of the print, an excellent plan when making use of two short lengths of material.

The accompanying diagram makes cutting easy. Straighten the ends of the material if they are not already straight. Then fold through the center lengthwise and place on the table with the fold next to you. To get the front and back sections, measure from the lower right corner to the left a distance equal to the length you

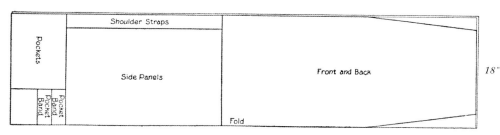

These older patterns are based on 36"-wide fabric.

wish the apron to be, for the average figure 36 inches. Trim off the section on a straight line. Then, trim off the triangular sections, as shown, cutting on each side from a point 2 inches from the edge to a point 18 inches from the end along both the fold and the selvage. This narrows the pieces at the top. Cut along the fold to separate the sections.

From the large section remaining, trim off a portion measuring 22 inches in length for the side panels, also cutting along the fold to make two panels of equal size. Along the selvage, cut off two shoulder straps, 2 inches wide.

Cut the pocket foundations from the section remaining, making them 11 inches wide and as deep as the material will allow, which should be about 9 inches. The remaining strip will permit the cutting of two pocket bands, which should each be 2-1/2 inches wide, their length to be determined later when you have decided on the finished width of the side panels.

Pin the shoulder straps in place and slip the apron on with front and back in proper position. Then pin the foundation pockets, arranging them so that the apron fits easily around the hips and their upper edges come at about the normal waist line. Remove the apron and pin the side panels in place to obtain their correct length, starting at the bottom. Gather to a size that measures 2 inches greater than the width of the pocket foundation and bind with the straight strips provided for this. Shape the lower edges of these as shown.

Bind the lower edges of both side panels and the upper edges of the pocket foundations. Then gather the side panels to fit the lower edges of the pocket foundations, baste in place, and stitch, forming the pockets. Bind the front and back pieces and the shoulder straps. Then baste the finished side sections in place and stitch just beyond the binding. With the apron on, pin the shoulder straps in place, and then attach them securely by stitching.

DEPARTMENT OF HOUSEKEEPING

Setting the Table

Fashion Service, November, 1927

Simplicity should be the keynote for the Thanksgiving table service, with the decorations and menu in harmony with the season. The artwork that leads off this chapter on November features a most attractive table, with its centerpiece of lovely autumn flowers and elegant candles accentuating the color scheme. A bowl or compote of harvest fruit would also be a pleasant arrangement, combined with lovely linens, china and silver.

Several menus are given here. Two are more suitable for a more elaborate company dinner, while the others are for informal home dinners. Recipes for most of these can be found in any good cookbook.

Autumn Expresses Its Colors

Thanksgiving is in the air
Turkey and mince pie at the family dinner table
Harvesting the crops
Pumpkins and corn roasts under a harvest moon
The first snowfall causes a shiver
Football games and warm plaid coats . . .
Autumn expresses its colors.

Informal Thanksgiving Dinners

Baked Loin of Pork   Apple Sauce
Browned Potatoes
Scalloped Turnips   Glazed Onions
Fruit Salad
Cranberry Meringue Pie   Coffee

Baked Ham
Southern Sweet Potatoes
Pickles   Relishes
Corn Pudding
Tomato Jelly Salad
Salad Rolls
Individual Pumpkin Pie Garnished
with Whipped Cream
Nuts   Candied Orange Peel
Coffee

❧ ❧ ❧

Roast Turkey or Chicken
Oyster Stuffing   Giblet Gravy
Mashed Potatoes   Stuffed Peppers
Squash Croquettes
Cranberry-Celery Salad   Cheese Straws
Pumpkin Pie   Coffee

❧ ❧ ❧

Formal Thanksgiving Dinners

Orange Mint Cup
Cream of Oyster Soup, Whipped Cream
Celery   Ripe Olives   Salted Almonds
Roast Stuffed Turkey   Giblet Gravy
Cranberry Sauce
Candied Sweet Potatoes   Baked Onions
Parsnip Fritters
Lettuce Hearts   Pimiento Dressing
Maple Mousse   Small Cakes
Raisins   Candied Pumpkin
Coffee

Fruit Soup
Celery   Radishes
Roast Goose   Potato Stuffing
Buttered Onions   Stuffed Tomatoes
Cauliflower and Peas
Endive   French Dressing
Toasted Saltines
Pineapple Cream Sherbet   Snowballs
Grilled Almonds   Mints
Candied Peel   Coffee

Testimonials

From a Factory to a Business of Her Own

Miss Ruth V. Carothers, a Connecticut student, is another woman who took up life where she found it and did the best she could with it, making her dream of a successful dressmaking career come true. "When I first heard of the Woman's Institute," she writes, "I was working in a factory, making anywhere from $8 to $18 a week. After reading your stories for some time, I spoke to my mother about taking up the Dressmaking Course . . . I started the course in July and by March was far enough along to give up my work in the factory and start dressmaking. The first week I made $10. That was nearly four years ago and I have never been without work from that time to this . . . My earnings have increased until I now make anywhere from $25 to $38 a week in town. . . . When I started, I worked in a small bedroom, but I outgrew this and last fall had a nice new room built on the house . . . and I had a hemstitching machine installed . . . and am thinking of adding a button-covering machine . . . Every one praises my work very highly . . . The Woman's Institute has a very warm place in my heart."

—*Women Who Succeed*, November 1926

From the Arctic Circle

The coming of winter weather makes many people thankful that they are no farther north than they already are and at least a little wistful regarding points South. But not so with Mrs. Lyman, who spent two years within the Arctic Circle . . . In the employee of the Hudson Bay Company, she reached Herschel Island, the "last word" in the North with little more beyond. The return trip took a whole season. Leaving the island May 1, by dog team, she traveled 75 miles over the ocean to King Point on the mainland. . . . Here, the party numbering ten, camped in tents for a month . . . arriving at Aklarik on June 11, she camped again until the arrival of the U. S. Arctic Distributor. . . . The lack of sun from November 26 to January 15 . . . did not keep Mrs. Lyman from working on her dressmaking lessons, nor did the fact that mail reached her only four times a year, twice in the summer, once after the ocean froze, and once in April. She completed the entire Course while there and made some 20 dresses for Eskimo women. These dresses were all of the finest silk available, for the Eskimos are very imitative in customs, manners, and dress.

—*Institute News in Brief*, November 1925

Modern Notions

One of my most cherished holiday traditions is trimming the tree—each year my family anticipates the careful unwrapping of the ornaments as much as the unwrapping of the gifts under the tree. We delight in rediscovering certain ornaments and each year we relish in the retelling of the life story behind each bauble and homemade trinket. We're particularly fond of the handmade decorations, whether it's a preschool project featuring a darling photo, a vintage ornament with each sequin attached by great-grandma, or the knitted stocking made by Mom so long ago.

Each year, in addition to the treasures from my kids and immediate family, I lovingly find spots for the ornaments given to me by my sorority sisters. They are family, after all—and it's a wonderful tradition we have going, having gathered every Christmas for almost twenty years for an ornament exchange. As years pass and life gets busier than our younger days, it's harder to find time to get together as a group. Nevertheless, we know we can count on this tradition to keep us connected, and I'm always excited to see the creative gift wrap and detailing that goes into our yearly exchange. This month's *Department of Instruction* is devoted solely to great gift wrap ideas, with inspiration for using all sorts of materials to whip up gorgeous packages in no time (and at little cost). The gift giving continues in the *Department of Sewing*, which answers the needs of readers of *Inspiration* magazine in 1924 (and our current needs) for affordable ways to give Christmas gifts. The results are amazing—gifts full of love and personality, from scarves and dishtowels to aprons and pincushions.

And in honor of The Woman's Institute, this Christmas I added something new to the mix of my holiday traditions—I posted our holiday family photo card on my Facebook page. As friends and loved ones from faraway cities—some in different countries altogether—posted comments and their own family photos in response, I felt a hint of what the students of The Woman's Institute must have felt receiving their newsletters every month, where women spoke directly to each other and shared their stories of strength, hope, and personal growth.

The holiday season is undoubtedly about connection with those who mean the most to us, and some of what social networking sites offer is exactly that—a new way to connect. When all of these web sites first began, I wasn't sure they were for me, but with my newfound appreciation of women bridging the distances, I'm hooked. My sorority sisters, both near and far, are privy to my life the way they were when they were only a bunk bed away. And looking at my tree all lit up on Christmas Eve, I see the love of friends, family, and everything in between decorating its branches, and I know that I am truly blessed.

Happy Holidays!

Amy B.

December

Be merry all, be merry all,
With holly dress the festive hall;
Prepare the song, the feast, the ball,
To welcome Merry Christmas.

— *Inspiration,* December 1920

A Thimbleful of Kindness

Christmas Kindliness

by Mary Brooks Picken

Excerpted from *Thimblefuls of Friendliness*, 1924

The other night, I sat with some friends, turning hems on some lovely, soft, white linen Christmas handkerchiefs. As the threads were drawn and the tiny hems turned, many thoughts came about Christmas giving.

Memories of old-time Christmases, snow-covered fields, long paths, star-studded skies, and the mysterious reindeers and Santa Claus that you yourself visualized into being—all these came fast to mind.

And then came the Christmas lesson of Jesus and the manger and the simplicity of the first Christmas. And these thoughts brought the realization that Christmas, instead of extravagant giving, should be a time of loving companionship, of tender memories, and of happily sympathetic appreciation of those we hold dear as friends and loved ones.

Christmas time should be wreathed in kindliness and candled with loving tenderness. The lonely heart should be sought and made to realize that there is unselfishness and that there is love at Christmas time. The person who is of good cheer and who really enjoys "Merry Christmas," who delights in the planning, making, buying, and tying of Christmas packages, is the one who has the best happiness and the most fun.

To receive a gift is not half such good fortune as to know real happiness in planning and giving one, especially if one is thoughtful enough to think up and procure something that even the "impossible" gift receiver will be delighted with. It always seems a mark of laziness for any one to say, "Oh, I haven't any idea what to give them because they are so hard to buy for," or "they have everything." Usually, the trouble in such cases is that we want the gift to seem sumptuous or generous, and we overlook the thoughtful thing that will be appreciated.

As a child, I remember a dear old lady who was greatly loved, outwardly for her delicious cookies and shining apples that she always had on hand for the children who visited her, and divinely for the loving spirit that made her plan to have these things ready when the eager-eyed little folks came. This old treasured woman seldom went to town, for her egg and butter money would not go far with all whom she delighted to remember.

Instead, she saved all the tin foil that came to her throughout the year and covered her luscious hickory nuts in it. Also, she made tiny bars of candied popcorn and wrapped them in bits of colored tissue paper; she made old-fashioned molasses drops; and baked delicious cookies for her little friends. These little packages amounted to no more than 5 or 6 cents in cost, but I know several of these children now grown-up, who treasure the thought that inspired them more than any gifts they have ever received.

Big, expensive, oftentimes impractical gifts are a financial problem to the giver and real responsibility for the recipient, for it is embarrassing to have gifts from those who you know have made a real sacrifice, and who put you in a position of obligation. Gifts should be as free as a mother's kiss.

The gift's responsibility is not to express money, but thoughtfulness. It should bring joy and tenderness to the hearts of all who are privileged to give and to receive.

Christmas time should be
wreathed in kindliness
and candled with
loving tenderness.

–Mary Brooks Picken

The Joy of Doing Things

Inspiration, 1922

Of all the joys that enter into our lives, it would be difficult to find one greater than that which brings from us the exclamation, "See, I did this all myself."

Can you picture the delight that comes to a child who has mastered the art of writing his own name for the first time? Can you conceive the joyful assurance that thrills the inventor who has perfected the plan of his dreams?

You can, because you know the joy that comes to you when you accomplish something you have set out to do. And be this something great or be it small, the joy that results from doing it is what makes life worthwhile because it arouses in us an enthusiasm for greater things.

I know of a woman who, until about a year ago, could not bake a loaf of bread. And well do I know the happiness that came to her—and her family, too—when she tried and persisted and found out that she could make bread as well as the next person. Her achievement meant not only good home-made bread, and then cakes and pies for her family, but a mother filled with an inward glow of happiness, and satisfaction in being able to do something she could not do before, a mother made more self-reliant with the assurance that she could do what she set out to do.

Yes, joy does come from discovering that we can do things, and it is the actual doing of them day by day that leads to worthwhile accomplishments. The daily performance of simple tasks closely akin to drudgery fits us for the performance of more important work without our being conscious of it. The making of a common apron, a simple waist dress, a plain hat, besides affording joy in the accomplishment at the time, produces in us the skill needed for making more elaborate wearing apparel. Even the studying of a lesson or section or single paragraph will enable us to claim for ourselves a bit of knowledge that we did not possess before.

Every greater act we perform is but the result of a lesser beginning. And our reward is not alone the joy that comes with doing things, but also the assurance, the confidence, we gain in our very selves.

Make Your Gift Wrappings Original and Artistic

Inspiration, December 1924

From the very simple to the most elaborate gift, let it express beauty and luxury and enchantment. And, best of all, let it come from your heart. Our gifts don't need to be costly or in any way beyond our resources. Just the simple little gifts that show we understand and appreciate not only the needs but the desires and hobbies of our friends will bring a warm glow to the heart such as the most expensive ones never could.

The personality of the one to whom the gift will go and the nature of the gift itself are the guiding stars of the successful wrapping of gifts. Perhaps you are intending to send a framed picture and you want to slip in a pretty cranberry pink chambray apron. Wrap the picture in the apron and tie it up with a white ribbon and attach a shower of flowers suspended from the center of the bow. Or consider that any child will appreciate a set of blocks twice as much if the ribbon that ties on the glazed chintz has a peppermint stick tucked in.

The days when the conventional white tissue paper, red ribbon, and Santa Claus seals were the universal wrappings for all Christmas gifts have so far passed that many persons wrap an entire season's gifts without the aid of a single one of these time-honored commodities. Red, green, and white—these were for years the only colors used—then someone introduced the silver of starlight and the gold of candle glow, and we had metallic papers. They opened the way for the glory of tint, texture, and design that is now available for this new art of beautifying the gift package.

Some of the most striking new effects in wrappings are attained by the use of familiar materials used in new ways. For example, we have all known how to cut snowflakes since our kindergarten days. But to cut them from silver paper and paste them on a white, blue or green tissue-wrapped box produces an effect that is original and distinctive. Even Christmas tree ornaments, such as tinsel stars and small-size ball ornaments, tied to the wrappings, are very festive.

Or tie to the top of the package a handkerchief corsage of three different-colored hankies, folded as shown, and tie several little tiny bottles of perfume to the ribbons' ends. A small lace paper doily may be used on this, too, or on this evergreen corsage.

Gift Baskets

Inspiration, 1920

The charming custom of dropping May baskets on the doorsteps of one's friends on May Day may be the inspiration for the sending of baskets at Christmas time. At any rate, the custom has become quite prevalent, and well it may, for a gift of this kind usually brings much joy to the one who prepares it and the one who receives it. There is really a splendid variety in basket gifts, for, while they always include food of some kind, they give, as shown here, the sender an opportunity to carry out any original ideas she may have in both the contents and the decorations.

Many persons send Christmas dinners to those who are a little less fortunate than they, but often they give very little thought to the way in which they send the food. A gift of this kind will be much more appreciated if it is arranged attractively in a large, substantial market basket, as shown, and it will carry with it much more of the Christmas spirit if it is decorated with holly, bitter sweet, a spray of evergreen, or a real potted plant.

Homemade candies and cookies are very popular, especially if you pack them artistically, in a somewhat unusual basket. Take, for instance, the round or heart-shaped basket. Baskets of this kind are very inexpensive when they are purchased in the natural color and then colored and trimmed at home according to one's fancy. Square baskets are somewhat of an innovation with their charming ribbon trimmings. Ribbon of good width may be used rather lavishly to tie up such a box after it is packed and you may complete the trimmings with a good-sized bow on top.

Or procure an open basket with a handle and in it place several small glasses of a variety of jellies, marmalades, and conserves. Fill in the spaces with such things as sweet chocolates wrapped in tin foil, tea balls made by wrapping in foil enough of her favorite tea for one brewing, and similar dainties. If the basket is large enough, some very fine fruit may be included.

A lovely box of fruit with a small box of homemade cookies in the center or a basket containing a sample of all the good things you are cooking at your home would delight any friend, neighbor, or a girl away from home.

The Allurements of Sweets

Fashion Service, December 1930

Christmas time without candy and cookies is like Easter without eggs. You just can't imagine either, can you? But you don't have to, so far as sweets are concerned, for they're so easy to make. If you've never made candy, there's a lot of excitement and pleasure ahead of you, for there is nothing more thrilling than to see tray after tray of these delicious concoctions and realize you've made them all yourself. These can also be packed attractively into boxes and baskets and wrapped gaily. Add much to the beauty of the boxes by using bonbon cups, which can be purchased from the store, waxed paper, and small paper doilies.

For the most part, you'll need only the ordinary utensils found in every kitchen, such as cooking kettles, a double boiler, measuring cups, knives, spoons, and spatulas. But most important of all, for the best results, is a candy thermometer, for it provides the safest method of determining when the candy is done. The cold-water test is successful in the hands of the experienced, but it cannot be recommended as absolutely sure in the hands of the novice.

 In the cold water method, the syrup forms a soft ball when drizzled in a glass of cold water.

Have you any fonder recollection of your youthful days than of hurrying home from school to make that batch of fudge that mother promised you could? The following recipe will produce excellent results in candies of this sort. Fudge is such a general favorite and this is the foundation recipe for it. Nuts, fruit, and marshmallow cream will produce different varieties when added to this recipe.

Creamy Fudge

1 tblsp. butter
2 cups sugar
3/4 cups milk or
   thin cream
1 tsp. vanilla
2 tsps. corn syrup
2 squares unsweetened chocolate
1/2 cup walnuts

Melt the chocolate and butter in a saucepan over hot water, add the milk or thin cream slowly and then the sugar and corn syrup. Stir until it boils and then occasionally, until a candy thermometer reaches 236 degrees, or the candy forms a soft ball in cold water. Remove from the heat and pour onto a large platter. Allow to stand undisturbed until cool (110 degrees), then add the vanilla and work with a spatula or wooden spoon until creamy. Pour into a buttered pan and allow to become firm. Cut in squares.

Candied Orange Peel

6 oranges
1 cup sugar
1/2 cup water

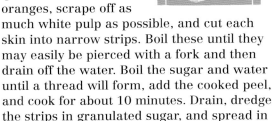

Remove the skin in quarters from the oranges, scrape off as much white pulp as possible, and cut each skin into narrow strips. Boil these until they may easily be pierced with a fork and then drain off the water. Boil the sugar and water until a thread will form, add the cooked peel, and cook for about 10 minutes. Drain, dredge the strips in granulated sugar, and spread in single layers to dry.

For a small cookie, nothing is nicer than having sand tarts. If decorated attractively, they may be used with confections in packing Christmas boxes and baskets. Blanched almonds are the usual decorations, but they may be replaced with English walnut halves, Southern pecan halves, or small pieces of candied pineapple or ginger—both palate-pleasing choices.

Sand Tarts

1/2 cup shortening or butter	2 tsps. baking powder
1 cup sugar	1/2 tsp. cinnamon
1 egg	1 egg white
1-3/4 cup flour	Nuts for toppings

Cream the shortening or butter and add the sugar and the egg. Sift together the flour, baking powder, and cinnamon, and add to the mixture. Fold in the beaten egg white. Roll very thin, cut into rounds, and place on cookie sheet. Decorate with nuts and bake in a hot oven at 400 degrees until light brown.

As soon as you have some sour cream on hand, try the following recipe. The texture is so fine and it can be decorated in such charming ways that it makes a much-desired dainty for festive occasions.

Sour Cream Dainties

2 eggs
1 cup sugar
Pinch salt
1 cup sour cream
1/2 tsp. soda
1-1/2 cups flour
1 tsp. baking powder

Beat the eggs very lightly. Sift the sugar and salt, and add them to the eggs. Then stir in the cream, to which the baking soda has been added. Combine the flour and the baking powder, and add to the mixture. Turn into petite-sized muffin pans, preferably with round bottoms, and bake 20 minutes at 350 degrees, or until toothpick inserted comes out clean. When cool, using the rounded bottom for the top, ice with Fluffy White Frosting (found on page 79) and sprinkle generously with fresh grated coconut. Or, you can omit the coconut and decorate with crushed nuts.

Be a Little Kinder

Inspiration, December 1921

A few days ago I ran across a little poem that impressed me so much that I should like to have you read it, think about it, and put it into practice.

I like the thoughts this little poem contains, for I know that kindness is a golden chain that binds us all closer together; that toleration is the real test of character—the test that shows whether we are big or petty; that praise, whether one has been successful or not, so long as one has tried, encourages success; that cheerfulness makes bearable conditions that seem unbearable; and that honest effort has its own reward in the satisfaction that comes to us in having done our best.

Each year as the holiday of holidays approaches, I wonder whether there really is anyone who fails to be carried away with the spirit of Christmas. It just seems that no matter where you look or where you go, you see someone planning or preparing to make someone else glad. Surely it would be an interesting experience if we could look into every heart at this time. I am positive we would find every one brimful of Christmas, and by this I mean gladness, for after all, Christmas is a synonym for gladness.

Nothing should be allowed to prevent us from doing all we can to relieve the hungry, to cheer the sorrowing, to brighten the depressed, to make more glad the glad. Nothing should deter us from giving of our store to the poor and needy, the children, and our friends. And if we can't give gifts, we can give cheerfulness and friendliness and a little bit of our time. Perhaps there's someone who'd appreciate a letter instead of a greeting card or another who'd be pleased if we dropped in to see them on Christmas day. Little attention these, but they gladden a spot in the human heart that responds to nothing quite so much as just real friendliness and interest. So my best wish for you during the coming holidays is that you allow Christmas to dwell in your heart, for once it is there it will remain with you—and you will surely let it—for all time to come.

Be a Little Kinder

Let me be a little kinder,
Let me be a little blinder
To the faults of those about me;
Let me praise a little more;
Let me be when I am weary
Just a bit more cheery—
Let me serve a little better
Those that I am striving for.

In Tune with the Holiday Spirit

Fashion Service, December 1925

Had Dame Fashion deliberately planned it months in advance, she could not have made our holiday dress more typical of the season. This is the time of sparkling tinsel, bright light and color, much gaiety, and festive activity. It is a time when beauty is uppermost in every mind, however dormant it may have lain through the rest of the year.

First of all, then, clothes for the holiday season are lovely from lingerie, with the charm of its silken daintiness, to the all-enveloping fur-trimmed coat, with its gay bit of a flare to the sides.

Next in importance are colors, with the reds and greens of holiday favor predominant in our apparel. Greens we wear, from the pale yellowish chartreuse for chiffon evening gowns, to the deep rich myrtle and epinard for tailored frocks of silk crepe or wool rep or twill through the day. Our reds are subdued, tending toward the purples or the browns. For variety, we add browns that are like winter woodlands, and blues as bright as the Christmas sky when the first star comes out.

But it is in its tinsel splendor that our clothing is most closely in tune with the holiday spirit. The long jumper blouse of shining silver brocade, worn with a brief circular skirt of velvet or satin for afternoon; the evening gown of supple metal lamé or of gossamer-sheer metallic lace; the evening wrap of rich, colorful metal brocade, or of velvet with metallic lining; the dainty silver shoes; the silver head bandeau studded with rhinestones—all of these reflect the light of the Christmas stars, the Christmas candles, or the Christmas sun, to the accompaniment of merry laughter as light and sparkling as the fabrics which make one look like nothing so much as a precious, tinseled Christmas package that one truly is.

The Fine Art of Giving

by Clarice Carpenter, *Inspiration*, 1924

Christmas giving is more than a lovely custom. It is an art—a fine art which you have mastered when your gifts are individual and thoughtful and fitted to the needs of those to whom they are given. Among the most welcome gifts we receive are simple things we never take time to make for ourselves. Judging from this, one way to insure a successful gift list is to include a number of articles that are simple but thoughtfully planned. The gifts shown here serve to illustrate the point.

Out of the sympathetic understanding of a little girl's longing for beauty in that most precious of places, her own room, grew the plan for the simple unbleached muslin bedspread and cur-

tains. Bands of checked gingham, 1-1/2 inches wide, in her favorite color, are applied. The edges are finished in rickrack of the same color.

A bride who loves pretty things but does not have a knack with a needle would be delighted with two aprons of unbleached muslin. Very simple embroidery stitches for trim are decorated with cotton-crepe flowers in blue, yellow, and gold whipped down with sewing thread.

Three lengths of coral pink and a half-yard of sea-blue crepe de Chine will make a gown and a slip for the "very best friend." Each has a half width inserted in the back.

To the left is a pair of dainty curtains for the

bathroom window of a friend who has a brand new house. They are made of striped dimity, edged with narrow lace, and embroidered in a very simple design.

Two pieces of linen joined on three edges with crocheting form a pocket for the piece of heavy cardboard that transforms them into a hot-dish mat. The open end is held in place with snaps. Three or four would make a nice set.

A card table cover that stays on is made of black sateen and has ribbon bands through which weighted tape is run.

With each gift at Christmas time, send a message done in rhyme.

Where sewing rooms are not so spacious
　　The pattern question is vexatious,
But with a pocket for each kind
　　They're very easy things to find.

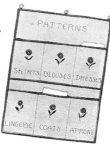

This pattern holder is made of plain gingham or Hebrides, embroidered in outline-stitch and appliqué, and bound with red bias tape. It is hung by ivory or brass rings.

When the door of your house is opened wide
　　And your guests find a cheery home inside,
You'll need for luncheon or afternoon tea
　　This set of extreme simplicity.

The luncheon set consists of a cloth and four napkins of pale yellow Hebrides cloth. Blue and black threads are drawn in to form the simple design. The edges are fringed and a row of machine stitching at the base of the fringe prevents further raveling.

Caesar, English, Chemistry, Trig,
　　A school girl's life is a constant dig.
But books lose their terrorizing powers
　　When encased in a strap that is
　　　　trimmed with flowers.

The strap is of black silk elastic, with the ends sewed together like a garter. Two glass bracelets make the handles, and crocheted wool roses add a charming personal touch that the school girl adores.

Needles and pins, needles and pins,
　　When you can't find them, the hunt begins,
But if you'll keep me on your dressing table,
　　You'll find my assistance
　　　　both constant and able.

A pin cushion of crepe de chine is stuffed with lamb's wool. A filet medallion tacked on at the corners is easily removed for washing. Very fine crocheted lace may be used instead of filet.

Just a dresser scarf
　　with a simple design
But it carries best wishes
　　to a friend of mine.

To make this as shown, pull out enough threads to leave a space as wide as is desired to fill with the design, with 1-1/2 inches being a good width. Hemstitch the hem in. Then, using soft colored cotton thread, weave in the design, running the threads across the entire width of the scarf and back again. Where the white threads of the linen show on one side, the colored embroidery thread will show on the other. It is interesting work and many original designs may be worked out. Decide on the width of the motifs and count the threads to keep the design even.

The Festive Touch at Yuletide

Inspiration, December 1924

When Charles Dickens wrote, "I will honor Christmas in my heart," he might have added "and in my home," too, for there is nothing that contributes so thoroughly to the joy of the season as a festive welcoming hall and living room. The means of obtaining the brightness and cheer characteristic of the season is within the reach of all of us, because the foundation of the most suitable decoration, evergreen, is usually available. If it cannot be found within walking distance, a trip by motor to the country, which can be made in the nature of a special treat for the children, will bring one near enough to the source of it to carry back the necessary quantity.

Ground pine, hemlock or pine boughs, and laurel combined with bright bittersweet are ideal and will give joy not only to the sense of sight

but, by their pungent odor, to the sense of smell, too. Holly and mistletoe are so much a part of the season that at least a small quantity of each should be procured and will provide needed variety.

The Tree

The Christmas tree is, of course, the focal point from which all the other decorations should radiate. It is an attractive idea to place it in the hall, or if there is not enough space available there, in a position where it will greet the eye of each visitor as soon as he or she enters the home. To obtain double pleasure from it, arrange to have it reflected in a mirror, as shown in this illustration, the reflection being even more alluring than the tree itself. Avoid any tendency toward an excess of trimming and do not obscure the shape of the tree entirely since its form is beautiful in itself and is truly decorative.

Garlands and Wreaths

Next in importance comes the wreaths for our windows and the garland for decoration. If there is time for it and one's fingers are deft, it really adds to the holiday feeling to make them. The foundation is a  stout wire joined in a circle. You will also need a length of fine wire for winding and a pair of sharp pliers. The material may be laurel, which keeps very well, pine, spruce, or boxwood, if it is available in quantity, or a combination of two or more of these. Clusters of bright berries will add an attractive touch. The wreaths should be covered quite closely with short sprays of the greens so that the circular effect will be retained. Fasten the fine wire or cord to the foundation wire and wind it carefully around each branch as it is placed in the proper position. A lightweight firm cord in dark green may be substituted for the wire.

Table Decorations

Table decorations at Christmas may be elaborate or simple, depending on your time and the formality of your dinner. Several unusual effects are shown here, each of which may be achieved with little effort. The centerpiece at the lower left consists of a low bowl of selected fruits wreathed with winter greens, such as pine and pinecones. Slender ropes of greens extend in star effect to the edge of the table, and tall, slender green tapers in flat candle holders, masked with greens, complete the picture.

For the table shown in the center, a candelabra, holding many red candles, is set in the center of a very full holly wreath. With such a decoration, a bowl of fruit and bayberry candles would be effective on the serving table. For the Christmas party, the centerpiece may be a silver or gold-covered box filled with favors from which ribbons may be run to the places of the guests. A large poinsettia, made of silver, red, and green paper may top the box so as to practically conceal its contents. Gay little skating figures with wire bodies, lollypop heads, and paper clothes, make timely place cards.

Magic Pattern

The Popular Circular Cape

Inspiration, 1926

Everywhere one sees capes—short ones, long ones, those of seven-eighths length, and some so short as to be nothing more than rather exaggerated collars. They furnish perhaps the freshest note in the season's fashions, and contribute no small amount of chic to the silhouette. Capes varying from shoulder to fingertip length are seen on many of the new coats. Illustrated here is a cape that is ideally suited to ensemble use, as it offers infinite possibilities for material, color, and fabric variation. Since it is cut in one piece, and hence is made without seams, the time required for completing it is a slight consideration. The width of the material used may be anywhere from 36 to 54 inches. If it is from 40 to 54 inches wide, 2 yards will be needed. If 36-inch material is used, supply 2-1/4 yards, the additional 1/4-yard being necessary for the ties.

The cutting of the cape is illustrated in Fig. 1 (*a*), which shows one-half of the material. If 54-inch material is used, first remove a 14-inch strip along one selvage by cutting along the line *ab*. This strip may be used in trimming a dress. Next, remove a 4-inch strip by cutting on the line *cd*. This will be used for the ties. If 36-inch material is used, cut 1/4 yard from one end, instead of along the selvage, to be used for ties. Then, with whatever width you used, you have a piece 2 yards long and 1 yard wide, one half of which is indicated by the shaded portion of Fig. 1 view (*a*).

Along the selvage edge, make a 5-inch fold toward the wrong side the entire length of the material, as shown by Fig. 1 (*b*). Then, beginning at the center back, measure 7 inches each way along the

 See Notes, page 232, for modern tips and techniques.

selvage and place pins to indicate the 14 inches thus laid off. Put in two rows of gathering threads, as shown by the double row of dotted lines at the lower right in (*b*), following a somewhat curved line from pin to pin. Leave long, unfastened ends of thread.

Next, put the material on the figure with the shirring at the back of the neck and a deep point dropping over each shoulder. Draw up the shirring threads to a length of 10 inches and wrap them around pins until you are sure this is the right adjustment. Fold over the double thickness of material above the shirring to form the collar. Adjust the

228

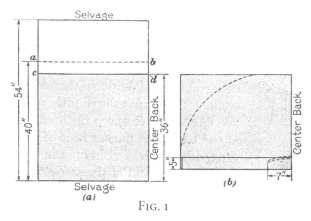

Selvage

54"

40"

Center Back 36"

5"

Selvage
(a)

Center Back

7"

(b)

FIG. 1

shirring until it fits well over the shoulders, and then fasten the threads.

Measuring up from the floor, mark an even line around the lower edge, which will take somewhat the curve shown by the dotted line at the upper left in Fig. 1 (b). Cut along this line, removing the points over the hips and giving the circular

 For lining the cape, see Notes, page 232, for instructions.

effect shown in the illustration. This completes the cutting of the cape. Remove it from the figure, fold it on the center-back line to make sure that the curves of the two sides are alike and blend smoothly into the straight edges of the front and back. Since bias edges have a tendency to stretch with wear, it is well to let the cape hang on a dress form for several hours, then measure and trim off the edges evenly once more.

If no lining is to be used, slip-stitch the selvage edge of the facing fold to the material invisibly. If heavy wool is used, the edges may be finished as shown in Fig. 2 (a). First make a 1/2- to 5/8-inch turn to the wrong side along the entire lower edge, and baste near the turn, as at a. To draw this turn in so that it will lie flat along the curves, run a row of gathering stitches near the raw edge, as at b. Provide a long bias strip of matching silk

about 3/4-inch wide and sew it to the raw edge, as at c, catching only the silk and turned edge, not the cape itself. Then turn under the free edge of the silk strip, and hem or slip-stitch it in place as at d, making the stitches as nearly invisible as possible. Remove the basting stitches along the edge, and press thoroughly.

With silk or light-weight wool, a narrow binding of self-material makes an attractive finish. Cut true bias strips 1 to 1-1/4 inches wide, using the corners that were cut off when the lower edge of the cape was shaped. Lay the right side of the bias over the right side of the cape, edges even, and stitch about 1/4 inch from the edge, as at a, Fig. 2 (b). Then fold the bias to the wrong side, turn under the raw edge, and hem or slip-stitch over the first row of stitches, as illustrated at b.

To make the tie, fold the 4-inch strip of material through the center lengthwise, right sides in, using the full 2-yard length. If 36-inch material is used, split the 1/4-yard strip lengthwise, sew the two pieces together, end to end, to get the 2-yard length; press the plain seam open, and fold the strip as just directed. Stitch across one end and the full length of

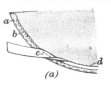

(a)

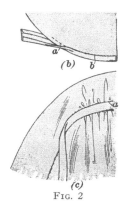

(b)

(c)

FIG. 2

the tie, having the seam 1/4 inch from the edge. Turn it right-side out, slip-stitch the open end together, and press. Put the finished tie over the shirring on the inside of the collar, as shown in Fig. 2 (c), having the center of the tie even with the center-back line of the cape. Hem or slip-stitch both edges of the tie to the cape, as at a, leaving the tie ends loose below the shirred line. If the material is heavy, cut away the under thickness of the tie through the short section where it is sewed over the shirring.

Testimonials

There's a song in the air! Did you hear it when you turned another leaf on your calendar and found December facing you? I did. Christmas is still many days away, but quite near enough for me to catch the lilting refrain of bells and laughter and gay, happy voices that will grow sweeter and clearer as the days slip away until they burst out in a world-wide chorus of joy on Christmas Day.

In the meantime, how busy you've been. We hear so much about hard times and scarcity of money that we are apt to become a bit depressed by it all, until we realize that right in our very fingers we have the skill and cunning to make this holiday as joyful as any other. One student has found it helpful to invite a group of her friends to her home for what she calls a "candy demonstration." She has several different confections made for exhibit for everyone to sample. Then she proceeds to show how to measure the ingredients and to use the candy thermometer for one of the recipes.

—*Inspiration,* December 1926

Here is what I hear from another reader:

"At Christmas time, I made a silk négligée for a friend for which I was very proud for it was the first sewing I ever did on anything so nice. It was not nearly so expensive as the ready-made ones and much better made."

—*Mrs. J. A. E., Massachusetts*

And another joyful letter from a resourceful reader:

"There are my Christmas gifts—all handmade. I call them rag-bag gifts, mainly because they are practically all made from pieces of cotton and silk from my piece bag, flour sack, bias tape, and confidence—thanks to you folks. I wish you could see them—scarves, fancy coat hangers, chemises, lunch cloths, and handkerchiefs, chiefly, also shoulder bouquets and boutonnieres.

"*Fashion Service* has inspired me to attempt so many things. When we invited some newly married cousins to dinner, I baked a fine white cake, put it on an old-fashioned cake stand, and decorated it with a tiny bride and groom . . . The Magazine just sets one thinking. It prompted us to have the little girls sing carols before the open fire on Christmas Eve and to finish up the day with Dickens's *Christmas Carol.* And we made every Christmas gift we gave and we tried to put our personality into each gift."

—*Mrs. R. H. F., Ohio*

A Final Word from Mary Brooks Picken

Aside from wanting to see everybody filled with gladness, my fondest hope this Christmastide is to see everyone making the best use of his or her opportunities. And particularly do my thoughts go to Institute students who are just beginning their courses of study. What a wonderful opportunity for progress lies before them if they only make every minute count. Do not be like the rich man who installed a library of books all bound in beautiful covers and then simply looked at the bindings through the glass door of his handsome bookcases. Open up your instruction books. Dig into them in earnest. There you will find a world of practical information that will give to you the knowledge so necessary for your real happiness and that of others as well.

My wish, then, at this glad time of the year is that you will be one who sows the seeds of happiness and prosperity for the year—yes, years—to come among your friends, acquaintances, and associates, seeds that will germinate and grow and multiply a thousand fold, so that in time to come you may look back and experience the satisfaction that comes to those who are aligned with the forces of good. May your Christmas deeds mean one more step toward the time when turmoil will vanish and peace increase. And may Christmas fill you with determination to make the best of your daily trials that beset you, with gratefulness for your opportunity to serve, and with the happiness that comes from serving.

Finally, a word about grandmothers—it seems as though they fill a special need in many households. Having reached a place where they no longer feel the rush and hurry of life, they have more time to devote to children and can enter into their little interests more understandingly sometimes than their too busy mothers. A former student of the Institute, Mrs. Annie Mills of Baltimore, Maryland, is a good example. She makes her home with a married daughter who has three little girls. A few weeks before Christmas last year, the steady hum of her sewing machine began to bespeak of unusual activity, but to repeated rappings of tiny hands upon the sewing-room door, there came only the response that she was working for Santa Claus and must not be disturbed.

So, on Christmas morning, to the complete surprise of three delighted youngsters, there appeared three perfectly appointed wardrobe trunks. Dolls' trunks, they were, fashioned under Mrs. Mills' skillful fingers. And in each trunk were complete doll outfits—twenty garments in all. We doubt if in all the state of Maryland there was a gift that gave more genuine pleasure or showed a truer, or more intimate, appreciation of what a little girl loves.

Magic Pattern Notes

We chose to republish the Institute's *Magic Patterns* in their original format, keeping the language as authentic as possible. We have tested the patterns and offered suggestions for the modern reader that are listed in this section. *Magic Patterns* are patterns you draw and cut yourself; or cut directly from the fabric using the measurements and diagrams that are provided as a guide. The patterns in the book have a range of skill requirements, from beginner to advanced. Women taking the Institute home study courses in the years that these patterns were first published were in various stages of school, so the patterns were intended to be accessible to women with diverse experience. These notes should help you with any questions that arise while you're making the patterns in the book. Please refer to the Vintage Notions website (www.vintagenotions.com) for further helpful tips, techniques, fabric suggestions, and photos of our finished *Magic Patterns*. Visit us often as we share our designs and those of readers who have made their own fashions using this book.

January
Men's Shirt Aprons
TIP
- Large-sized men's long-sleeved shirts, in plaids or stripes, work best for creating these aprons.

February
Lingerie
TIP
- Before beginning, finish all the raw edges of the pattern pieces with a zigzag stitch or serger.

TECHNIQUES
- When cutting the pattern pieces, remember that these instructions were cut from 40" wide fabric, not 44" wide fabric.
- The approximate finished measurements of the vest using the original cutting instructions from 40" wide fabric:
  - Bust: 36"
  - Waist: 36"
  - Hips: 42"
- The approximate finished measurements of the panties using the original cutting instructions from 40" wide fabric:
  - Waist: 30"
  - Hips: 30"
- The approximate finished measurements of the nightgown using the original cutting instructions from 40" wide fabric:
  - Nightgown Band: 40"
  - Hips: 60"
- Use a 1/4" seam allowance for lingerie construction.

- When gathering the top edge of the panties and before joining the waistband, make sure you can easily pull them over your hips before you stitch the waistband in place.
- "Slashes" at the center-front and center-back refer to cuts that are 4" long; which is half the panty flap width.
- Hem the nightgown to desired length.

March
Apron
TIPS
- We used 1-1/4 yards of 44"-wide fabric, with the selvages cut off and the fabric squared.
- We used purchased 1/4"-wide double-fold bias binding or make your own from 1"-wide bias fabric strips.

April
Flower
TIP
- Cut fabric circles using a rotary circle cutter.

TECHNIQUES
- To draw the paper circle pattern pieces you can also use a circle template.
- Purchase a pin-back at the crafts store or jewelry supply store and stitch it to the back of the finished flower.

May
Magic Scarves
TIP
- Fabrics used to create these scarves should to be lightweight or sheer and double-sided, making them completely reversible.

June
Summer Purse
This is a more complicated pattern recommended for advanced sewers.

TIPS
- Use temporary spray adhesive instead of machine or hand basting.
- If, when attaching the gusset or stitching on the foundation, the piece does not move easily under your presser foot, then decrease the tension on the foot and lengthen the stitch.
- Make the 2-3/4" interior pocket deeper to accommodate a cell phone, etc.
- Replace the 1" wide by 6" long handle with cotton belting or a braided strap using a commercial cord maker.
- An alternative method to construct this purse would be to cut the outside fabric and lining fabric to the same size as the buckram and eliminate the binding around the pieces in the initial steps. Construct the entire purse as written and then use bias binding around the outside edges as a final step. This makes for fewer steps and a cleaner, more accurate finish.
- For the coin purse, we used bias tape binding for a more finished look. First bind the bottom 3-3/8" edge (see view G). Next, fold this edge up to form a pocket. Then, bind remaining three raw edges to finish.

TECHNIQUES

- Fabric Requirements: Three fat quarters
  – One for exterior
  – One for lining
  – One for bias trim and interior pocket
- Use 3/8" seam allowance for gusset construction.
- When it says, "join straight edges" of gusset it refers to the straight ends at the top of the "U." Stitch them right-sides together, turn, and press.
- To attach the gusset to the large lining piece, first turn under 1/4" on the lining. Then match up the bottom of the lining with gusset piece and turn under the gusset over the lining 1/4". Stitch to foundation.
- Press under 1/4" of small foundation section edges. To attach the gusset to the remaining lining and foundation, stitch the lining to the foundation on the top straight edge as on the large section. Fold the gusset over the lining, then pin to small foundation edge matching bottom. Stitch.

July

Bias Slip

This is a more complicated pattern recommended for advanced sewers.

TIPS

- To draw the first large curve (*c-e*) it is helpful to have a partner hold the string or tape the end to a table.
- To draw the second curve (*f-g*) try a flexible ruler
- Before beginning, finish all raw edges of the pattern pieces with a zigzag stitch or serger.

TECHNIQUES

- Approximate finished slip measurements using original cutting instructions:
  Bust: 38"
  Waist: 38"
- "A seam's width" refers to a 3/8" seam allowance for slip construction.
- Cut shoulder straps 1-3/4" wide.
- Cut the top edge facing piece 2" wide.
- After you stitch the center-front and center-back skirt section, stitch the side seams.

August

Kimono

TIPS

- If using one-way directional fabric, be aware that the design on either the front or the back will finish upside down.
- You will also need 3 yards of 1-1/2" wide soft satin ribbon, cut in two equal pieces for the belt.
- Make sure the fabric is straight at the cut edges.
- Practice the fabric folds, marking and cutting on a piece of 8-1/2" x 11" paper. This will help to avoid a costly error with your fabric.
- Use chalk or your favorite marking system to mark all the lines before you cut.
- After marking, and before cutting, pin the layers together to prevent slipping.
- Shoulder tucks: Hang the garment from a door to be sure the tucks follow a straight line down the back of the garment. Measure the front tucks to be sure they are equidistant from the binding.

TECHNIQUES

- Use one length of 44" wide fabric, by measuring from your shoulder to the floor and doubling this measurement to determine the complete yardage needed. For an average person, 3 yards is required.
- "Plain seams" refer to a 5/8" seam allowance for Kimono construction.
- Stitch down the back tucks on the shoulders (at *k*) when inserting the ends of the waist ribbon belt pieces.
- Hem the bottom and the sleeves.

September

Economical Apron

TIPS

- Instead of placing a line of pins from point *c* to *d*, use a ruler and a chalk-marking pencil to mark this line.
- Before beginning, finish all raw edges of the pattern pieces with a zigzag stitch or serger.
- Make the side sections of the apron skirt equal when gathered.

TECHNIQUES

- We recommend not cutting the pocket from the 6" fabric strip, instead cut a pocket from the fabric piece you cut from the bib section. This will allow for a longer bib strap and waistband/belt to adjust to your figure.
- We recommend a wider bib for better coverage. Measure across your bust for a bib width measurement that suits your figure and divide that measurement in half and add 1/2" for seaming. This will be your new distance from *a* to *b*.
- Use 1/4" seam allowances for apron construction.
- Before you gather the top edge of the side sections and baste the bands in place, you will need to hem the sides of the apron by turning the raw edges in a 1/4" and topstitching.

October

Practical Nightgown

TIPS

- For measuring and marking the placement of the decorative scallop design, use a circle template and a chalk pencil.
- Use a size 4.0 twin needle to stitch down both sides of the decorative bias binding simultaneously.

TECHNIQUE

- Use 1/2" seam allowances for nightgown construction.

November

Apron—no additional notes needed

December

Cape

TIPS

- Use a flexible ruler and chalk-marking pencil to mark the 14" curved line at the center-back neckline as a guide to follow for the two rows of gathering threads.
- Instead of using matching silk bias strips to finish the lower edge of the cape as in Fig. 2a, you could use hem tape or bind the edges with a contrasting material as in Fig. 2b.
- Leave both ends of the tie open and use a tube turner to turn right-side out then slipstitch both ends closed.
- On Fig. 1a and b, note that the center-back is the "fold" of the fabric.

Cape Lining Instructions:

If the cape is to be lined, sew the lining to the selvage edge of the turned-back facing before shirring the collar. Pin all other edges together firmly, and, after the lower edge of both cape and lining are evened off together, turn the edges in and slipstitch them together. In doing this, make the turn of the lining deeper than that on the cape material, so that the seam will not show on the right side.

GLOSSARY OF STITCHES

The following dictionary of stitches appeared in the widely acclaimed book, *The Language of Fashion: A Dictionary and Digest of Fabric, Sewing, and Dress*, written by Mary Brooks Picken and published in 1939.

Stitch. 1. Single turn or loop of the thread, yarn, etc., made by hand or machine in sewing, crocheting, embroidery, knitting, lace-making. **2.** Particular method or style of stitching. All eye-needle types, whether for embroidery, tapestry, lace, or sewing, are based approximately upon the seven basic stitches; running, back, overcast, cross, blanket, chain, knot. Type of design, weight and kind of fabric and thread, length of stitch, and position of thread at right or left of needle provide the many variations.

afghan-s. Simple crochet stitch worked with long, hooked needle to produce a plain design. See TRICOT-STITCH.

applique-s. (ap li *kay*). Any stitch used to fasten applied piece to fabric article or garment.

arrowhead-s. Series of stitches placed to resemble arrowheads, one below the other, all pointing in the same direction. Can be used as border or filling stitch.

Aubusson-s. (oh boo sonh). Type of needle-tapestry stitch. Same as REP-STITCH.

back-s. Basic stitch, second in importance, from which combination-stitch, seed-stitch, etc., were developed. Made by inserting needle about 1/8 inch back of end of previous stitch and bringing it out about 1/8 inch beyond end. Under stitch is thus twice length of top stitch. Top resembles machine-stitch. Used for strength in plain sewing, also for embroidery.

basket filling-s. 1. Stitch with lengthwise threads alternately passing over and under cross threads, as in darning. **2.** Couching stitch worked alternately over and under cords. Used in embroidery.

basket-s. Embroidery stitch resembling series of overlapping cross-stitches, each stitch overlapping the one before by about half. Varies in appearance from close, braid-like line to cross-stitch effect, according to whether stitches are placed close together or spaced. Used as filling or outline where heavy, solid effect is desired.

Basket-Stitch

basting (ba*ist* ing). Long, loose stitch used to hold fabric in place until final sewing. — **diagonal-b.** Diagonal on top side; short, straight, crosswise stitch underneath. Used to hold two thicknesses of fabric together and to prevent slipping. — **even-b.** Long running-stitches. Used for seams before fitting gar-

ment, and for exacting machine work. — **uneven-b.** Twice as long as even-basting, with short stitch underneath and long stitch on top. Quickest method of basting.

blanket-s. Basic stitch, fifth in importance, from which buttonhole-stitch, feather-stitch, etc., were developed. Essential characteristic is single purl, formed by bringing needle out over thread so as to cross it. Blanket-stitch is widely spaced; single-purl buttonhole is the same stitch worked close together. Used for simulated buttonholes, cut work, ornamental edging.

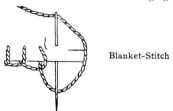

Blanket-Stitch

blind-s. Concealed stitch like slip-stitch, but shorter.

braided-band-s. Embroidery stitch made by weaving threads in diamond shape to fill in band or border.

bredstitch (*bred* stitch) or **bredestitch** (*breed* stitch). Old embroidery stitch that appears same on each side of fabric.

brick-s. or **brickwork. 1.** Blanket-stitch arranged to resemble brick formation. Used for bands and borders and for covering large surface. **2.** Embroidery stitch in which flat stitches are laid in alternate rows as bricks are laid, end of one stitch coming under middle of stitch above.

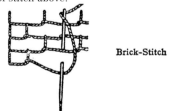

Brick-Stitch

brier-s. (*bry* er). Type of feather stitching made to resemble thorns on a stem.

broad chain-s. Same as SQUARE CHAIN-STITCH.

bullion-s. (*bool* yun). Decorative stitch made by twisting needle around thread several times before inserting it into material. Short bullion-stitches sometimes called *knots*.

bundle-s. Group of parallel stitches laid on fabric and tied together at the middle. Sometimes called *fagot filling-stitch* or *sheaf filling-stitch*.

burden-s. Flat couching.

buttonhole-s. 1. Stitch with a double purl. Used to finish the edges of tailored buttonholes; also, to form a secure edge, as in cut work.

Also called *close-stitch* and *feston*. **2.** Same as blanket-stitch, but worked close together. Used in laces and open-work embroidery.

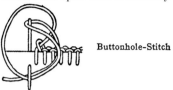

Buttonhole-Stitch

buttonhole tied-s. Open-seam stitch made by working from four to six single-purl-stitches on a bar. Used to join ribbons.

Byzantine-s. (*biz* an teen). Slanting satin-stitch worked on canvas over four vertical and four horizontal threads in diagonal zigzag pattern.

cable-s. Embroidery stitch of chain-stitch type, differing from ordinary chain-stitch by having small stitch connecting one link to the next.

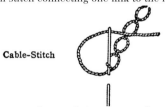

Cable-Stitch

canvas s. Cross-stitch or any of various stitches used in canvas work.

catch-s. Large, easy cross-like stitch made with sewing thread. Used to hold edges too bulky for hem turn, and as finish for seam edges in fabric that does not fray.

catstitch. Same as CATCH-STITCH.

chain-s. 1. Basic stitch, sixth in importance, from which lazy-daisy and link-powdering were developed. Made of connecting loop stitches that form links, as in a chain. Also called *loop-, picot-, railway-stitch*. Used in embroidery. **2.** In crochet, stitch made by catching thread around hook and pulling it through thread loop, catching thread again to form another loop, and repeating process. There are many other stitches used in crochet that are not given here, since they are all variations of this and are used chiefly in following a pattern.

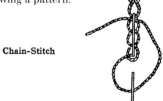

Chain-Stitch

chequered chain-s. Same as MAGIC CHAIN-STITCH.

chevron-s. (*shev* ron). Embroidery stitch

made in somewhat the same manner as catch-stitch, but instead of a small cross at each angle, a short, straight stitch covers the joining.

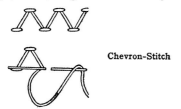

Chevron-Stitch

closed feather-s. Single feather-stitch, always made by putting needle in vertically instead of diagonally.

close-s. (cloce). Same as BUTTONHOLE-STITCH.

cloth-s. Close stitch, used in making pillow lace, in which threads are woven as in a piece of cloth. Also called *whole-stitch*.

combination-s. Back-stitch combined with two or more running-stitches. Used when more strength is needed than given by running-stitch.

continental-s. Type of stitch used in canvas work; made the same as tent-stitch, but worked on double-thread canvas.

coral-s. Blanket-stitch worked backward with heavy thread and embroidered close together. Used as outline or filling stitch.

cord-s. Fine stitch closely worked over laid thread to give effect of raised line or cord.

couching-s. (cowch ing). Overcasting or ornamental stitches taken at regular intervals to fasten down one or more strands of thread, yarn, or cord. Used as ornamental work on dresses, linens, hangings, etc.

Couching-Stitch

Cretan-s. (creet an). Variation of feather-stitch made by taking shorter underneath stitch, so that, instead of a straight center line, a braided effect results.

crewel-s. Outline-stitch used in crewel work. Sometimes called *stem-stitch*.

cross-basket-s. Two groups of parallel threads laid perpendicular to each other and fastened by cross-stitches where the threads intersect. Used as filling.

crossed blanket-s. Blanket-stitch made so that one stitch slants diagonally to right and next crosses in diagonal slant to the left, resulting in series of crosses above the purled line.

cross-s. Basic stitch, fourth in importance, having many varieties. Made by one stitch crossed over another to form an X. Used on dresses, children's clothes, linens. Also used on canvas in needle-tapestry work, in which each cross is completed before the next is begun.

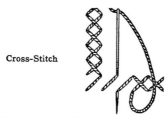

Cross-Stitch

cushion-s. (coosh un). **1.** In embroidery, same as TENT-STITCH, I. **2.** Short, straight stitch producing effect of weaving. Used on coarse canvas; formerly used in embroidery to fill in backgrounds, especially in imitating painted designs. Loosely, any stitch used in canvas work as filling stitch.

darning-s. Stitch done in imitation of weaving, used to reinforce or replace fabric and for allover decoration. Used as a filling stitch in embroidery.

detached chain-s. Same as LAZY-DAISY-STITCH.

diagonal cross-s. Oblong cross-stitch, with a vertical stitch connecting the two ends on the same side of each cross, giving a boxed-in effect.

double back-s. Same as SHADOW-STITCH.

double chain-s. Chain-stitch combining two links or thread loops. Gives a heavier line than single chain-stitch.

double cross-s. Canvas stitch consisting of one ordinary cross-stitch with another made upright on top of it.

double running-s. Running-stitch done twice on the same line to make continuous line on both sides of fabric. Also called *two-sided-stitch, Holbein-stitch, Italian-stitch*. Used for embroidery and needle tapestry.

drawn-fabric-s. Any stitch producing an open-work effect by drawing fabric threads together in groups to form a design or pattern. Done with coarse needle and strong thread for best results. See ITALIAN HEMSTITCHING, PUNCH-WORK-STITCH.

embroidery darning-s. Even-basting-stitches in alternating rows. Used for filling in bands and borders, etc.

etching-s. Same as OUTLINE-STITCH.

fagot filling-s. Same as BUNDLE-STITCH.

fagoting-s. Open-seam stitch similar to single feather-stitch. Used to join ribbons, bands, or folds. Also called *insertion-stitch*. — **Bermuda f.** Fagoting-stitch on the wrong side of sheer fabric. Similar to SHADOW EMBROIDERY. — **drawn-work** or **hemstitch f.** Fagoting done on open sections of fabric from which certain threads have been drawn. Stitches used are of hemstitch type, placed to gather fabric threads in various designs. See DRAWN WORK. See HEMSTITCH. — **single f.** Fagoting made by inserting the needle at right angles to the

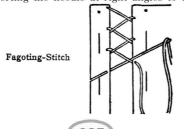

Fagoting-Stitch

edges to be joined. — **twisted f.** Fagoting made by inserting the needle parallel to the edges to be joined.

feather-s. Variation of short blanket-stitch, in groups alternating from one side of an unmarked line to the other.

fern-s. Stitch worked on same principle as arrowhead-stitch, but done in groups of three stitches instead of two, so that third stitch of each group forms continuous stem line.

fiber-s. Stitch used in making bobbin lace, for indicating central vein of a leaf design.

filling-s. Any embroidery stitch used to fill in part of a design.

fishbone-s. Embroidery stitch like the backbone of a fish; made with a series of single-purl-stitches worked diagonally and alternately to the left and to the right of an unmarked line. Used as braid or border stitch.

Fishbone-Stitch

flat-s. Stitch worked on same principle as satin-fishbone-stitch, but needle is put in at less of an angle with shorter underneath stitch, giving more overlapping on surface.

Florentine-s. (flor en teen). Canvas stitch made upright, usually in zigzag or oblique lines rather than horizontal rows. Stitch usually covers four horizontal threads.

fly-s. Same as Y stitch, with shorter tail.

French knot. Ornamental knot made by twisting needle around thread from three to five times and putting needle back at approximately same point it came through. When the thread is pulled through, a shapely knot is formed. Used for embroidering centers of flowers, etc.

French Knot

garter-s. Usual simple stitch used in hand knitting. Also called *plain knitting*.

German-s. Stitch formed by working long and short slanting stitches alternately across canvas in diagonal line. Used in BERLIN WORK.

glove- or **glover's-s.** (gluv erz). Stitch made by alternately drawing thread through one side of seam, then other, always from inside outward. Used in sewing seams of gloves.

Gobelin-s. (gob a lin). Canvas stitch laid upright over two horizontal threads and worked horizontally on the canvas. Sometimes called *tapestry-stitch*. — **encroaching G.-s.** Same stitch worked on slant over one vertical and five horizontal threads, with each succeeding row beginning in the same row of squares as the bottom of the preceding row, giving over-lapped effect. — **oblique G.-s.** Same stitch worked on slant by laying it over one vertical thread as well as the two horizontal threads.

Gothic-s. Same as CHAIN-STITCH, I.

gros point (gro pwanh). Needle tapestry stitch as used for canvas work. French term meaning large point.

half back-s. Stitch similar to back-stitch, but having longer under stitch so that there is space between the top stitches. Not as strong as back-stitch, but gives more strength than running-or combination-stitches.

half cross-s. Stitch used in canvas work, worked diagonally from left to right, the needle being put through from one square to the square immediately below. Usually on double-mesh canvas with trammé laid first.

half-s. 1. In crocheting or knitting, two stitches taken as one to contract edge. **2.** In pillow laces, loose open stitch used in delicate parts of design; in contrast to cloth stitch. Also called *lace-stitch, shadow-stitch.*

hemming-s. 1. Quick stitch made with short, slanting stitch on right side and slightly longer slanting stitch on wrong side. Also called *whipping*. **2.** Same as VERTICAL HEMMING-STITCH. See under STITCHES.

hemstitch or **hemstitching.** Ornamental stitch, as at top of hem, made by drawing out number of parallel threads and fastening together those remaining in open sections, in successive small groups.

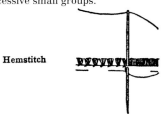

Hemstitch

herringbone-s. Name of catch-stitch in embroidery. Used to form bands, fill borders and motifs. Close herringbone used for heavy stems.

Holbein-s. (*hole* bine). Same as DOUBLE RUNNING-STITCH.

hollie-s. Type of buttonhole-stitch with a twist. Used in making hollie point lace.

honeycomb-s. Blanket-stitches so connected as to form a honeycomb design. Similar to BRICK-STITCH, I. Used for filling.

huckaback-s. (*huck* a back). Surface stitch darned into the weft threads of huckaback toweling; often placed to form designs or make zigzag borders. Generally in multi-colored effects.

Huckaback-Stitch

Hungarian-s. (hung *gay* ri an). Alternating long and short upright stitches; worked horizontally on plain canvas. Covers four and two threads.

insertion-s. Any open-seam stitch. See FAGOTING, I.

Irish-s. Long stitch taken in upright direction across several threads of canvas; worked diagonally across canvas. Used in BERLIN WORK.

Italian hemstitching. 1. Drawn-fabric stitch made with alternating vertical and horizontal stitch, forming line similar in appearance to blanket-stitch but with open-work effect caused by use of large needle to punch hole and fine thread to draw fabric threads apart. May be worked in any direction on fabric. Often used as seam-finish on sheer fabrics, in same manner as machine hemstitching, to give flat, strong, decorative finish, for which no preliminary stitching is needed. **2.** Same stitch used in embroidery on linen or other fabric for line or for filling, but done on counted threads.

Italian relief-s. Single-purl-stitches used in flower designs to fill in petals and leaves. Often seen in combination with punch work.

Italian-s. Same as DOUBLE RUNNING-STITCH.

Kensington-s. (*ken* zing ton). Same as LONG-AND-SHORT-STITCH.

knot-s. Basic stitch, seventh in importance. Made by twisting thread around needle in any way that forms a knot in the thread on the fabric surface when the thread is drawn through. See FRENCH-KNOT, LIBERTY KNOT-STITCH, SIMPLICITY KNOT-STITCH.

lace-s. Stitch used in making bobbin lace to fill inside and lighter parts of designs. Also called *half-stitch.*

ladder-s. 1. Embroidery stitch over open seam or drawn or cut-out fabric, resembling fagoting. Done with over-casting, buttonhole-stitch, or catch-stitch. **2.** Embroidery stitch with ladder-like effect, generally square chain-stitch.

laid-s. Long, loose stitch laid on surface of fabric; usually held down by stitches worked over it. Used for outline and filling.

lattice-basket-s. Lattice-work embroidery made by laying close, parallel threads and weaving the eye of the needle in and out of these threads as in darning. Used for square, diamond, or basket motifs and border effects.

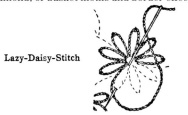

Lazy-Daisy-Stitch

lazy-daisy-s. Elongated, detached chain-stitches, grouped to form a daisy. Used in embroidery.

leviathan-s. (le *vy* ath an). Stitch used in canvas work. Same as DOUBLE CROSS-STITCH.

liberty knot-s. Embroidery stitch worked by inserting needle perpendicularly to line to be decorated, carrying the thread around the needle, and then pulling needle through, thus forming a knot. Used for outlines.

link-powdering-s. Series of chain-like stitches not linked together, but completed separately. Usually worked in spaced design. Used for filling. Sometimes called *washable knot-stitch.*

lock-s. Sewing-machine stitch formed by locking top and bobbin threads together at each stitch.

long-and-short-s. Alternating long and short stitches used as a filling- or darning-stitch in embroidery. Also called *Kensington-stitch.*

long-leg cross-s. Cross-stitch made with one long and one short stitch. Used in linen and canvas embroidery.

long-s. Satin-stitch without padding.

looped-braid-s. Embroidery stitch made by bringing the thread around in a loop and taking one stitch through the loop, length of loop and stitch regulating width of braid. Used chiefly on things that are not laundered.

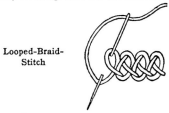

Looped-Braid-Stitch

loop-s. Same as CHAIN-STITCH, I.

magic chain-s. Chain-stitch worked with two threads of different colors in one needle. Colors made to alternate by looping one thread under needle for one stitch, the other thread for the next stitch.

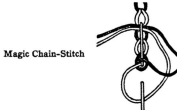

Magic Chain-Stitch

marking-s. Same as CROSS-STITCH.

mark-s. Same as TAILORS' TACKS.

needle-point s. 1. Term used to designate any stitch used in needle tapestry. **2.** Any stitch used in making needle-point lace.

oblong cross-s. Cross-stitch made long and narrow instead of square.

open chain-s. Same as SQUARE CHAIN-STITCH.

open-s. Any embroidery stitch that produces open work.

Oriental-s. Series of long, straight, parallel stitches intersected at center by short, diagonal stitches. Sometimes used as open-seam stitch. Also called *Rumanian-stitch.*

ornamental buttonhole edge-s. Stitch made by forming series of loops along an edge and working over each loop with buttonhole-stitches. Used to decorate plain edges.

outline-s. Slanting back-stitch used for outlines, stems, and as padding foundation under other stitches. When thread is kept to left of needle, a straighter line is obtained.

Shorter stitch is taken and thread is kept to right of needle when broader effect desired. Latter method used in crewel embroidery and known as *crewel-* or *stem-stitch*. Weight in line gained by size of thread and closeness of stitches.

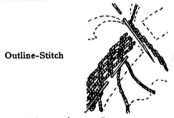

Outline-Stitch

overcast running-s. Same as TWISTED RUNNING-STITCH.

overcast- or overcasting-s. Basic stitch, third in importance, from which outline, satin, and many canvas stitches were developed. Slanting stitch used mainly to protect raw edges from raveling or to hold two edges together.

overhanding. Short over-and-over stitches placed close together, with needle always put in vertically. Used chiefly to join selvage or finished edges; also, for eyelets.

over-s. Stitch used to bind raw edge or hem, giving ornamental finish; usually made on sewing machine.

padding-s. 1. Outline-stitch used as filling to form foundation or base over which other stitches are worked. Also, plain stitch laid on fabric as base for raised design. Padding is always concealed by the embroidery stitch. 2. Diagonal-basting-stitch used to hold padding to an interlining.

Pekinese-s. (pee kin *eez*). Stitch made by looping thread through a line of back-stitches, couching, or machine-stitches. Used in shading or as outline. Sometimes called *threaded back-stitch*. Illustration shows line made by machine with heavy thread on bobbin.

petal-s. Series of chain-stitches laid along one side of a line. Stitches connecting these and forming stem give appearance of outline-stitch.

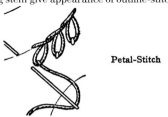

Petal-Stitch

petit-point-s. (*pet* i point). Term from French for TENT-STITCH.

picot-S. (pee co). Loop of thread extending down between groups of buttonhole-, blanket-, or crochet-stitches. Used in lacemaking, for decoration, and for edge finishes.

plain knitting. Basic stitch used in hand knitting. Made by putting right-hand needle through first stitch on left-hand needle, throwing thread around point, and drawing loop through, thus transferring stitch to right needle. This process is repeated until all stitches

are worked off left needle. Needles are then exchanged in hands and process repeated as before. Stitch may also be made on circular needles or on several small needles used for circular knitting.

plaited s. (*platt* ed). Any stitch giving braided or interwoven effect, as herringbone or basket-weave.

plush-s. Stitch used in Berlin work; made to form loops on surface in plush effect. Loops may be cut and combed or left as stitched.

Portuguese knot. Outline-stitch knotted at center of each stitch. Used as outline.

prick-s. Very short stitch taken in heavy material or where stitches are not to show. Made by putting needle in on right side very close to where it came out.

punch-work-s. Stitch worked on a loosely woven fabric which has been stamped with dots in rows about 1/8 inch apart. Rows of dots must run straight with fabric threads. Horizontal stitches are done first and then connected by vertical stitches, thereby giving square effect. Stitch is always worked from top to bottom.

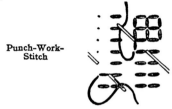

Punch-Work-Stitch

purl-s. 1. Stitch made by bringing needle through from underside out over thread so as to cross it. Commonly called *blanket-stitch*. Double purl, which is used in making tailored buttonholes, made by throwing thread over needle as it crosses, forming knot or double purl. Commonly called *buttonhole-stitch*. 2. In knitting, stitch made backward, giving ribbed appearance.

raccroc-s. (ra *cro*). Very fine stitch used by lacemakers to join net. Done so cleverly that it can not be detected by naked eye.

railway-s. 1. Same as CHAIN-STITCH, I. 2. In crochet, same as TRICOT STITCH.

rambler-rose-s. Stitch made by laying back-stitches of bulky thread around and around a center to form a compact flower. Used for clover blossoms, roses, and small flowers.

Rambler-Rose-Stitch

ray-s. Same as SPOKE-STITCH, 2.

rep-s. Canvas stitch worked vertically on double-thread canvas. Covers one horizontal and two vertical threads. Also called *Aubusson-stitch*.

Roman-s. Same as ORIENTAL-STITCH, except that intersecting stitches are shorter and straighter.

rope-s. Overlapped, twisted blanket-stitch used to give rope-like line.

Rumanian-s. (roo *may* ni an). Same as ORIENTAL-STITCH.

running hem. Same as VERTICAL HEMMING-STITCH.

running-s. Basic stitch that is first in importance. Made in series of short stitches of same length, several run on needle at once. Used for seaming, gathering, tucking, quilting, etc.

saddle-s. Simple overcasting-stitch, used as decoration. Often made of narrow strips of leather.

satin-fishbone-s. Slanting satin-stitches worked alternately from side to side and meeting at an angle, the stitches overlapping slightly at center. Gives effect of backbone of fish.

satin-s. Over-and-over stitch laid in straight or slanting parallel lines close together so as to produce a satiny effect. May be worked flat or over padding. One of most widely used embroidery stitches.

Satin-Stitch

scallop buttonhole-s. Single- or double-purl-stitch made in scallop design, often over padding.

seam-s. Same as PURL-STITCH, 2.

seed-s. Short back-stitch made with long underneath stitch which allows for a space between top stitches. Similar to half back-stitch but irregularly placed. Used for outlining and filling.

Seed-Stitch

shadow-s. 1. Catch-stitch worked on wrong side of sheer material. Also called double back-stitch from appearance on right side. Compare SHADOW EMBROIDERY. 2. In pillow lace, same as HALF-STITCH, 2.

sheaf-filling-s. Same as BUNDLE-STITCH.

sheaf-s. Open-seam stitch having appearance of a sheaf. Bar threads, which join the two edges, are gathered into groups and tied together with a knot.

shell-s. Stitch crocheted along an edge to produce scalloped effect; made with groups of stitches radiating from certain points placed equal distances apart.

short-and-long-s. Satin-stitches of uneven

length put side by side within an outline design so as to form irregular inner edge and even outer edge. Used in half-solid work.

simplicity knot-s. Two small back-stitches laid side by side to resemble a knot. Made of heavy thread. Used for outlines and borders.

slip-s. Loose stitch concealed between two thicknesses of fabric. Made by taking up thread of fabric, then catching needle in hem edge. Used for hems, facings, folds, etc., wherever it is desired that stitches be invisible on right side.

smocking-s. Any one of several decorative stitches used for gathering cloth in regular folds, usually to form honeycomb or diamond pattern.

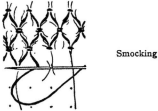

Smocking

spider-web-s. Embroidery stitches so combined as to form spider web. Made by laying threads in spoke effect over fabric; then, weaving a thread over and under these threads, around and around the center. Used in place of medallions and as a filling in drawn-work corners.

split-s. Long outline-stitch in which needle is brought up through thread itself. Used for stems and outlines and in needle-tapestry work.

spoke-s. 1. Drawn-work embroidery stitch by which threads are held together in pattern resembling spokes of a wheel. **2.** Straight stitches placed so as to radiate from a center. Also called *ray-stitch.*

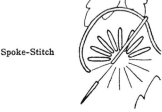

Spoke-Stitch

square chain-s. Chain-stitch made with slanting underneath stitch instead of straight. Squared effect made by putting needle in at some distance from where it came out instead of in same hole. Also called *open chain-* and *broad chain-stitch.*

star-s. Embroidery stitch in shape of eight-pointed star, made like double cross-stitch.

stem-s. 1. Slanting overhanding-stitch embroidered over a padding thread. Used for fine, definite lines, as in stems. **2.** Outline-stitch used in crewel work; called *crewel-stitch.*

Stem-Stitch

stroke-s. Same as DOUBLE RUNNING-STITCH.

surface darning-s. Stitch laid on fabric with short even- or uneven-bastings. Often used in huckaback work.

sword-edge-s. Elongated stitch so twisted at top that irregular cross is formed. Used for borders and to soften edges of leaves.

tailor's tacks. Basting stitches, with large loops left at intervals, taken through two pieces of fabric, then cut apart, leaving threads on both pieces. Used as marking of seam lines and perforations. Also called *mark-stitch.*

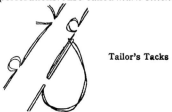

Tailor's Tacks

tambour-s. (*tam* boor). Loop-stitch made with crochet needle. Resembles chain-stitch.

tapestry darning-s. Over-and-over stitch giving solid effect in stitches alternating to left and right and so laid as to resemble darned work. Used as border for coarse materials.

tapestry-s. Short, upright stitch used in canvas work to imitate weave in woven tapestries. See GOBELIN-STITCH.

tassel-s. Embroidery stitch in which loops are made and cut to form fringe. See PLUSH-STITCH.

tent-s. 1. Short outline-stitch worked on slanting line. Used for filling in linen embroidery. Sometimes called *cushion-stitch.* **2.** Canvas stitch worked on single-thread canvas so that each stitch lies across one vertical and one horizontal thread. When worked on double-canvas, paired threads are separated before working. Can be worked horizontally or diagonally on the canvas. Also called *petit point.*

thorn-s. Embroidery stitch similar in appearance to feather-stitch or fern-stitch, but worked by alternating flat stitches over long laid stitch that forms stem.

threaded back-s. Same as PEKINESE-STITCH.

three-sided-s. 1. Drawn-fabric stitch worked on fine material by using heavy needle to punch hole and fine thread to draw fabric threads apart, giving openwork effect in bands of adjoining triangles. Need not be made to follow grain of fabric. **2.** Same stitch worked horizontally on coarse fabric over counted threads, each stitch covering from four to six threads.

tie-s. Stitch made by first taking small stitch, leaving ends of thread several inches long, then tying these in a knot. Used mainly in millinery work; sometimes in dressmaking.

tramé underlay (tram ay). Needle-point stitch made by laying long, parallel threads on narrow mesh of canvas in preparation for stitches that will hold them in place.

trellis-s. Cord-stitch worked in parallel lines, latticed with threads, knotted at each crossing of cord. Used for diamond and square motifs. Also, any combination of stitches so worked as to give trellis-like effect.

triangular blanket-s. Blanket-stitch worked diagonally to form small triangular sections. Used for edging or filling.

tricot-s. (*tree* co). Simple crochet stitch suitable for plain work. Usually done with long hooked needle and fleecy wool. Also called *Tunisian crochet, afghan-, railway-,* and *idiot-stitch.*

trio filling-s. (*tree* o). One vertical and two diagonal stitches grouped in a design. Also called thousand-flower-stitch.

twisted-bar-s. Open-seam stitch made by twisting thread several times around a bar that connects two edges. Space between stitches usually about two-thirds of that between edges. Two ribbons often connected in this manner.

twisted chain-s. Variation of chain-stitch made by taking diagonal instead of straight stitch on underside, then bringing thread over needle and around point to obtain twisted effect. Used for trimming on non-washable garments.

twisted running-s. Stitch made by overcasting series of running-stitches so as to produce twined effect. Also called overcast running.

twist-s. Same as CORD-STITCH.

two-sided cross-s. 1. Cross-stitch enclosed on two sides: left side and bottom; so that when it is worked in adjoining rows, cross appears to be boxed in on all sides. Used on loosely woven linen or canvas. **2.** Cross-stitch worked so as to appear the same on both sides.

two-sided-s. Same as DOUBLE RUNNING-STITCH.

upright-s. Satin-stitch made vertically in combination with another stitch or as filling-stitch.

vertical hemming-s. Hemming-stitch made perpendicular to hem. Used for inconspicuous hem turn. Sometimes called *running hem.*

washable knot-s. Chain-like stitch used for filling. See LINK-POWDERING-STITCH.

wheat-s. Series of slanting stitches connected at center by means of line of loops. Resembles full wheat ear. Used for border or outline effects.

wheel-s. Stitch used in making design similar to spider's web; done on material, not over space.

whip-s. Short, easy overcasting. Used over rolled edge, drawing up thread to form gathers; or over two selvages laid together to form a flat seam; or to fell down an appliqué edge.

whole-s. Same as CLOTH-STITCH.

Y-s. Decorative blanket type of stitch with each loop fastened down to form series of unconnected Y's.

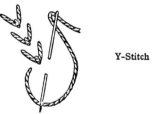

Y-Stitch

zigzag chain-s. Chain-stitch made by inserting needle at an angle and alternating from side to side.

RESOURCES

Gordon, Sarah A., *"Make It Yourself:" Home Sewing, Gender and Culture,* 1890-1930. New York: Columbia University Press, 2009.

Malloch, Douglas, *The Heart Content: "Lyrics of Life,"* 1926, 1927. New York: Doubleday, Doran & Co., Inc.

Picken, Mary Brooks, *Sewing for Profit.* Scranton, PA: International Educational Publishing.

Picken, Mary Brooks, *Singer Sewing Book.* New York: Singer Sewing Machine Co., 1949.

Picken, Mary Brooks, *The Language of Fashion: A Dictionary and Digest of Fabric, Sewing, and Dress.* New York: Funk & Wagnalls Company, 1939.

Picken, Mary Brooks, *The Mary Brooks Picken Method of Modern Dressmaking.* New York: The Pictorial Review Company, 1925.

Picken, Mary Brooks, *Thimblefuls of Friendliness: One Woman's Everyday Philosophy.* Scranton, PA: Woman's Institute of Domestics Arts and Sciences, 1924.

Woman's Institute of Domestic Arts and Sciences, "Fashion Service: Woman's Institute Magazine." Scranton, PA: 1920 to 1934.

Woman's Institute of Domestic Arts and Sciences, "Inspiration: Woman's Institute Magazine." Scranton, PA: 1920 to 1928.

Woman's Institute of Domestic Arts and Sciences, "Making Beautiful Clothes." Scranton, PA: 1918, 1921, 1922, 1923, 1925.

Woman's Institute of Domestic Arts and Sciences, *Sewing for Profit.* Scranton, PA: International Educational Publishing, 1924, 1929.

Woman's Institute of Domestic Arts and Sciences, *Smart Individuality,* course work from the correspondence school.

Woman's Weekly, "Home Craft: The American Woman's Handibook." Chicago: The Magazine Circulation Co., Publishers of Woman's Weekly, 1918.

Woman's World, "The Patchwork Book." Chicago: The Woman's World, 1931.

Wright's Bias Fold Tape Sewing Books. New Jersey: Wm. E. Wright & Sons, Co., Inc., 1930, 1931. Illustrations from these books are featured in several places throughout the book.

In addition to the books and magazines listed above, a great deal of information was gathered from the following sources: *Who's News and Why, 1954,* which featured the biography of Mary Brooks Picken; numerous letters, stories, and notices that were shared by her nephew Rick Greener and niece Gretchen Warren; her obituary that appeared in the *New York Times*; and material that was purchased from many sources during the editing of this book.

Acknowledgments

1916   1920   1924   1928   1932

To my husband Bob, who gave his whole-hearted support in this intense research and writing endeavor, and to my children, Jack and Emma, who agreed to come along for the ride.

To my mother, Donna Martin, whose style, creative energy and enthusiasm for sewing I believe matches that of Mary Brooks Picken. You have always been there to support and promote my entrepreneurial endeavors and you set a wonderful example for me to follow.

To Jean Lowe, my editor and publishing consultant—your involvement and talent was key to this project's success. Thank you for your belief in my vision and seeing me through every detail of the publishing process.

To Desiree Mueller, a gifted graphic designer and art director whose design of the book and sensitivity to this material has made this book a reality; to assistant designer Nancy Premer for all of her help and countless contributions.

To Erin Hill for her beautiful designs for the art on the cover and end papers.

To Kevan Gibbs for your business consultation and enthusiasm for this book and your coordination of our brand-building activities surrounding the launch.

To Bridget Lowe, whose charming writing and editing brought my words and ideas to life.

To my team at Indygo Junction and The Vintage Workshop—Cheryl Pinkman, Secely Palmer, Dian Stanley, Annette Waisner, and Erin Hill—your contributions have allowed me the freedom I needed to take on this project.

To Rick Greener and Gretchen Warren—great nephew and niece of Mary Brooks Picken who have shared their wonderful stories of Mary with me.

The following friends and family members have so generously contributed their time and professional experience: Hollis Barickman, Barbara Barickman, Karen Strauss, Linda Flake, Jenny Spencer, Alexis Ceule, Tom Wurster, and members of Briarwood Elementary's Second Grade Mom's Book Club. And to the countless others whom I may not have recognized here who have given me counsel and advice through this exciting and challenging process.

I am deeply grateful to all of you for your enthusiastic support of this project!

About the Author

Amy Barickman, founder and owner of Indygo Junction and The Vintage Workshop, is a leader in the sewing, needle arts, fashion pattern and retail crafting industry. Amy grew up spending hours at her mother's creative arts retail store working and watching the business evolve along with the trends. The seeds of entrepreneurism took root in Amy, and she started her own business designing and marketing collectible teddy bears while still in high school.

After graduating from the University of Kansas with a degree in art and design, Amy founded Indygo Junction in 1990 to publish and market sewing books and patterns in the fabric arts. Amy's knack for anticipating popular trends has led her to discover more than 35 innovative designers and, over the years, publish over 800 sewing pattern titles, selling nearly two million. In addition, she has licensed her craft kits and fabric lines with top fabric, fashion and novelty craft suppliers and has published 80 books that have sold at stores throughout the U.S. and internationally. Through her published works, business websites and her e-newsletters, Amy inspires countless crafters to explore their own creative spirit and experiment with the newest techniques.

With her keen eye for innovative design and market trends, Amy spotted the emerging vintage art movement and collected an impressive archive of vintage ephemera. On the heels of Indygo Junction's success, Amy founded The Vintage Workshop in 2002 to create products that allow crafters online access to timeless vintage artwork, which may be printed on fabrics. Her digital vintage designs are available to download from her website at www.thevintageworkshop.com.

Named one of America's most creative women entrepreneurs by *Country Living* magazine, Amy has made frequent guest appearances on television, including HGTV's "The Carol Duvall Show," "America Sews" and "Sewing with Nancy" on PBS. *Amy Barickman's Vintage Notions* is the latest addition to her best-selling book titles, which include *The Vintage Workshop's Art-to-Wear, Indygo Junction's Needle Felting, Button Ware, Denim Redesign, Bag Boutique, The Sew-It Book* and *Hankie Style*. She lives with her family in Prairie Village, Kansas.